Untouchable

Untouchable

How Powerful People Get Away with It

ELIE HONIG

HARPER

An Imprint of HarperCollins*Publishers*

HarperCollins books may be purchased for educational, business, or sales promotional use. For information, please email the Special Markets Department at SPsales@harpercollins.com.

FIRST EDITION

Designed by Bonni Leon-Berman

Library of Congress Cataloging-in-Publication Data has been applied for.

ISBN 978-0-06-324150-3

23 24 25 26 27 LBC 5 4 3 2 1

To Rachael, Aaron, and Leah

CONTENTS

Untouchable

Chapter 1

"DO WHAT YOU HAVE TO DO"

Frank Hydell had no idea that the beer he drank at Scarlet's strip club in Staten Island on a cool spring night in 1998 would be his last.

It was, he believed, just a casual, two-guys-with-nothing-better-to-do Monday night out. John Matera, Hydell's longtime pal, had called early that evening and proposed they grab a drink at the club. Hydell, then thirty-one years old, half-heartedly agreed. He hardly even bothered to get dressed, wearing navy-blue sweatpants and white sneakers to the scene of his own murder.

Inside Scarlet's that night, Hydell and Matera took a table and ordered some beers. At one point Matera got up and made a call from a pay phone. Around midnight, seeing that things were headed nowhere in particular, Hydell called it quits. He gathered up his wallet and keys, walked out to the parking lot, and opened the driver's-side door of his white Camry.

There's no way to know whether Hydell ever saw Eddie Boyle coming. Either way, it all happened too fast for Hydell to resist or even react. Hydell knew Boyle from the streets. Both hovered on the periphery of the Gambino family. Boyle was a "capable" guy (capable of violence, that is, in mob parlance), while Hydell was a bit player who dabbled mostly in after-hours bank burglaries. That night in the parking lot at Scarlet's, Boyle strode briskly up to Hydell, pulled out a .357 Magnum revolver, and shot him three times in the head and chest. Hydell fell dead to the asphalt next to his car, driver's-side door still flung open.

..

When I first met Ted Otto in 2006, he was obsessed with the Hydell murder. Otto, a brilliant, incorrigible, relentless FBI special agent with the Queens-based Gambino squad, had investigated and solved plenty of mob cases over his career, often deploying unorthodox techniques. He once typed up pages of phony transcripts, put them in a binder, and showed them to a Gambino soldier to try to convince him that the FBI had been wiretapping his phone and he needed to flip; didn't work, but it was a hell of an effort. Otto was a world-class pain in the ass—beloved by prosecutors, tolerated with a wince by his FBI supervisors, despised by the mob. Think Detective Jimmy McNulty from *The Wire*, only with reddish-blond hair.

Despite Otto's many investigative successes, the Hydell murder gnawed at him. Maybe it was the sheer cold-bloodedness of the Gambino family mobsters who plotted Hydell's death, who exploited the cover of Matera's friendship to lure him to Scarlet's and execute him in the parking lot. Perhaps it was that Hydell was targeted because he had begun to cooperate with the FBI, providing valuable information about crimes committed by other gangsters right up until he was silenced. It could have been that Otto refused to accept the unimaginable grief of Hydell's mother, who found herself mourning the loss of a second child to the mob; her older son, James, had been lured to his death at the hands of a different Mafia family, the Luccheses, twelve years earlier, in 1986. Whatever it was, the Hydell murder bothered Otto so deeply, and for so long, that he carried in his own wallet a funeral card bearing Hydell's image.

Over time, Otto doggedly chipped away at the Hydell murder. I worked with him as the lead prosecutor during the latter phases of this effort. A few years before I got involved, Otto and a team of my colleagues at the Southern District of New York (SDNY) got their first break when they flipped powerhouse Gambino family captain Michael DiLeonardo (known on the streets as "Mikey Scars," referring to facial scars he had sustained as a child from a dog attack).

The mob was in DiLeonardo's blood. He was the grandson of a Sicilian-born member of the original "Black Hand" faction of Italian immigrants to the United States that staked its claim to criminal dominance in Brooklyn in the early 1900s. As he rose through the Gambino family, DiLeonardo excelled across the criminal spectrum. He was an "earner and a burner," in the parlance: he brought in millions through construction rackets, and he could hand out a beating, or worse, as necessary to intimidate or eliminate anybody who posed a problem. His decision to flip, when faced with a slate of charges that threatened to keep him behind bars for the rest of his life, sent tremors through the mob world.

When he started to cooperate, DiLeonardo gave prosecutors and the FBI reams of information about crimes that he and others had committed over decades. Ultimately, he would testify in a dozen trials and contribute to the convictions of about eighty gangsters. But when it came to the Hydell murder, DiLeonardo had only a few precious dribs of actionable information. Most importantly, a fellow Gambino family member, Thomas Carbonaro, once told DiLeonardo that he had driven the shooter, Boyle, to and from the Hydell hit. Carbonaro also boasted that they had enlisted Matera to lure Hydell to the scene and to alert the hit team that the target was in place, through that pay-phone call from inside Scarlet's.

After years of investigation, Otto and the team started to get results in court. Based largely on DiLeonardo's information, the SDNY charged and convicted Matera (who admitted he was part of the conspiracy to kill Hydell, pled guilty, and received a sentence of twenty years), Carbonaro (who was convicted of plotting to kill Hydell, among many other crimes, and sentenced to seventy years behind bars), and even DiLeonardo himself (as part of his cooperation agreement, he pled guilty to murder conspiracy for passing word within the Gambino family about the plan to kill Hydell, and other crimes).

Later, when I joined the SDNY's Organized Crime Unit, we charged and secured guilty pleas from two other Gambinos, Tommy Dono and Lenny DeCarlo, who were at the scene of the murder in the designated "crash car." (It's common Mafia practice to have a nearby car waiting to create a diversion if the actual hit man's getaway car encounters any trouble. If, for example, a police officer had stopped or pursued the shooter's getaway car, then the Dono-DeCarlo car would have crashed into something to pull focus and allow the assassin to get away.) Both were sentenced to fifteen years in prison.

Eventually the SDNY charged and tried Boyle, the shooter. The jury, somewhat bizarrely, found Boyle not guilty of murdering Hydell but guilty of racketeering conspiracy charges—meaning that Boyle was part of the Gambino family, and knew that the family was involved in multiple crimes, including murder. The judge sentenced Boyle to the maximum of twenty years, specifically finding at the sentencing hearing that he had in fact killed Hydell. (This can and does happen in our criminal justice system; even if the jury acquits a defendant on a particular count, the judge still can find at sentencing that the charge was proven by a "preponderance" of the evidence—essentially, more likely than not—and sentence accordingly.)

Sounds like a clean sweep, or nearly that. All the main players who carried out the murder of Hydell that night in the parking lot at Scarlet's were charged, convicted, and sentenced to prison terms, though some of them ultimately felt a bit light. Fifteen or twenty years is a long time behind bars, but didn't seem fully adequate for such a cold-blooded, premeditated murder.

But even after all these convictions, there was still one thing we couldn't ignore, one thing that simply had to be true: Daniel Marino—Hydell's own uncle, married to his mother's sister—was behind it all. (This Dan Marino was, of course, not the rifle-armed Miami Dolphins quarterback from the 1980s and '90s, but the cold-blooded Gambino family powerhouse from the past six decades.)

We knew Marino had to have been involved, purely by dint of his position near the top of the Gambino family and his familial relationship with Hydell. Indeed, according to DiLeonardo, when he learned that Hydell was cooperating with the FBI and would need to be eliminated, he sent word to Marino, who was then in federal prison in Pennsylvania. (This is why, years later, as part of his cooperation deal with the SDNY, DiLeonardo pled guilty for his part, small as it was, in the murder conspiracy.)

As a savvy mob veteran, DiLeonardo recognized that nobody could put hands on Danny Marino's nephew, never mind kill him, without Marino's blessing. To kill Hydell without permission would land any gangster squarely in Marino's own crosshairs—a place nobody wanted to be, not even a powerhouse in his own right like DiLeonardo.

So, DiLeonardo told us, he instructed an intermediary to go discuss the matter with Marino. DiLeonardo couldn't go himself because he wasn't on Marino's list of approved prison visitors. In any event, it would have been too conspicuous to have two notorious Gambino family leaders sitting together chatting in the prison's visiting area.

The intermediary took the order. Weeks later, he reported back to DiLeonardo that, during the in-person prison visit, he told Marino that Hydell was a "rat." Marino showed little reaction other than to ask, "Are you sure?" The intermediary confirmed that yes, the Gambino family was sure. "Do what you have to do," Marino responded flatly. He never specifically said "Kill him"—powerful mobsters typically don't need to be so explicit—but his meaning was plain to all involved.

To be clear: this isn't much to go on in terms of a criminal charge— never mind a murder conspiracy charge against one of the most powerful, wealthy, and feared members of the mob. It was a convoluted game of whisper-down-the-lane, hearsay-upon-hearsay (the type that can be legally admissible but isn't supremely persuasive to a jury). And the star witness would be DiLeonardo, a self-professed criminal, without meaningful corroboration from other witnesses or documents or recordings.

Further complicating matters, Marino didn't pull the trigger, and wasn't even at the crime scene; heck, he was locked up in another state when the hit went down. The entire crux of the case would come down to nine words, give or take—"Are you sure?" and "Do what you have to do"—uttered during a jailhouse visit. But federal law enabled us to charge Marino as part of a broad conspiracy to commit the murder (a conspiracy is just an agreement to commit a crime), and we knew that the hit never could have happened without his permission. He was, after all, the most powerful person involved. He was a boss.

As the prosecutor on the case, I asked myself countless times: Did we have enough to charge Marino? Maybe, barely. But was it enough to prove the case to a jury, unanimously and beyond a reasonable doubt? Even I had to acknowledge, in my heart of hearts: probably not. Otto was characteristically a bit more gung-ho, but he recognized that it was an uphill climb.

Ultimately, Otto and I decided to give it a shot. (We tended to mutually reinforce one another's more aggressive instincts, for better or worse.) We charged Marino, who was then seventy years old, with conspiracy to murder his nephew, Hydell. We knew our case was shaky. We knew that Marino and his attorney—one of the best criminal defense lawyers in the country, Gerald Shargel—knew that too. But we also knew trial would present enormous risks to both sides. An acquittal would be a devastating blow to Otto, to me, to the SDNY, and, most importantly, to the Hydell family. But a conviction would land Marino behind bars for the rest of his life.

As trial approached, Otto and I scrambled to bolster our case. We tried to flip Matera and the intermediary who spoke with Marino in prison, without success. (We actually had the US Marshals transport Matera back to New York from the prison where he was serving his time; he met with us, and was quite open about his role in setting up the murder, but politely declined to cooperate against anyone else.) We canvassed our stable of Gambino family cooperators, but none had any usable information. When Otto and I talked to one new Gambino cooperator, we asked him eagerly if he knew anything about the Hydell murder. "I'd love to be able to help you with that, but I just don't have anything on it," he replied, instantly deflating us. As time passed and the trial approached, it became increasingly clear that we needed to get to the bargaining table and work out a deal.

In the end, we agreed to a guilty plea that would send Marino to prison for—and I still cringe even now, years later, as I write this—five years. The judge on the case was thoroughly unimpressed. When he saw our proposed plea deal, he took the rare step of publicly expressing dissatisfaction and making us explain on the record why we believed it was justified. In one of my least glamorous court appearances, I stammered through an explanation that boiled down, in essence, to "This is the best we can do."

To this day, I have regrets about the Marino case. It still bothers me. I feel like we let him off too easy. The rational part of me understands that it was a minor miracle that we scraped up enough evidence and had the guts to bring a charge against him in the first place. Five years isn't nothing, and partial justice is preferable, after all, to no justice at all. But it never felt right, or adequate. Marino took his plea, did his time, and was released from prison in 2014. At this moment, he is still alive at eighty-one, still wealthy, still a Gambino, and as free as you and me.

So how did Marino do it? How did he end up with the lowest sentence, by far, of all the people involved in the Hydell murder? Marino's approval was absolutely necessary for the hit to go down, a condition precedent, yet every other participant got at least a decade longer behind bars. The man authorized the murder of his own nephew, and he did just five years (less, actually, because federal inmates get 15 percent off their sentences for good behavior in prison).

Ever since I prosecuted the Marino case, this conundrum has plagued me: How did the most powerful person get off the easiest?

· ·

That question has become even more resonant, and more broadly applicable, over the past half decade. Through my work in the media, I receive questions constantly from viewers and readers. The most common by far is this: "How the hell does he get away with it?" The "he" can vary, but it always refers to somebody who is powerful, or rich, or famous, or some combination of those things—and it's almost always a "he." The most frequent subject of inquiry, by a lot, is the former president of the United States: Donald J. Trump.

Few if any people in American history have flouted the law in as many ways, over as many years, in as public a manner as Trump has. He has been impeached twice, tried twice in the Senate, and acquitted both times. He has been sued, subpoenaed, and deposed dozens of times. He has been the subject of countless adverse findings in reports issued by prosecutors, judges, Congress, and other investigative bodies. But as of this writing, Donald Trump has never been charged with a crime. His rap sheet is blank.

That could change, of course. Given several long-pending investigations, some prosecutor at some level might finally take a shot. In my view, the Fulton County, Georgia, district attorney is the most likely to indict Trump, perhaps even by the time of this book's publication in early 2023. But the prime opportunities to hold Trump criminally accountable for his actions have passed. Prosecutors, federal and state alike, have fumbled away their best chances and inexcusably allowed years to lapse without meaningful action. And, as we'll examine throughout this book, Trump has long displayed an uncanny ability to exploit the advantages afforded by our criminal justice system to powerful people in general, and the president in particular. At this point, the cold reality is that Trump is unlikely ever to be convicted and imprisoned, even if he eventually does face a criminal charge.

For years this one extraordinarily powerful man, unburdened by ethics, shame, or even a logical sense of self-preservation, has floated above the law, often while pissing down on it—first as president and then, more confoundingly, as a private citizen stripped of the unique protections afforded only to the sitting occupant of the Oval Office. He is a lawless Houdini, repeatedly escaping (and at times being rescued from) the clutches of law enforcement. Meanwhile, a staggering parade of his henchmen and personal, political, and business associates have been indicted, and in many instances convicted and imprisoned: Michael Cohen, Roger Stone, Paul Manafort, Michael Flynn, Steve Bannon, Peter Navarro, Rick Gates, George Papadopoulos, Lev Parnas, Igor Fruman, Thomas Barrack, Elliott Broidy, Sam Patten, George Nader, Allen Weisselberg, and the Trump Organization itself.

Yet the boss somehow stands at the epicenter of the carnage, untouched, undeterred, and, if anything, emboldened. Picture the famous scene from the old black-and-white movie *Steamboat Bill, Jr.*, where the facade of a house blows loose in a windstorm and collapses, seemingly about to crush the character played by Buster Keaton—yet as the building falls around him, he miraculously escapes unharmed, standing in a void created by an open window.

Trump is hardly the only powerhouse in recent memory to get off easy. We've seen other giants of politics, finance, and entertainment either skirt the law altogether or escape with meager punishments. In some instances, justice came about belatedly and imperfectly, only after intense media scrutiny focused on the prosecutors and police who'd initially given their powerful subjects a generous pass. In other cases justice never arrived at all. Not every boss gets away scot-free, of course. Many crooked kingpins, billionaires, politicians, and CEOs have faced meaningful accountability in the criminal courts. But on the whole, powerful people tend to fare better in our criminal justice system than normal folks, if they even wind up in court at all.

On some level, it's obvious how this happens. The rich and powerful get away with things that an ordinary person can't. It's a truth so widely accepted as to be axiomatic. But consider: How exactly do they pull it off? If you suddenly had vast power and limitless resources, how would you go about protecting yourself? Would you know where to start in your (hypothetical) quest to insulate yourself from prosecutors and cops? You need more than money, fame, and power. You need to know how to use those resources the right way. And once you know how to exploit those advantages—once you start to *think like a boss*—you can shape the world around you.

On the flip side, how do we hold accountable those people who know how to game the system? The best place to start is by understanding the tactics of the powerful and the ruthless. Any decent prosecutor learns—over many years, often by painful firsthand experience (like mine in the Marino case, and others that we'll examine)—that bosses can wreak havoc in our criminal justice system. So we need to get inside the heads of the savviest kingpins, and turn their tactics against them.

For example, I worked on a case involving a large labor union that was under the control of the Genovese organized crime family. We knew from experience that the moment we served subpoenas on the people who were being shaken down through the union, the family's leadership would spring into action, tampering with the victims to keep them from telling us the full truth.

We also knew they'd likely discuss those plans at a specific place:

the back corner table at Don Pepe's restaurant in Queens, where the powerful Genovese captain who controlled the union regularly held court with his fellow gangsters every Tuesday and Thursday over plates of whatever was good that night. (I learned over the years that a real gangster never orders off the menu; you just walk in and say to the server, "What are we eating tonight?") So before we sent out the subpoenas, we got court permission to wiretap the key mob players' phones and have the FBI drop a bug—a hidden recording device—within the actual table where they ate, in that back corner at Don Pepe's. We then served the subpoenas, sat back, and listened. Sure enough, we immediately started picking up conversations in which the Genovese family players explicitly discussed their plans to thwart our investigation—"Make sure that guy doesn't talk to the feds," "We need him to say he never paid," and the like, all audible over the clatter of silverware and chewing of food. Those wiretaps enabled us to charge the mobsters not only with the union shakedown but also with witness tampering and obstruction of justice. It was like throwing bread crumbs into a lake and then scooping up the fish as they bubbled to the surface. Prosecution doesn't always lend itself to such tidy solutions, of course. But there are countless ways prosecutors can use creativity and aggression to topple even the most ruthless criminals.

I don't aim here to diagnose or cure all the ills of inequality in our justice system; libraries have been written on this sprawling subject, and there is, of course, no magic bullet. But a careful examination of recent legal sagas around Trump and other powerful players can help us identify and understand how they try to exploit fundamental flaws (or perhaps features) of our legal system and the people who hold power within it.

I was one of those people. I worked for fourteen years as a federal and state prosecutor, from 2004 through 2018. I spent eight-plus years with the US Attorney's Office for the Southern District of New

York (SDNY), where I eventually became co-chief of the Organized Crime Unit, and then five and a half years at the New Jersey attorney general's office, where I led over five hundred prosecutors, detectives, and staff at the Division of Criminal Justice. That experience certainly hasn't given me all the answers. But it enables me to understand the criminal justice system and the human element of it—the power dynamic between prosecutors, cops, defense lawyers, defendants, and judges, the culture inside prosecutors' offices and courthouses, and the impact of politics, money, the media, and other outside influences on prosecutorial and judicial processes.

In chapter 2 of this book, I report for the first time on the behind-the-scenes story of the investigation by my former office, the vaunted SDNY, into hush money payments that Trump and his associates made shortly before the 2016 election to silence two women, former *Playboy* model Karen McDougal and adult film star Stephanie Clifford (screen name Stormy Daniels), who had allegedly had sexual affairs with Trump. In the end, somehow, the SDNY ended up charging only one person: Michael Cohen, the attorney who essentially served as a bag man in the scheme. While Cohen went to federal prison, Trump managed not only to avoid criminal charges but also to take on minimal political damage—with help from the bosses at Justice Department headquarters, who forced SDNY prosecutors to remove crucial information about Trump from their public legal filings.

As we'll see, the SDNY's hush money prosecution of Cohen offers a case study on how powerful people—particularly the president—get away with it, often while others around them don't. In retrospect, we can see how, if conditions had been a little different and if key players (including prosecutors) had made different decisions, Trump might have faced justice (or at least meaningful consequences) years ago.

"Justice is blind," we are taught in law school, and reminded often.

But if you look at the statue of Lady Justice as she holds the scales of justice in her hands, you'll notice that she's not actually blind. She wears a blindfold. Occasionally, it turns out, she takes a peek to see who's in front of her. But as much as the institutional deck is stacked in favor of powerful, wealthy, famous people, all is not lost. This is no defeatist eulogy for our justice system. This is, rather, a guide to navigate it. If we understand how bosses exploit systemic vulnerabilities, then we can meaningfully call upon the people who make the big decisions—primarily prosecutors—to fight back and pursue justice, no matter how daunting the challenge.

Chapter 2

THE SOUTHERN DISTRICT OF
NEW YORK AND "INDIVIDUAL-1"

*Behind the Scenes in the Department of Justice's
Internal Struggle over Trump*

If you ever get a chance to walk the halls of the exalted US Attorney's
Office for the Southern District of New York, you'll be thoroughly
unimpressed. Located right where the Brooklyn Bridge comes down
from its span over the East River into Manhattan, the SDNY's main
office building is at once somehow both nondescript and ugly. Short
and misshapen, with cloudy windows and a faded brick exterior, it
sits awkwardly wedged between a dignified old church to the west,
the NYPD headquarters to the east, and a drab but menacing federal prison to the north.

Inside the building you'll find claustrophobic hallways that barely
permit two people to pass without brushing shoulders. The tables
and chairs in the conference rooms are mismatched and appear
salvaged from flea markets. The water fountains are long dead,
marked off as sources of non-potable water only. Various wildlife
inhabit the office space, from routine New York City mice (occasionally I'd hear one of my hallmates shriek, grab a manila folder,
bend it like a taco, and scoop the offending rodent out of her office)
to the invisible but insidious bedbugs that visit the building every
few months (prosecutors would at times come in to find yellow po-

lice tape on their office doors, if the bedbug-sniffing dog indicated a localized infestation).

And there are, of course, papers, files, and boxes *everywhere*—piled on desks, jammed into and on top of overstuffed filing cabinets, stashed in closets, crammed into copy-paper boxes, and stacked up in common areas. At one point we converted a boiler room into an improvised filing area of sorts; nothing ever caught fire, though the documents sometimes were warm to the touch. The paper mess would get so bad that every few years, just before auditors came up from Justice Department headquarters in Washington, DC, to inspect the office for compliance with DOJ administrative rules, the SDNY office manager would walk around with a hand truck, load up stray boxes and files, hide them away in the sub-basement, and then return them after the audit team left town. (Prosecutors know how to clean up the scene, when necessary.)

There is no way to know how many documents are inside the SDNY's main office—how many printed pages, how many binders and manila folders and Redwelds, how many gigabytes of electronic data. There are more search warrants, prosecution memos, FBI 302s, wiretap transcripts, complaints, indictments, sentencing memos, and appellate briefs than could ever be reliably counted.

Within that innumerable mass of documents, somewhere inside that SDNY building—on one of the overburdened, blinking servers that keep the computer network running, perhaps printed out and stuffed in a folder in a sealed-up box—is a draft indictment that would have shaken Donald Trump's presidency and the country. The document didn't name Trump as a defendant, but it would have done him incalculable damage.

That draft indictment never got out of the building. But it was close—closer than anybody outside the SDNY and the Justice Department has previously known.

The reporting in this chapter is based on interviews with over a half dozen people who were directly involved in the SDNY's 2018 prosecution of Michael Cohen. All played different roles in the case, viewed it from different perspectives, and represented different interests. Some know most or nearly all of the story, while others know pieces relevant to their own work. These varied accounts, taken together, reflect a fundamental consistency, and this bottom line: while SDNY prosecutors believed they had evidence sufficient to establish that Trump had participated in campaign finance crimes, they never charged him. And leadership at the Justice Department stepped in to prevent the SDNY from taking actions in the prosecution of Cohen that would have damaged Trump's public image and political standing, and could have made it difficult for prosecutors to walk away from a post-presidency indictment of Trump himself.

..

Robert Mueller's investigation of Russian interference in the 2016 presidential election and obstruction of justice reached its zenith during the summer of 2018. By that point Mueller had racked up indictments of key players in Trump's orbit: Michael Flynn, Paul Manafort, Rick Gates, George Papadopoulos, and others. But the big question was whether any of those charges would implicate Trump himself in any appreciable respect.

It was already clear that Mueller would not immediately charge Trump, due to long-standing DOJ policy against indictment of a sitting president. Still, the world was on the lookout for two things that could damage Trump and potentially foretell his eventual fate. First, would the Mueller investigation and its various spinoffs yield evidence explosive enough to support Trump's impeachment? And second, were prosecutors laying a foundation to indict Trump *after* he left office and became fair game for criminal charges?

The answer to both questions would be contained between the lines. Whenever Mueller's team filed any document in the courts, it was intensely scrutinized for any implications for Trump. Even routine, boilerplate motions prompted frenzied analysis and speculation. For example, Mueller submitted several requests to postpone Flynn's sentencing (while Flynn was cooperating and before the cooperation, and Flynn himself, went haywire). These were entirely standard and unremarkable requests. Prosecutors constantly push back the dates of sentencing hearings for cooperators; at times, I'd postpone them for years. Nonetheless, each delay evoked a barrage of questions: What could this mean? Was this bad news for Trump? Did it mean that Flynn was cooperating successfully against Trump, or was there some problem behind the scenes? Similarly, when Manafort went to trial in late July 2018, court watchers kept their ears perked for any testimony implicating Trump. Alas, the charged conduct related almost entirely to Manafort's own private fraud schemes, unconnected to Trump or the campaign.

In fact, seemingly all of the defendants charged by Mueller had committed crimes in the vicinity of Trump, but not directly and provably involving him. Gates, like Manafort, mostly participated in frauds not touching on Trump or the campaign. Flynn lied to the FBI about his contacts with a Russian official during the presidential transition, but nothing in the case directly implicated Trump himself. Similarly, Papadopoulos lied to the FBI about his contacts with Russians on behalf of the campaign, but not in any way that could be linked squarely to Trump. (Trump nonetheless tried to distance himself from Papadopoulos, dismissing him as a mere "coffee boy.")

But the Michael Cohen case was different. The investigation and prosecution of Trump's longtime personal attorney posed a unique threat directly to Trump himself.

The Cohen investigation landed with the SDNY because Mueller determined that it did not fit within his core mission to investigate

Russian interference in the 2016 election. (Mueller referred at least fourteen spin-off cases to various US attorneys across the country.) While an ordinary SDNY prosecution of a crooked lawyer might be staffed by one or two assigned "line" prosecutors, reporting up to a deputy chief and ultimately chief of a unit, the team on the Cohen case ran at least nine deep: four line prosecutors from the Public Corruption Unit (Andrea Griswold, Rachel Maimin, Thomas McKay, and Nicolas Roos); the unit's chiefs and deputy chiefs (Tatiana Martins, who left the office during the investigation in the ordinary flow of business, Russell Capone, and Ted Diskant); the chief of the criminal division, Lisa Zornberg; the executive US attorney, Audrey Strauss; and the deputy US attorney, Rob Khuzami. The SDNY's top-ranking official at the time, US attorney Geoffrey Berman, was recused from the Cohen investigation at his own request, with approval from senior DOJ officials, because he had donated to and been selected for the office by Trump, who could conceivably wind up in the investigation's purview—and perhaps its crosshairs. That could have created a conflict of interest for Berman, or at least the appearance of one. In Berman's absence, Khuzami stepped into the top position on the Cohen case.

Khuzami was a heavy hitter in law enforcement circles, well known and widely respected for his work ethic and intensity by New York prosecutors, federal agents, and defense lawyers. He had spent over a decade, from 1991 to 2002, as a prosecutor with the SDNY, where he became chief of the Securities Fraud Unit. He later became a top regulator at the Securities Enforcement Commission (SEC), sandwiched between stints as an in-house lawyer for Deutsche Bank and as a partner at the private law firm Kirkland & Ellis. Khuzami then returned to the SDNY as Berman's deputy in January 2018. The Cohen case landed on his desk almost immediately upon his arrival back at the SDNY.

Building off a base of evidence provided by Mueller and aided by their own execution of search warrants on Cohen's home, office, hotel, and cell phones, the SDNY team by mid-2018 had assembled ample evidence to charge Cohen with a spate of federal crimes, including tax evasion and bank fraud. Those frauds related to Cohen's own finances, however, without any connection to Trump.

But Cohen also participated in a scheme, just before the November 2016 election, to pay a total of $280,000 in hush money to two women, Karen McDougal and Stephanie Clifford (also known as Stormy Daniels), who had allegedly had sexual affairs with Trump about a decade earlier. If those payments related to the Trump campaign—if they were intended in significant part to prevent McDougal and Clifford from going public and harming Trump's electoral prospects—then they could be illegal, undisclosed campaign expenditures or donations, far in excess of federal limits. If Cohen participated in the scheme to make the payments, and understood their purpose, then he could be charged with a federal crime. The same went for Trump, or anybody else.

Because of the DOJ policy against indicting a sitting president, Trump plainly would not be charged then and there, in the summer of 2018. But SDNY prosecutors had a unique opportunity to lay down a marker in the Cohen case that would memorialize for the American public—and potentially for Congress and prosecutors who someday might be able to charge Trump after he left office—the full extent of Trump's involvement in the criminal payoff scheme.

Although they were fully aware of the long-standing DOJ no-indictment policy, the SDNY team, true to the office's reputation for headstrong independence, nonetheless decided to do their own research on the issue, just to make sure the Justice Department had gotten it right. (The Justice Department is comprised of the attorney general and his centralized staff at headquarters in Washington, DC—often referred to collectively as "Main Justice," in the lingo—

plus ninety-four US attorneys' offices, including the SDNY, one in each federal geographic district across the country.)

A seasoned SDNY prosecutor, Thomas McKay, did the primary research and ultimately landed in the same place as DOJ, concluding that the SDNY indeed had no authority to indict the sitting president. McKay's supervisors agreed. The SDNY also considered whether it could indict the sitting president "under seal"—filed secretly with a court and then made public later, after the president left office. Consistent with a footnote in one of the original DOJ memos establishing the no-indictment policy, the SDNY concluded that it could not go this route, either. (Various pundits speculated publicly in 2018 that the SDNY might already have indicted Trump under seal; they were wrong.)

As reflected by the SDNY's decision to do its own (arguably overcautious and unnecessary) double check of long-standing DOJ policy, the Cohen prosecutors understood the stakes—particularly as they related to Trump. The SDNY team fully expected that their work someday would be scrutinized intensely and publicly, perhaps even by Congress. They discussed the need to be careful in texts and emails, mindful of embarrassing revelations about inappropriate electronic communications between members of Mueller's team. Most famously, FBI special agent Peter Strzok responded to a colleague's concern that Trump might win the 2016 election by texting, "No. No he won't. We'll stop it." The SDNY team explicitly discussed the need to avoid making any comments, even jokes, that could reflect poorly on the team's prosecutorial efforts and motives.

While the SDNY team recognized they could not indict Trump while he held office, they had no intention to let him slink away untouched. The prosecutors on the hush money case resolved early on and unanimously to investigate the matter fully and aggressively, as they would any other case—as to Cohen himself, and as to Trump and any other participants.

Opinions on the team varied about the strength of the evidence against Trump. As one SDNY prosecutor put it, "We wouldn't even bat an eye about charging Trump, if it was somebody who was less known." Others on the team agreed they had more than enough to charge Trump, but for the DOJ policy against charging the sitting president. Still others felt the evidence against Trump, though substantial and theoretically enough to charge, was a bit close to the line for such a high-stakes (potential) case. Good prosecutors always consider what the defense will be, and the concern was that while Trump plainly knew about and directed the payments, he might not have adequately understood the criminal purpose to evade campaign finance laws. On balance, however, even considering that likely defense, the majority of SDNY team members felt they had a chargeable case against Trump. Even the more skeptical prosecutors thought it was at least a close call.

The SDNY indeed had substantial evidence against Trump. Prosecutors had a series of checks—some signed by Trump himself—from Trump-controlled organizations to Cohen, to reimburse him for the hush money payments. The SDNY team also could point to Trump's own false public denial that he knew anything about the payoff scheme, which suggested a guilty state of mind; why lie about something if there's nothing to hide? The team had a publicly available recording made secretly by Cohen in 2016 (which Cohen's lawyer gave to the media in 2018) in which Cohen and Trump discussed setting up a shell company to make the payments, and whether it would be best to pay with cash. The SDNY obtained phone records showing communications between Trump and others in the scheme at critical moments. And, on the key issue of intent, SDNY prosecutors believed the conspicuous timing of the payments was particularly incriminating; the payments were made just weeks before the election, while the underlying affairs had allegedly happened many years before.

On top of that documentary evidence, the SDNY had what it

believed to be credible, incriminating testimony from David Pecker, chairman of American Media, Inc. (AMI), the parent company of the *National Enquirer*, and from other AMI employees. AMI served as a conduit for the payments to McDougal, using money from a Trump-controlled organization to buy the rights to her story and then burying it (a practice sometimes known as "catch and kill"). Recognizing the value of Pecker's testimony, the SDNY granted him immunity from prosecution in exchange for his testimony, which prosecutors believed implicated Trump in campaign finance crimes. The SDNY also spoke with the Trump Organization's longtime chief financial officer, Allen Weisselberg. But the prosecutors ultimately concluded that Weisselberg had shaded the truth in Trump's favor, and was unusable as a witness; the SDNY did not, however, believe that Weisselberg had lied in a provable and direct enough manner to sustain a separate prosecution for perjury. (Weisselberg's reluctance to come clean in the SDNY case reflected his loyalty to Trump, and foretold his eventual refusal to cooperate against Trump personally years later, in 2021, when the Manhattan district attorney's office charged him with tax fraud in an unsuccessful effort to flip him.)

It's important to understand this, however: Michael Cohen's testimony was never going to be part of the SDNY's case against Trump, or anyone else. As a rule, cooperation in the SDNY is all-or-nothing. The office does not enlist any defendant as a cooperator unless and until prosecutors are convinced that he has fully and truthfully disclosed all of his own wrongdoing, and all crimes that he knows any other person committed. The SDNY eventually made clear in its formal sentencing submission that, in its view, Cohen did not pass muster. While Cohen "did provide information to law enforcement," the SDNY team wrote, his "description of those efforts is overstated in some respects and incomplete in others. . . . While he answered questions about the charged conduct, he refused to discuss other uncharged criminal conduct, if any, in which he may have participated." The SDNY's bottom line: Cohen was neither entirely truthful nor fully forthcoming, and maybe worse than that. Any case against Trump would not rest in any part on Cohen's testimony.

Even without Cohen as a star witness, however, the SDNY team believed it had a solid core of evidence in place against Trump. But they also sought to bolster their case, as they would against any other person. The team even considered, briefly, the possibility of pursuing a wiretap that might have enabled them to listen in, live, to phone calls involving Trump himself.

· ·

One of the great things about being a prosecutor is that you'll get these moments where real life—*your actual job*—feels like a scene in a movie.

I had one of those moments early on in my career, the first time I walked into a wire room. Ours was on a high floor of 26 Federal Plaza, the forty-one-story tower across the street from the SDNY's main offices. "26 Fed," as we'd call it, housed all manner of federal agencies, from immigration to a post office to the FBI. The building was also a target for terrorist plots; the SDNY over the years has charged and convicted defendants affiliated with al-Qaeda and Hezbollah for conspiring to attack and destroy the federal complex.

If you've ever seen a movie where the cops are monitoring a wiretap, the FBI wire room was just like that, only with a couple dozen monitoring stations set up around a massive, open floor space. Each wiretap was staffed by an investigative team for long hours, sometimes around the clock. The vibe of the wire room is erratic: long periods of boredom, reading the sports page and eating terrible snacks, punctuated by sudden bursts of adrenaline whenever the target phone rang. Suddenly an FBI agent would drop whatever he was doing, throw on a set of headphones, and listen in through a computer in real time, as the actual conversation took place on the streets. I got a charge out of it. There was a voyeuristic thrill to listening in, live, as criminals discussed drug deals or fraud schemes, unknowingly handing us devastating evidence that eventually would be used to seal their convictions in the federal courthouse across the street.

To obtain a wiretap, prosecutors must establish in a written affidavit that they have probable cause to believe that a crime was committed and that the wiretap likely will yield evidence of that crime. A judge then reviews the documents and can either grant or deny the application. Judges sometimes ask questions or request more information, but they almost always end up authorizing any wiretap requested by prosecutors.

Over the years, I had wiretaps that busted and boomed. The first time I ever got a judge's permission to go up on a wire, the FBI agents on the case and I quickly realized that by the time we started monitoring, the phone was already dead; our targeted drug trafficker had likely become suspicious and simply dropped the hot phone. I had other wiretaps that were duds. I once did a case with the FBI where we went up on a burner phone that, it turned out, the target used not for drug deals but only to talk on the side with his girlfriend.

But when wiretaps went right—and they usually did—they'd provide devastating proof of the subject's guilt. When a wiretap hit, there was no better source of dead-bang, game-over incriminating evidence. What could be more compelling than a recording of a subject, in his own words, discussing his own crimes? It was rare to go to trial on a wiretap case; those defendants typically pled guilty, quickly.

Savvier targets might use code words to try to hide their illegal activities, though they sometimes slipped up. Mob wires invariably would yield conversations about how "that guy" saw "the other guy" at "the place" about "the thing." Still, these conversations could be helpful in providing leads and in establishing who dealt with whom—and in a sense they sounded even more incriminating when played for a jury. Drug traffickers often used superficially innocuous words to discuss how many kilograms they needed or had for sale: "I've got fourteen tickets right now," or "Hey, do you have five T-shirts I can buy?" My personal favorite: one clever wholesaler referred to his kilos as "cars," but in one recording he offered to sell his prospective buyer "two and a half cars." He pled guilty, quickly.

As you walk around that vast wire room at 26 Fed, teams of FBI agents at each cubicle are monitoring a different type of criminal, or suspected criminal: a drug trafficker at this station, a Wall Street inside trader at the next stop down the row, then perhaps a mobster, an illegal firearms dealer, a credit card fraudster. If the Cohen prosecution team had been given a green light on a wiretap that they briefly considered, one of those stations might have picked up live phone calls to and from the sitting president of the United States.

During his presidency, Trump was notoriously erratic in his phone habits. A former Trump official told CNN, "Trump hated people knowing who he spoke to, including from the residence at night when they went through the switchboard." Trump often used nonsecure phone lines from inside the White House, to the consternation of security officials, at times telling people who dialed in through secure lines to call back on his cell phone instead. He reportedly cycled through various cell phones during his presidency, at times owning two phones at once, and he resisted handing them over to government security experts for routine inspections, which were, in his view, "too inconvenient." Trump infamously had a habit of grabbing his advisors' cell phones—including those of deputy chief of staff Dan Scavino, aide Keith Schiller, and others—and making calls that were not recorded on any official White House log.

Members of the SDNY's frontline prosecution team discussed internally whether they could make the required showing of probable cause relating to any of Trump's advisors' phones. The team knew that during the early stages of the investigation in 2018, Trump would still speak with Cohen over the phone. Indeed, Cohen confirmed to me that Trump last called him on April 9, 2018—the day the FBI conducted the search warrant at Cohen's home, office, and hotel room as part of the SDNY prosecution. According to Cohen, Trump told him over the phone to "stay strong," that "nothing is going to happen," and that "this is all bullshit." A prosecutor might see those comments by Trump as evidence of an attempt to keep Cohen quiet, which could constitute witness tampering—a predicate crime that a prosecutor could use to obtain permission for a wiretap.

Unfazed by Trump's status as the sitting president, the frontline team working the Cohen case raised internally within the SDNY the possibility of seeking a wiretap on one or more cell phones of key Trump advisors. The team understood that such a wiretap might yield evidence of conversations involving Trump himself. If granted, the wiretap would have been a historic first. No sitting president, or former president, has ever been captured speaking on a court-ordered wiretap. (Richard Nixon taped himself in the Oval Office, as we'll discuss later, which stands on different legal and political footing.) Importantly, any evidence gleaned from the wiretap would have survived Trump's presidency, and would have been usable against him once he became subject to indictment upon leaving office.

But Strauss quickly rebuffed the proposed wiretap, unwilling to take the historic if precipitous step of bugging a phone that might capture conversations with the sitting president. Without question, such a move would have been extraordinarily controversial and explosive. If the SDNY team had pursued the wiretap, they first would have needed approval from Main Justice; all wiretaps must go down to DOJ headquarters for review, and this one surely would've received particularly intense scrutiny. It's doubtful in retrospect that Main Justice would have signed off, given how DOJ bosses would later water down the SDNY's work on the Cohen case (as we'll see in a moment), or that a federal judge would ultimately have authorized the wiretap. And if the SDNY did somehow get up on a wire, they eventually could have faced public and political backlash for intruding on the confidential, political, and personal communications of the sitting president. (Wiretaps are secret while they are ongoing, of course, but typically are unsealed and become public after their conclusion.)

There's simply no way to know just how much additional evidence of criminality or other misconduct, if any (by Trump or others), a wiretap might have revealed. Strauss quickly snuffed any chance of finding out.

. .

Even without the wiretap, the SDNY had assembled more than enough evidence to support a charge against Cohen by summer 2018. And in the impending indictment of Cohen, the SDNY had a potent vehicle to expose to the public the full extent of Trump's criminal conduct. They intended to do just that—originally, at least.

A little background here. Generally, there are two types of indictments. First, there's the bare-bones indictment, which essentially just names the defendant and then recites the technical language of whatever laws he allegedly violated. It's dry and conclusory, and it provides little to no detail.

And then there's the "speaking indictment," which, well, speaks. Prosecutors often use speaking indictments to lay out the facts supporting the charges. Sometimes speaking indictments give the basic who-what-when-where, and sometimes they contain driving narratives and vivid detail. The SDNY routinely issues speaking indictments that run dozens of pages; my personal longest was fifty-six pages. The bottom line: in any charging document, prosecutors can say as little or as much as they want. And it's all available to the public.

One natural consequence of the speaking indictment is what prosecutors sometimes call "collateral damage." People almost never commit crimes alone, at least not the complex crimes that typically land in the federal system. So in laying out the charges against a defendant, prosecutors inevitably—and sometimes intentionally—include language about the actions of other people who are not directly charged in that indictment. The prevailing norm is to refrain from specifically naming those people in the charging document itself. You'll notice that in most federal indictments, the only people identified by proper name are the charged defendants. Everyone else gets a generic label. Sometimes those labels are descriptive but benign: the Accountant, the Clerk, the Bystander. Prosecutors will attach a number where there are multiple generic names in the same indictment: Person-1, Victim-2, Individual-3.

But there's a subset of these generic labels that can be more charged, that indicate some level of wrongdoing. Prosecutors sometimes must refer to people who were involved in a crime, but are not charged in the indictment itself. This can happen if, for example, the uncharged person has committed bad acts, but the evidence doesn't quite support specific criminal charges. Sometimes the generically labeled wrongdoer cannot be charged because he has already been prosecuted, or because he has died, or because he has been given immunity—or, in a very narrow category of cases, because he is the sitting president of the United States.

Accordingly, the SDNY team had to decide how it would refer to Trump in the Cohen indictment. The nuclear option would've been to label Trump as an unindicted co-conspirator: "co-conspirator 1," abbreviated as "CC-1." In 1974, the same grand jury that had indicted seven defendants in the Watergate scandal created a report (not an indictment) that formally labeled Richard Nixon as an unindicted co-conspirator. The grand jury issued its report secretly in February 1974. When the public learned in June that Nixon had been identified as a co-conspirator, the impact was seismic. Two months later, following a series of devastating public revelations and setbacks in court, Nixon was a goner.

A similar "co-conspirator" designation for Trump would have hit like a bomb. The "CC-1" label would convey to the world that, in the eyes of the SDNY, Trump was liable for the charged campaign finance crimes, and would have been charged but for his status as sitting president—and perhaps that he *should* be charged when he no longer held that status. It would have put Trump on the same historical plane as Nixon.

Of course, we know Trump wasn't ultimately labeled a co-conspirator. What's less known is why the SDNY held its fire.

As the SDNY was gearing up to charge Cohen, Trump's own legal representatives got involved to try to limit the collateral damage. One of Trump's attorneys, Joanna Hendon, requested and was granted an in-person meeting with prosecutors to make her pitch on her client's behalf. This accommodation was unusual, though not unreasonable. While prosecutors almost always will grant an audience to the attorney for a person who is about to get charged, it's far from a given that prosecutors will afford the same opportunity to lawyers for third parties who are at no risk of a charge but want to minimize the damage done by the indictment of some other person.

Hendon had worked as an SDNY prosecutor from 1995 until 2001. During much of that time, Khuzami was her colleague and supervisor. By 2018, Hendon was a veteran litigator at a private law firm. She was widely respected in New York legal circles, and at the SDNY itself. (I can attest as an SDNY alum that the office tends to give its own former members a favorable presumption of credibility.) Hendon was assertive when necessary, but uninterested in causing needless conflict, particularly with the SDNY prosecutors who held her client's fate in their hands. She had no interest in media attention, or in Trump's politics, or in any politics. To Hendon, it was a legal representation to be handled zealously and professionally, like any other.

Hendon was a notable departure from some of Trump's other chosen legal representatives over the years. She was no Rudy Giuliani or Alan Dershowitz, in style or substance. It's one thing to go on Newsmax and screech that your client is being persecuted, but it's another to walk into the SDNY and convince a group of hard-driving federal prosecutors to see things your way.

Hendon met with Khuzami and the team of SDNY prosecutors late in the summer of 2018, as the Cohen indictment was in the latter stages of construction. She had a multi-tiered pitch. First, she argued to the team of SDNY prosecutors on the Cohen case that, given DOJ policy, they could not indict Trump while he held office. This argument ultimately wasn't necessary, of course, because the SDNY had already reached the same conclusion on its own. But Hendon, understanding the SDNY's history of headstrong independence, wanted to make absolutely sure the office wouldn't go rogue and charge her client, DOJ policy be damned. Khuzami assured her that the SDNY agreed it could not indict a sitting president and had no plans to indict Trump while he was in office.

With an imminent indictment off the table, Hendon focused on the damage that the SDNY might do to her client, Trump, through the Cohen indictment. She first argued that the SDNY should not charge Cohen at all with campaign finance crimes, primarily citing the Justice Department's failed prosecution of former Democratic presidential candidate John Edwards on similar charges in 2012. Trump's legal team pushed for this outcome not because they wanted the best for Cohen, but rather because a decision not to charge Cohen would suggest that the hush money payments were simply not criminal at all. If there was no campaign finance charge against Cohen, then Trump would have little if anything to worry about.

This pitch, ambitious as it was, fell flat. The SDNY prosecutors were confident that theirs was a different, and stronger, case against Cohen than the Justice Department's against Edwards years before. The team consulted with David Harbach, who had once worked at the SDNY and later became the lead DOJ prosecutor in the Edwards trial. Nobody understood the nuances of campaign finance law, and the problems with the Edwards case, better than Harbach. He agreed that the case against Cohen (and by extension, potentially Trump) was stronger than the Edwards case. There was no way the SDNY was going to walk away from holding Cohen accountable for his role in the illegal payoff scheme.

Hendon next argued that if the SDNY was going to charge Cohen with campaign finance crimes, they should indict him only on what prosecutors call a "substantive" count (a completed violation of the law) rather than a conspiracy count (an agreement with some other person to violate the law). Here's why that distinction mattered to Trump's team. One person can commit a substantive crime—a campaign finance violation, or any other offense—by himself. But a conspiracy charge necessarily requires an agreement between two or more people to commit a crime. Trump's representatives might be able to spin a substantive charge as "Cohen committed the crime alone," whereas a conspiracy charge would mean "Cohen committed the crime along with at least one other person." Ultimately, the SDNY charged Cohen only with substantive campaign finance crimes, but not conspiracy—a subtle but meaningful win for Trump.

Hendon also urged the SDNY team not to identify Trump in any documents relating to Cohen as a co-conspirator, "CC-1." She argued that to label Trump as "CC-1" would do untold damage to his reputation, and that because he could not be indicted, he would have no forum available in which to defend himself and clear his name. This argument paralleled the rationale that Mueller would offer months later when he explained in his final report that he would not explicitly state whether Trump had committed any crimes: "Fairness concerns counseled against potentially reaching that judgment when no charges can be brought. The ordinary means for an individual to respond to an accusation is through a speedy and public trial, with all the procedural protections that surround a criminal case. An individual who believes he was wrongly accused can use that process to seek to clear his name." Note the bootstrapping of benefits accruing to Trump here: *We can't indict him because he's president, and we can't name him as a co-conspirator because we can't indict him.*

The SDNY shared those concerns, to an extent. The Cohen prosecution team gave serious internal consideration to branding Trump as "CC-1," but ultimately the prosecutors concluded that it was a close call and that the bosses at Main Justice almost certainly would squash it anyway. Instead, the SDNY drafted an indictment of Cohen that identified Trump as "Candidate-1." That seemed to be a fairly innocuous label; there's nothing wrong with being a candidate, after all. But Main Justice saw it differently. In the view of the DOJ bosses overseeing the case from Washington, DC, it would be too direct a swipe at Trump to label him "Candidate-1." Who else but Trump could fit that description? Main Justice preferred a bit more circumspection. The SDNY team joked internally that, just to be obstinate toward Main Justice, they should revise the indictment to refer to Trump as "President-1."

Rebuffed by DOJ bosses, the SDNY instead settled on the now-infamous moniker: "Individual-1." It's hard to think of anything less inflammatory; every human being is, after all, an individual. At the same time, the draft Cohen indictment would leave zero doubt about the true identity of this mysterious Individual-1. The final charging document specified that "in or about January 2017, COHEN left the Company and began holding himself out as the 'personal attorney' to Individual-1, who at that point had become the President of the United States." Only one person on the planet became president of the United States in January 2017.

But Main Justice's downgrading of Trump's generic label was just the start. A bigger fight loomed: regardless of how the SDNY labeled Trump in the indictment, how much detail would they include about his criminal conduct?

The SDNY team decided to lay it all out, in detail, in the impending indictment of Cohen. "Whether we were going to charge him [Trump] or not, this was a matter of public importance, and we felt the public had to know," one member of the SDNY team told me. If the SDNY couldn't indict Trump, the prosecution team believed it was imperative that they at least inform the American public of the extent of his conduct. And the team feared that if they did omit the details of Trump's wrongdoing, the public would think they pulled their punches on the president.

Accordingly, the SDNY team put together a draft indictment of Cohen that laid out in extensive detail Trump's central involvement in the hush money scheme. The draft Cohen indictment was a full accounting, running over fifty pages in one iteration—essentially both a formal indictment of Cohen and a public excoriation of Trump, only without charges attached. In the SDNY team's view, the whole story needed to be told, and there was no way to do that fully and honestly without detailing Trump's conduct. The SDNY's draft indictment left no doubt: Trump wasn't merely a bystander or an unwitting beneficiary of the campaign finance crime. He was the driving force behind the scheme, and likely criminally liable for it.

But the bosses at Main Justice shut it down.

· ·

The SDNY is famously the most independent of the Justice Department's ninety-four US attorney's offices. Lawyers and judges commonly refer to the SDNY as the "Sovereign District of New York"—only half-jokingly, if that much, and not always affectionately. Google the phrase "fiercely independent SDNY," and you'll get pages upon pages of search results.

As an insider, I can proudly confirm: the SDNY absolutely does view itself as its own sovereign entity, unbound by the rules and restrictions that apply to other prosecutors or to other governmental agencies in general. During my time at the SDNY, we clashed regularly with our distant bureaucratic tormentors at Justice Department headquarters in Washington, DC. On smaller matters, we'd sometimes flatly ignore DOJ's guidance. I was informally instructed early on to just blow off some petty DOJ administrative requirements—monthly time sheets and pedantic training requirements. Or we'd simply decline to consult with Main Justice, even if technically required to do so on certain types of cases. For example, we were supposed to get pre-approval from Main Justice before taking major steps on any racketeering case; often we just didn't. At one point we learned that the attorney general and other top officials would be coming to New York to attend a press conference on a Mafia case of mine. When I casually said something like, "So, the big bosses are coming to town for this," one of my supervisors snapped, "They're not our bosses. We don't work for them, and they don't tell us what to do." Lesson learned.

But we also understood that in the end, like it or not, the SDNY is part of the US Department of Justice. We could resist Main Justice and fight for our turf, and battle to bring the most important cases, and generally be headstrong and difficult and maybe even a wee bit arrogant. But we also knew that we were ultimately subject to the direct orders of the attorney general and other top DOJ brass. We SDNY prosecutors are stubbornly independent, but we're not anarchists.

While the SDNY ran the Cohen investigation, its leadership fully understood that they had to send any potential indictment to Main

Justice for pre-approval. DOJ's *Justice Manual* specifically requires notification by US attorney's offices to department brass for any "major developments" on any "significant investigations" or on any case with a "high likelihood of coverage in national news media." An indictment on the Cohen case would qualify, obviously.

Shortly before the anticipated arrest of Cohen, Khuzami sent the draft indictment—complete with a full accounting of Trump's wrongdoing—down to DC for review by DOJ bosses. A few days later, he got word back from Main Justice: no go.

Ed O'Callaghan was another SDNY alum—we truly are everywhere—who had served as co-chief of the office's Terrorism and National Security Unit before he left the office in 2008. While the vast majority of SDNY prosecutors leave for lucrative law firm gigs, O'Callaghan took an unorthodox path when he went to work for Republican presidential candidate Senator John McCain. Among other duties, O'Callaghan served as part of vice presidential candidate Sarah Palin's self-titled Truth Squad, which purportedly would set the record straight as scandals swirled around the former Alaska governor. O'Callaghan later worked at a private law firm until he returned to the Justice Department in 2017 in the Trump administration, where he eventually became the principal associate deputy attorney general—PADAG, to insiders—typically a primary point of contact for Main Justice with US attorneys across the country.

O'Callaghan and Khuzami were former SDNY colleagues, overlapping there in the late 1990s and early 2000s, and now Khuzami was running the Cohen case in Manhattan while O'Callaghan was a boss down at Main Justice in DC. After reviewing the SDNY's draft indictment of Cohen, O'Callaghan told Khuzami that the SDNY needed to remove the language detailing Trump's role in the hush money scheme and the charged campaign finance crimes. In DOJ's view, the Trump-specific language was superfluous and threatened to harm the reputation of an unindicted party. It would be unfair to Trump, and potentially damaging more broadly to the country, to effectively accuse the sitting president of a crime without affording him a formal mechanism to defend himself. (This mirrored the argument made by Hendon, Trump's own attorney.)

Khuzami—known by colleagues to be serious, aggressive, and headstrong—was furious, as were other members of the SDNY's prosecution team. In the prevailing view at the SDNY, DOJ brass sought to sanitize the indictment by pulling out all substantive references to Trump's involvement. Khuzami pushed back, with eager support and encouragement from the SDNY team. He contended that details about Trump's involvement were necessary to establish the charges against Cohen. And the SDNY team argued that DOJ could not and should not hide vital information from the public about the sitting president's role in a federal felony. If the outside world ever learned that the Justice Department held back on Trump-specific content, the SDNY team argued, it would appear that they had taken a soft touch on a powerful target—anathema to SDNY tradition and to strong prosecutorial practice generally.

Ultimately, the resistance effort by Khuzami and his team was unavailing. After a series of occasionally heated but substantive discussions, Main Justice held firm, and the SDNY acceded. No matter how vehemently the SDNY disagreed, their will could be, well, trumped by the bosses down at DOJ headquarters.

In the end, virtually all of the vital details about Trump's participation in the crime were stripped out of the Cohen charging document before it was filed publicly. The final version of the document—technically called an "information" rather than an indictment because, by then, Cohen and his attorneys had agreed to plead guilty to it immediately—referred to Trump as Individual-1 rather than Co-Conspirator-1 or even Candidate-1.

More importantly, the document was essentially devoid of substance relating to Trump's conduct. The final Cohen information uses the term "Individual-1" seven times total, mostly in passing. The information specifies that Individual-1 owned the "Company" (the Trump Organization); that Cohen worked as a private attorney to Individual-1; that Individual-1 ran for office and became president of the United States in 2017; and that Cohen made the hush money payments to protect Individual-1's political interests. Notably absent: any mention whatsoever of Individual-1's central participation in the scheme itself. If a person entirely unfamiliar with public reporting around the hush money scheme read only the Cohen information, he could reasonably conclude that Trump was an unwitting beneficiary of the hush money payments, entirely uninvolved in the criminal scheme's formulation or execution—that Cohen and others decided on their own to make the payments to benefit Trump, but without Trump's knowledge or participation.

Cohen pled guilty to the Trump-sanitized charging document, including campaign finance crimes and other offenses, on the same day it was unveiled publicly, August 21, 2018. (Three months later, in November 2018, Cohen pled guilty to another charge, for lying to Congress about Trump's efforts to build a skyscraper in Moscow.)

SDNY prosecutors didn't say anything meaningful about Trump's involvement in the illegal hush money scheme until they filed a sentencing memorandum in the Cohen case on December 7, 2018. This time the SDNY—frustrated by and wary of how Main Justice had stifled the original charging document—declined to consult with DOJ bosses at all. As a practical matter, and on any reasonable reading of internal policy, the SDNY should have obtained pre-approval from Justice Department brass. But this time, the SDNY hewed to its own tradition of independence bordering on defiance, and filed its sentencing memo in the Cohen case, Main Justice be damned. Easier to ask for forgiveness than permission.

Even then, though, the SDNY provided minimal detail about Trump. The crux of it came in a single sentence, toward the bottom of page 11 of the Cohen sentencing memorandum: "In particular, and as Cohen himself has now admitted, with respect to both payments, he acted in coordination with and at the direction of Individual-1."

On one hand, this was just about as clear a statement as possible that the SDNY believed Trump was part of, and likely criminally liable for, the scheme to make illegal hush money payments. There's little ambiguity about it: Cohen committed a campaign finance crime (he had by that point been charged and pled guilty), and he did it "in coordination with and at the direction of" Trump. It's essentially a mathematical equation, a prosecutorial near-certainty: Person A committed crime + "in coordination with and at the direction of" Person B = Person B committed the same crime. Prosecutors would still have to establish that Trump had the necessary criminal state of mind, but the SDNY's statement put the ball on the one-yard line, right at the brink of criminality.

The SDNY gave the world its bottom line in the sentencing memo. But once again, it left most of the detail on the cutting-room floor: nothing about the specific nature or extent of Trump's involvement in the criminal scheme, and no detail about the evidence against him. The SDNY calculated that it could get away with one summary sentence about Trump's involvement, but that it would be too aggressive, too insubordinate, to lay out the precise details that Main Justice had vetoed earlier. The SDNY was willing to push back against DOJ bosses, but only so far.

Even after Cohen was sentenced in December 2018, Justice Department leadership kept up the effort to undermine the SDNY's campaign finance case. The *New York Times* reported in 2020 that shortly after William Barr took over as attorney general in February 2019, he questioned SDNY prosecutors about their decision to charge Cohen with campaign finance violations (but, conspicuously, not on the other tax fraud and bank fraud charges—which had nothing to do with Trump). According to the *Times*, Barr "instructed Justice Department officials in Washington to draft a memo outlining legal arguments that could have raised questions about Mr. Cohen's conviction and undercut similar prosecutions in the future."

Barr took this unusual step even though Cohen's case was over. Members of the SDNY team confirmed to me that they immediately recognized that Barr's goal was to limit the eventual damage the SDNY might do to Trump by casting doubt on the applicability of campaign finance charges to the hush money scheme, writ large. As one SDNY team member noted, the Justice Department had already approved the campaign finance charge against Cohen before Barr's arrival, so Barr's determination to re-examine the case was facially suspect and looked like political protectionism toward Trump. The SDNY's prosecution team, true to the office's tradition of independence, pushed back, and DOJ's Office of Legal Counsel (OLC) concluded that the SDNY's charges against Cohen were in fact legally supported. Ultimately Barr—seeing his gambit to undo Cohen's conviction on campaign finance charges cut off at every turn—backed down.

But a few months after Barr's near-intervention, the SDNY subtly undermined its own ability to eventually bring charges against Trump. In early 2019 a group of national media outlets, including CNN (where I work as an on-air senior legal analyst), requested that the court unseal—make public, essentially—certain confidential documents relating to the Cohen case. The SDNY initially advised the court that the documents should remain sealed because its investigation was ongoing, and the court obliged. But in July 2019 the judge wrote in an order, "The Government now represents that it has concluded the aspects of its investigation that justified the continued sealing of the portions of the Materials relating to Cohen's campaign finance violations."

In other words, the SDNY stated on the record that it was done with the hush money investigation, or at least some large part of it, and the documents therefore could be made public. This didn't necessarily foreclose an eventual Trump prosecution by the SDNY. It's possible prosecutors believed they had already amassed sufficient evidence to charge Trump, and didn't need to keep investigating—though the prevailing ethic at the SDNY is that an investigation isn't over until the jury comes back with its verdict. Or the SDNY might have believed it had enough evidence, and that public disclosure of the documents did not compromise any ongoing investigation. There's nothing necessarily binding about the SDNY's statement that part of its investigation had concluded; prosecutors could have reopened the investigation at any time, at their own discretion. But as a practical matter, it's difficult for any prosecutor's office to revive a case after it has already formally told a judge that the investigation is closed, and after the judge has relied on that representation to give the public access to materials from that case. Trump wasn't technically in the clear, but the SDNY's statement undoubtedly made a future prosecution less likely.

It's easy enough to cast the SDNY as the righteous crusader, eager to speak truth to power and expose Trump's criminal malfeasance to the public, only to be stifled by the weak-kneed, in-the-bag bosses at Main Justice. There's some truth to that narrative, but it also oversimplifies matters. Even the staunchest SDNY advocate must grapple with this difficult question: If the SDNY felt so confident singling out Trump, and specifying in a public filing that he played a key role in a federal crime, why didn't they ever charge him? We know that DOJ policy precluded an indictment while Trump held the presidency. But why didn't the SDNY charge him after he left office in January 2021?

We'll circle back to this question at the end of this book. The answer, as you'll see, is complicated. Trump always claimed that the SDNY had no case against him, but we know that's not true, and we now know that the SDNY knew it wasn't true. It says much about our criminal justice process, the inherent advantages afforded to the most powerful among us, and Trump's unique capacity to exploit the system to his own advantage that the former president got away with it—even when under scrutiny by the fearsome SDNY.

BOSS TACTICS

How Criminal Kingpins
Play the System

Chapter 3

CONTROL THE LAWYERS, CONTROL THE GAME

"I just talked to Hootie's girlfriend," FBI special agent Rob Herbster said when I picked up the phone. Herbster was doggedly even-keeled, but I could detect some giddiness in his voice. "He wants to talk. But he's scared shitless."

This was, potentially, a huge break. We had charged Anthino "Hootie" Russo—apparently the nickname was a reference not to the 1990s pop band but rather to Russo's habit of greeting friends by yelling, inexplicably, "Hootie-hoo!"—as part of a Gambino family takedown. Russo was a mid- to lower-level player in the case, listed fourteenth of the twenty-one names on our indictment; typically, we'd order the defendants not alphabetically but according to their Mafia ranks, powerhouses up top and mopes down below.

Russo was a Gambino "associate," meaning he had not yet been formally "made," or initiated as a full member. But he was on the rise. He was well connected on the streets and helped the mob run its drug, gambling, and loan-sharking rackets. Most intriguingly, Russo might be able to deliver valuable information about the top handful of names on the indictment—the Gambino family's acting boss Bartolomeo Vernace, the consiglieri (advisor and third overall in charge) Joseph Corozzo, and a powerful captain who ran the family's fastest-growing crew, Alphonse Trucchio.

But there was one catch. Ordinarily, when a defendant wants to cooperate, he tells his lawyer, who then contacts prosecutors to set up the initial meeting. In this case, however, Russo had sent word to the FBI through his girlfriend because he knew he couldn't tell his own lawyer that he wanted to flip. The problem, you see, was that Russo's lawyer didn't exactly work for Russo exclusively. Rather, as often happened in the mob, the lawyer had a conflict of interest arising from his long-standing relationship with the Gambino family's leadership.

The deal was simple, if typically unstated. The powerhouses have the money, so they provide and pay for lawyers for everyone on the indictment. It can get costly, but the benefits are enormous. First, by carefully selecting and controlling the attorneys, the bosses get to call the shots—who brings what motion, who pleads guilty, who goes to trial. More importantly, it is nearly impossible for lower-ranking guys to flip. How can they, if their lawyers will report back up the chain of command that their client is interested in talking to the feds? A marginal player like Russo typically doesn't even have the option of choosing his own counsel. Rather, he'll find out on the day of arrest that he has been "given" a certain lawyer by the Gambino powers-that-be. We sometimes called these lawyers "house counsel" because they represent the mob's institutional interests, such as they are, above those of the individual client.

Certain defense lawyers were well attuned to this dynamic. They understood that if they did advise their clients about the possibility of cooperating—which typically could result in enormous sentencing benefits—they might be branded a "rat lawyer" and henceforth banned from the list of trusted (and paid) house counsel. More than once, when I suggested that a lawyer might want to discuss the possibility of cooperation with his client, I got this indignant response: "I don't do cooperation" (or, as I occasionally heard it put more bluntly, "I don't do rats"). This is, of course, entirely unethical. Any lawyer has a duty to advise his client of all available options. To omit or foreclose one of those options—often the best one for the client, cooperation—to preserve the lawyer's own ability to get a certain line of future work is ethically indefensible but often overlooked by judges, prosecutors, and attorney licensing bodies.

The phenomenon of house counsel was so predictable that we'd sometimes play this parlor game around it. Anytime we were preparing for a takedown, I'd try to predict which defense lawyers we'd see in court the next morning to represent the newly arrested mobsters. I wouldn't get them all, but usually I'd accurately predict a solid majority, sometimes to the astonishment of younger prosecutors. How'd I pull off this little prosecutorial Nostradamus routine? Easy. I knew it was all about power and money, and the bosses had both. If we had, say, twenty-one Gambino defendants, as in Russo's case, I'd tick off the names of about that many defense lawyers we knew to be house lawyers—those who understood how the game was played, who would take the money from the bosses (sometimes funneled through other sources, usually without asking too many questions), and who understood that their true mission was to keep their less powerful clients from breaking rank and talking.

So despite his apparent interest in cooperating, Russo was essentially blocked. If he told his lawyer he wanted to cooperate, word would quickly reach the top of the family, with potentially dire consequences. Russo understood that, so he tried a back-channel approach.

Despite the difficulty of Russo's situation, we had one available countermove: shadow counsel. I had heard of this exotic, little-known legal procedure, but I had never tried it myself before. Here's how it works. The prosecutor writes a motion and files it "under seal" (secretly, that is) with the judge. The motion explains that the defendant apparently wants to cooperate but can't because his lawyer has an undisclosed conflict of interest—namely, loyalty to the bosses or the family rather than to the defendant himself. The motion requests that the judge secretly appoint a separate, independent lawyer (the so-called shadow counsel), who then meets quietly with the defendant, determines if the defendant is in fact being blocked from cooperating, and then reports back to the judge and prosecutor.

I drafted up the motion, feeling a bit of a charge from the cloak-and-dagger nature of it all. Herbster and I then walked it over personally to the judge's chambers. No electronic filing on this one, too risky. As the judge read over our papers explaining Russo's predicament, his face lit up at the unusual scenario. As he signed his name, he said, "I'll be interested to see how this one turns out." The judge assigned Jim DeVita—a respected veteran defense lawyer and former SDNY prosecutor who had, decades before, tried and convicted the notorious socialite tax cheat Leona Helmsley—to serve as Russo's shadow counsel.

A few days later, my phone rang. It was DeVita. "You guys were right," he said in his gravelly but amiable voice. "He's in if you want him."

This was, of course, great news. But now we had another problem. Russo was being held at the Metropolitan Correctional Center (MCC), a run-down, overcrowded federal prison in Lower Manhattan, along with about a dozen of his Gambino codefendants. I can attest, having spent hours and days inside the MCC, that the place was downright claustrophobic; I would gulp the outdoor air every time I left. And in those tight quarters, everybody is in everybody else's business. As another cooperator once put it to me, "If you take a piss in a different urinal than usual, everyone knows about it."

We had to get Russo out of there, quickly and quietly. To leave him in the MCC and hope nobody noticed that he had switched lawyers, or that he was being pulled out of the general population to meet with prosecutors, would expose him to near-certain retribution—perhaps the kind that comes on the sharpened butt end of a toothbrush.

Fortunately, the MCC was physically connected to the adjacent courthouse, and the SDNY's offices, by a series of old underground tunnels and aboveground bridges controlled by the US Marshals. Those walkways had been sealed off years before due to security concerns, but they could still be used in emergencies. So we put in a discreet word with the Bureau of Prisons and the US Marshals, who helped us execute a delicate, coordinated extraction.

First, a prison guard called Russo's name, told him he had a "take-out" for an attorney visit, and walked him out of the general holding area. (I eventually learned that we had nearly flubbed this part; another inmate later told us, "As soon as I heard them call for Hootie, I knew he was flipping—you don't get attorney visits at that time of day.") The prison guard then took Russo directly to Herbster, who was waiting in the prison's administrative wing. Herbster took custody of Russo and walked him right out of the MCC, through one of those old tunnels (which the marshals had opened specially for us), and into the SDNY's offices.

I had only a few minutes to speak with Russo before the FBI whisked him away. I remember asking him, "You're sure you want to do this, right?" He responded, flustered, "Yeah, but you almost got me killed with that takeout." He also asked if somebody could go back and get his personal belongings. "We'll grab whatever we can, and you'll get new stuff soon, don't worry," I told him. The FBI then transported Russo to a prison several hundred miles away, where he was held safely while we began the cooperation process.

Russo ultimately did cooperate, quite productively. He gave us incriminating information about most of his codefendants, including the bosses. All twenty of his codefendants pled guilty and did prison time, due largely to Russo's cooperation. I eventually wrote Russo a sentencing letter—called a 5K letter, after the relevant section of the sentencing guidelines—and he received a major break from the judge.

Russo's cooperation was key to the case, and to taking down the top-ranking Gambinos on the indictment. But it wouldn't have

happened without the extraordinary measures we took to outma-
neuver the bosses—getting special permission to assign "shadow
counsel" and then the coordinated removal of Russo from the MCC.
The bosses had made it as difficult as possible for Russo to cooperate, and for prosecutors to gain the benefit of his cooperation. They
were able to do so because they had the ability to pay for lawyers to
control Russo and the entire slate of defendants, primarily to keep
them quiet.

There's no way to know how many times some lower-ranking
player in a case involving a larger organization—the Mafia, or a
drug trafficking organization, or a political outfit—has wanted to
cooperate but effectively been prevented because some powerhouse
was paying for his lawyer. But I'm certain that Russo, who managed to break through those barriers, was more the exception than
the rule.

• •

Donald Trump is famous for using his money to buy glitzy country
clubs, schmaltzy casinos, and gilded hotels. But he also harnessed
the power of his wealth to protect himself, and others around him,
from criminal prosecution.

During the 2016 and 2020 presidential runs, the Trump campaign
and pro-Trump political action committees raised well over a billion
dollars. Some portion of that money paid for the traditional campaign assets: lawn signs, staff salaries, television ads, MAGA hats.
But Trump also spent his campaign funds on something decidedly
less get-out-the-vote than get-out-of-jail: lawyers.

The *New York Times* and the nonpartisan Campaign Finance Institute determined that from 2015 to 2020, Trump and his affiliated
political entities spent over $58 million in campaign donations on
legal fees. To put that in context, Trump's two presidential prede-

cessors, Barack Obama and George W. Bush, each spent less than $11 million on lawyers.

Of course, any major political campaign incurs fees for standard election-related legal work—compliance, review of ads, FEC filings, and the like—and some of Trump's $58 million went to such uses. (It's impossible to tell from those FEC filings, which contain limited detail, precisely how much Trump spent on conventional legal costs.) But campaign money also funded a flood of litigation designed to advance and protect the personal interests of Trump and his allies.

For example, the *Times* noted that the Trump campaign and the Republican National Committee spent $1.8 million to challenge a California law requiring candidates for office to publicly disclose their tax returns. Team Trump spent $1.5 million of campaign funds to sue a former campaign worker who claimed she had been sexually harassed by another staffer. One major law firm, Jones Day, collected over $18 million from Trump-affiliated political entities to defend him in various lawsuits, including one filed by demonstrators who claimed they were assaulted at a Trump rally, and another by a man who claimed he was wrongly arrested at a Trump rally. Trump spent millions in campaign money to sue former employees of his businesses, campaign, and administration who publicly criticized him, including former White House staffers Omarosa Manigault Newman and Cliff Sims. And Trump used political donations to fund defamation lawsuits against media outlets including CNN, the *Times*, and the *Washington Post*.

Trump even took a page out of the mob's playbook. Just as the Gambino family powers-that-be funded Russo's lawyer to try to keep him in line, Trump used campaign money to protect himself in ongoing criminal matters. The Trump campaign and associated political entities used tens of millions of dollars in donations to pay for lawyers who represented potential witnesses in criminal investigations relating to Trump, including Donald Trump Jr., Jared

Kushner, Hope Hicks, and Corey Lewandowski—all of whom witnessed potential criminality by Trump, according to the Mueller report. Trump campaign funds also covered legal fees for his advisor
Boris Epshteyn and bodyguard Keith Schiller, both of whom gave
testimony favorable to Trump in the House's investigation of Russian election interference.

Trump deployed the cash reserves of his private business, the
Trump Organization, to similar effect. According to Michael Cohen, the corporation picked up legal fees for Eric Trump, longtime
Trump Organization chief financial officer Allen Weisselberg, and
controller Jeffrey McConney, among others. In its fraud investigation, the Manhattan district attorney targeted and tried to flip Weisselberg and McConney in particular, given their familiarity with the
inner financial workings of the Trump Organization. Prosecutors
ultimately charged Weisselberg with fraud, and while he agreed to
cooperate against the Trump Organization as a corporate entity, he
refused to cooperate against Trump or any other individual. And
prosecutors granted immunity to McConney by compelling him to
testify in a state grand jury, though his testimony didn't hurt Trump
badly enough to result in an indictment. The Manhattan DA, left
without an effective insider witness who could directly tie the organization's frauds to Trump himself, ultimately declined to indict
him; the state attorney general eventually filed a civil lawsuit alleging fraud, but no criminal charges.

Cohen's saga nicely illustrates the implicit bargain. "Donald would
never part with a dollar from his own pocket. He'd pay for lawyers
using campaign money, Trump Organization money, insurance,"
Cohen told me in an interview for this book. "It was the ultimate
piggybank." Cohen further described Trump's methodology for
keeping his confidants beholden to him: "He'd always be a step or
two behind on payments. Miss the payment for the first month, then
make a partial payment in the second month," Cohen explained.

"Before you know it, you're so deep in legal fees that you can't stop and you need his money to get out of the hole."

That financial pressure to rely on Trump's largesse had the practical effect of preventing people from cooperating, lest they lose Trump's financial backing and meet a fate like Cohen's. When the Mueller investigation began—and before Cohen gave any public indication that he might flip—Trump used campaign funds and Trump Organization money to pay over $1.7 million for Cohen's attorney fees. But when the FBI executed a search warrant on Cohen's office and home in April 2018, it suddenly seemed that he might get arrested—the ultimate incentive to flip. At first Trump tried the sweet-talk approach. He called Cohen a "good person" and a "great guy" on Fox News, and he tweeted that Cohen was "a fine person with a wonderful family . . . who I have always liked and respected," adding that he did not think Cohen would flip (wink, wink). Less visible to the public in the immediate aftermath of the search warrant, but perhaps more resonant, Trump also made a payment of over $48,000 to Cohen's legal team.

Cohen eventually did provide information about Trump to prosecutors and Congress, of course. Trump quickly turned against him, and the money dried up. In an effort to recoup some of his attorney fees, Cohen sued the Trump Organization for $1.9 million in outstanding legal costs that he claimed he was owed as a former employee, alleging that Trump cut him off because he cooperated, in violation of the Trump Organization's original contractual promise to cover his legal fees. But a New York state judge dismissed Cohen's lawsuit in November 2021, and Cohen was stuck with his own massive legal bill.

Only the wealthiest and most powerful people can reach the level of the mob boss, or Trump, who can pay not only for his own legal team but also for lawyers to represent other people who need to be kept in line. While Cohen managed to break away, he did so only at great financial and personal cost. And very few people have the independent financial means and the straight-up chutzpah of a Michael Cohen, making it difficult or impossible to cut the financial leash and cooperate against the boss.

• •

Trump similarly used the power of the purse strings to selectively pay for counsel for potential witnesses in the House of Representatives' January 6 Select Committee's probe.

American Conservative Union chairman Matt Schlapp confirmed to CNN in January 2022 that his organization had raised "over seven figures" from donors, and that he was "in communication with [Trump's] team" about who would receive assistance from this pot of money to pay for legal fees. Trump reportedly was "more than aware of this fund," and encouraged people to make use of it. Schlapp openly admitted—bragged, even—that the money was reserved for those who stonewalled the committee. "We are certainly not going to assist anyone who agrees with the mission of the committee and is aiding and abetting the committee," he told CNN. The deal was right out in the open: Trump might authorize payment for your attorneys, but only if you keep quiet.

The committee's probe hit its stride during the summer of 2022, when it held a series of public hearings that revealed explosive evidence of the effort by Trump and other powerful players to steal the 2020 presidential election. In June 2022, over 13 million people watched on television as Cassidy Hutchinson, a former Trump White House aide, testified that Trump knew that some people in the crowd at the rally held immediately before the January 6 Capitol attack were armed, that Trump nonetheless directed that mob to the US Capitol, and that Trump wanted desperately to accompany them there. Hutchinson also testified that her former boss, White

House chief of staff Mark Meadows, and Trump's personal attorney Rudy Giuliani had sought presidential pardons. Among those in the television-viewing audience were Justice Department prosecutors who, seemingly beaten to the punch by the committee, were "astonished" at Hutchinson's revelations, according to the *New York Times*.

Hutchinson emerged as a star witness for the committee only after she shook loose from her original attorney, Stefan Passantino, a former Trump White House ethics advisor who had been selected and paid for by Trump's political action committee. Hutchinson testified before the committee, behind closed doors, three times while Passantino was representing her. But only after she fired Passantino and retained independent counsel of her own choosing, former federal prosecutor Jody Hunt, did she come forward with additional damning information and agree to testify publicly. The committee, seemingly wary of losing Hutchinson to the sway of Trump-world attorneys again, on June 27 called an emergency hearing—despite having previously declared a two-week recess—to have her testify the next afternoon.

Hutchinson was not the only witness who received legal counsel originally paid for by Trump and his allies. The *New York Times* reported that Trump's "political organization and his allies have paid for or promised to finance the legal fees of more than a dozen witnesses called in the congressional investigation into the Jan. 6 attack, raising legal and ethical questions about whether the former president may be influencing testimony with a direct bearing on him." The *Times* noted that "the episode raised questions about whether Mr. Trump and his allies may, implicitly or explicitly, be pressuring witnesses to hold back crucial information that might incriminate or cast a negative light on the former president."

While it is not necessarily illegal for Trump, or any third party, to recommend a lawyer or to pay for another person's legal fees, the undeniable practical reality is that this makes it more difficult for the recipient to turn against the benefactor. Hutchinson managed to break free, despite enormous financial and political pressure to the contrary. But many other potential witnesses over the years took their assigned counsel, paid for by Trump and his political organization, and either toed the party line or stayed mum altogether.

. .

In the broader view, it is not unusual for a company to pay for attorneys for its employees. This happens regularly, across industries, and lower-ranking individuals or employees often *want* the boss or the corporation to pick up their tab for legal expenses, which can run well into the six figures in major investigations. As a natural consequence, however, it becomes difficult for those employees to cooperate against their superiors and colleagues (or former colleagues)—particularly when the employee understands that the benefactor will cease paying his legal fees if he flips.

In fact, the Justice Department once formally recognized that witnesses are less likely to cooperate when a corporation is paying their attorney's fees. According to long-standing DOJ policy, when prosecutors were determining whether to bring criminal charges against a corporation, "the Department reserved the right to consider such payments negatively in deciding whether to assign cooperation credit to a corporation." In other words, DOJ recognized that it is inherently more difficult for an employee to cooperate with prosecutors when a company pays for that employee's attorneys, and it was formal department policy to discourage and potentially punish this type of arrangement.

But in 2008 the Justice Department reversed course, instead declaring that it generally would *not* penalize companies that paid legal fees for their employees. In announcing the policy change, DOJ declared optimistically that "the Department shares a common cause with responsible corporate leaders: we are both committed to promoting the public's trust and security in our capital markets." The Justice Department enacted this pro-corporation, anti-cooperation policy change through a simple internal memo, which garnered minimal mainstream public attention. And this permissive policy has been on the books at DOJ ever since.

· ·

So what can we learn from this? If you're a boss, it's vital to keep your co-conspirators—employees, colleagues, henchmen, what have you—under your thumb to prevent cooperation. One remarkably effective way to do that is by choosing and paying for their lawyers. An unsophisticated boss might resort to open threats against prospective cooperators, but those tactics are obvious, and likely to provide evidence of obstruction of justice if discovered by prosecutors.

But paying legal fees for others is generally perfectly legal—DOJ is just fine with the practice now—and can even look charitable on the surface. Few people can afford to pay their own attorneys' fees in a major case. And if they're reliant on the boss's money, it becomes difficult to flip. It's a clean, common, and remarkably effective (but often overlooked) tactic that the savviest bosses use, across industries, to protect themselves from prosecution. As the saying goes, "Take the king's coin, do the king's bidding."

Chapter 4

DEFENSE, AT A COST

As Michael Cohen's case illustrates—his total legal bill exceeded $3 million, and he didn't even go to trial—criminal defense lawyers aren't cheap. It can be difficult for a person who doesn't frequent the criminal justice system to imagine how much it can cost just to retain a top-tier private attorney. And it's almost unimaginably expensive, often prohibitively, for any defendant to go all the way to trial.

Prices vary, of course, as does quality (and the two do not necessarily correlate). There's no centralized data on the cost of private defense attorneys, but I informally surveyed former colleagues and other friends who now work as private defense lawyers, mostly at elite New York City firms. For a criminal case with any degree of complexity, fees often start off in the mid- to high six figures, and that's just for the preliminaries—arraignment, discovery, perhaps a guilty plea. If a defendant wants to put up a fight in pretrial motions or exercise his right to go to trial, he'd better be prepared to pay $1 million, and in some instances far more. Plenty of top-shelf defense lawyers routinely (and appropriately) tell prospective clients, "You can't afford me." It's not about arrogance; it's a practical reality.

To be sure, our Constitution guarantees all criminal defendants the right to counsel, even if the defendant is poor. It's the whole "You have the right to an attorney; if you cannot afford an attorney, one will be provided for you" part of the Miranda warnings that cops give upon arrest. On one hand, I reject the common misperception that public defenders are mediocre, overburdened hacks just looking to plead out their client and reduce their caseloads. Of course quality varies—as it does in any profession, including prosecution—but it's untrue in my experience that public defenders are subpar on the whole. In the Southern District of New York, the federal public defenders were excellent trial lawyers, often as good as we were (and that's saying something, coming from an SDNY prosecutor famously self-assured about the office's talents).

The problem was, there were so few of those public defenders. The SDNY federal defenders' office typically has only about 15 public defenders at a time, compared to about 150 federal prosecutors across the street. (Of course, prosecutors represent the government in all criminal cases, while public defenders represent only a fraction of all criminal defendants.) And, candidly, the quality of public defenders at the state level varies more widely. When I was with the New Jersey attorney general's office, we dealt with plenty of superb advocates, but we also encountered some county-level public defenders who could just barely keep their heads above water, and were eager to take quick guilty pleas to manage their caseloads.

Public defenders are only part of the story. Whenever a defendant can't afford private counsel, a judge will assign either a public defender or a private attorney from the Criminal Justice Act (CJA) pool of private attorneys. CJA attorneys are paid a modest hourly rate set by the courts. In 2021, in the SDNY, for example, CJA attorneys were paid $155 per hour—pocket change compared to most private counsel, some of whom charge $1,000 per hour or more. So when a private lawyer draws an assignment off the CJA wheel, she's not quite working for free, but close to it. The incentive to put in the hours is therefore, shall we say, limited. Talk to any private lawyer on the CJA panel, and they'll tell you: it's honorable and important work, but you don't get rich billing time on CJA cases.

Even with the availability of reasonable court-appointed options, rest assured: money matters. A person with means can fully exercise that constitutional right to effective legal counsel, while a poor person gets one roll of the dice and is essentially stuck with the court-appointed public defender or CJA lawyer, for better or worse. And there's no such thing as a court-appointed legal team; it's mostly just the one attorney, on his own, perhaps with basic administrative support if he's lucky.

Even among those who can afford to pay for private counsel, means vary widely. I've had more than one private defense lawyer grumble to me outside an SDNY courtroom that a client was behind on payments or had no money left. "Sure, I'll file that motion to dismiss, but I need to get a visit from Mr. Green first," the old courtroom half-joke went ("Mr. Green" being a euphemism for cash). Simply put, wealthy clients can pay for more service, and they often receive it. And once a prosecutor knows that the defendant cannot afford to go to trial, that tips the plea negotiating table firmly in the prosecutor's favor and drives up the price of a guilty plea. It tends to fall flat when a defense lawyer pounds the table and proclaims, "Well then, we'll see you at trial!" if the prosecutor knows the defendant can't actually afford it.

But rich defendants don't have these concerns. They can pay as many lawyers as they need to spend as many hours as necessary fighting the case as aggressively as possible. Data about total legal bills in specific cases is scarce, but recent examples that have bubbled to the surface help illustrate the point. Notorious drug lord Joaquín "El Chapo" Guzman reportedly spent "at least $5 million" on his defense team in 2018 and 2019, according to the *New York Post*. The *Wall Street Journal* reported that billionaire Raj Rajaratnam spent about $40 million for his legal defense on insider trading charges in 2011. Both went to trial and were convicted and sentenced to long stretches in prison. (Like I said, cost of lawyering does not necessarily correlate to quality.)

I once tried a case against a big-time New York law firm that assigned two partners, two associates, three paralegals, an investigator, and at least one other person whose job apparently was to provide the other staffers with energy bars, highlighters, and Post-it notes. At trial, the defense team spilled over two long tables, and into the first row of the gallery. For weeks leading up to trial, the defense team bombarded the court, and us, with requests, demands, and questions. They filed endless motions in the days leading up to trial, and then seemingly every night during trial, often at absurdly late (or early) hours. One morning I ran into a paralegal at a convenience store outside the courthouse at around 7:00 a.m. and joked to him, "Hey, no motion last night?" He said flatly, "Check your email." Sure enough: a new motion to dismiss, filed at 6:40 a.m. The jury ultimately convicted the defendant, but he received a brand and intensity of legal representation far beyond what any person of normal means, or certainly any poor person, could ever dream of.

· ·

Sometimes even those defendants who have ample money and resources ultimately face justice. But other times, money can make all the difference. Take Jeffrey Epstein, for example.

When the billionaire serial child rapist first faced potential federal criminal charges in Florida in 2006, he assembled a team of high-priced, high-powered, famous (or infamous) defense attorneys to represent him.

Alexander Acosta, then US attorney for the Southern District of Florida, could and should have brought federal charges that would have landed Epstein in prison for decades. Instead, Acosta ultimately gave Epstein an absurdly lenient deal requiring him to plead guilty only to low-level state charges, which resulted in him serving just over one year in a minimum security prison, much of it out of custody on a dubious "work release" program. (More on Acosta's galling mishandling of the Epstein case later in this book.) Only after intense media focus on the injustice of the first Epstein case did the SDNY, more than a decade later, bring the heavy federal charges that Epstein's conduct merited. Epstein, of course, died in prison while awaiting trial in New York in 2019.

Acosta attempted to explain his own disgracefully lenient handling of the original Florida case by whining that Epstein had put together "an army of legal superstars." While I take issue with Acosta's fawning description—several of Epstein's lawyers were past their prime, and have since proven themselves more sputtering hacks than skilled practitioners—the team was certainly stacked with lawyers who were both famous and expensive.

Epstein's legal team featured Ken Starr, the former independent counsel whose sex-fixated investigation led to the 1998 impeachment of Bill Clinton, and famed Harvard professor and criminal defense attorney Alan Dershowitz. (Both Starr and Dershowitz would later represent Trump in his first impeachment.) Dershowitz was personal friends with Epstein, and had socialized and traveled with him. One of Epstein's victims, Virginia Giuffre, alleged in court filings that when she was a minor, she had sex with Dershowitz at least six times. Dershowitz furiously denied those claims and attacked Giuffre as a liar; Giuffre later withdrew her lawsuit and said she "may have made a mistake in identifying Mr. Dershowitz." He conceded only that he did once receive a massage at Epstein's home, purportedly given by a "fifty-year-old Russian woman named Olga," but that "I kept my underwear on."

Beyond the smarmy if imposing one-two punch of Starr and Dershowitz, Epstein also hired legendary Miami-area criminal defense lawyer Roy Black, who had represented a string of celebrities and privileged powerbrokers including Kennedy family member William Kennedy Smith in a rape trial that captivated the nation in 1991, ending with Smith's acquittal; Acosta's predecessor as Miami-area US attorney, Guy Lewis; a former federal prosecutor who once had worked with Acosta, Jay Lefkowitz; and a top-shelf New York–area defense attorney, Gerald Lefcourt. I prosecuted cases against defendants represented by Lefcourt. He was seen as one of the most expensive, influential attorneys in the city, representing celebrities including actor Russell Crowe, hip-hop mogul Irv Gotti, and comedian Tracy Morgan. Yet for Epstein, Lefcourt was a supporting player, several names down on the legal defense roster.

Epstein's team staged an intense legal and investigative blitz. They launched an all-encompassing effort to convince Acosta and his prosecutors not only to give Epstein a pass on federal charges but also to hide the sweetheart deal from Epstein's victims. Epstein's legal team took their case directly to Acosta, and they eventually went over his head to the bosses at Main Justice. At one point Acosta had a private one-on-one breakfast with Lefkowitz, at which Acosta agreed to the defense team's request to hold off on notifying Epstein's victims of the impending sweetheart deal. Acosta later claimed that Epstein's team played dirty and engaged in intimidation tactics: "Defense counsel investigated individual prosecutors and their families, looking for personal peccadilloes that may provide a basis for disqualification." (Dershowitz denied this.)

There's no real doubt that Epstein's powerhouse legal team overwhelmed Acosta, to Epstein's enormous benefit. Maria Villafaña, one of the prosecutors in Acosta's office who spearheaded the Epstein investigation, wrote an internal email to a supervisor expressing her concern that she "didn't want to get to the end and then have the Office be intimidated by the high-powered lawyers"—which is precisely what ultimately happened. Spencer Kuvin, an attorney for three of Epstein's victims, later said publicly of Acosta and his prosecutors, "I think that they just felt overwhelmed. They shirked their responsibility. They weren't up for the fight. They were afraid." A federal court of appeals in 2020 sharply criticized Acosta's handling of the case, finding that he and his prosecutors "seemingly . . .

defer[red] to Epstein's lawyers" at key junctures. And lest there be
any lingering doubt, Acosta himself later bemoaned "a year-long assault on the prosecution and the prosecutors" by Epstein's defense
squad of boldface names.

Acosta himself bears primary fault here. He didn't have to wimp
out and cower before Epstein's legal team. But he did. Epstein had
enough money to pay for a swarm of aggressive, famous defense
lawyers, hoping to overwhelm federal prosecutors and win a lenient
outcome—and it worked.

. .

Smart, wealthy bosses know the importance of playing both sides
of any case: protect yourself by hiring the best defense available—
and, if possible, use some cash to soften up the prosecution. Now,
straight-up bribery of a prosecutor is absurdly obvious, and exceed-
ingly rare. But there's a more subtle way to funnel cash to powerful
prosecutors, and it's perfectly legal.

The highest-ranking federal prosecutors—the US attorney general,
his top deputies, and the US attorneys throughout the country—are
appointed by the president and confirmed by the US Senate. But
the vast majority of top prosecutors in the United States are elected.
Forty-four state-level attorneys general (including the AG for the
District of Columbia) are popularly elected, while only seven are appointed by the governor or other entity. And the vast majority of the
thousands of county-level prosecutors (often called district attorneys
or state's attorneys) across the United States are elected. Only three
states do not hold elections for top county-level prosecutor positions.
In total, over two thousand top state and local prosecutors in the
United States are elected.

Unavoidably, candidates for elected prosecutor positions must
raise money to fund their campaigns. That intersection of prosecu-

tion, politics, and money is inherently fraught. You've got a system in which candidates can accept money from the very same people who could at any time end up in the investigative crosshairs, or who might represent those targets. At an absolute minimum, the presence of money in the prosecutorial system creates the public appearance of conflicts of interest. Any time a prosecutor makes any decision that touches on somebody who has donated to his campaign—or to his electoral opponent's campaign—the public might rightly wonder whether campaign cash played any role in prosecutorial decision-making.

For a worst-case scenario, take the longtime New York County (Manhattan) district attorney Cy Vance. In a remarkable piece of journalism titled "How Ivanka Trump and Donald Trump, Jr., Avoided a Criminal Indictment," the *New Yorker* in 2017 exposed how Vance had, years before, declined to file fraud charges against two of Trump's adult children but only after granting access to a Trump lawyer who was one of Vance's biggest campaign donors.

Starting in 2010, a team of Vance's prosecutors spent two years building a fraud case centered on the Trump Soho, an apartment and condo complex in Manhattan that was intended to establish the Trump kids as major players in New York real estate, despite their lack of professional qualifications. But initial sales lagged at around 15 percent of total occupancy. Unbowed by reality, Don Jr. claimed to potential buyers that far higher numbers—ranging from 31 to 55 percent—had been sold. Ivanka, too, crowed publicly about robust (but nonexistent) sales. These false claims were intended to draw in more investors, and to save the financing deal for the project in its entirety, which required 15 percent occupancy for the closing to occur. Some buyers concluded they'd been cheated and filed a civil lawsuit seeking damages. The building eventually went into foreclosure and was taken over by a creditor.

It's a crime under New York state law to induce a sale by fraudulent

representations. In the case of the Trumps, the conduct likely con-
stituted a felony, given its broad scope and high dollar amount. And
the proof seemed compelling. During their investigation, Vance's
prosecutors reportedly obtained dozens of emails showing that
Don Jr. and Ivanka knew about false information given to potential investors, coordinated on how to use those claims to lure in
prospective buyers, and eventually worried that their grift might be
uncovered.

If you're the Trump kids in this situation, you'll start by trying to
make the whole thing go away. Lawyers for Don Jr. and Ivanka met
several times with the frontline prosecution team, without success.
These meetings are a standard move, called a reverse proffer or a
pitch, in which defense lawyers try to preemptively convince prosecutors not to file charges. Defense lawyers argued that the false statements by Don Jr. and Ivanka were harmless bluster, and that some
buyers did not consider themselves victims. But their arguments did
not persuade the prosecutors in the DA's office who had built the
case.

The Trumps would need to try something else. It was around that
time that their father got involved. According to the *New Yorker*,
Donald Trump, furious at the inability of Don Jr. and Ivanka's lawyers to obtain a favorable result, sent in his own longtime attorney,
Marc Kasowitz. Kasowitz was an accomplished civil litigator, but
he had little experience in criminal matters. He had also, in January
2012, donated $25,000 to Vance's reelection campaign.

In May 2012, just months after making his contribution, Kasowitz
met directly with Vance at the DA's offices in Lower Manhattan.
Shortly before the meeting, Vance returned Kasowitz's donation,
contending that this was his standard practice when dealing with an
attorney who had given money to the campaign.

Typically, a defense lawyer has to work his way up the chain before
getting a sit-down with the top prosecutor. The lawyer first has to

meet with the line-level prosecutors, then the unit chiefs, and then maybe (if granted an audience, which is not a given) with the top prosecutor himself. While lawyers for Don Jr. and Ivanka had already met with prosecutors on the lower rungs on the DA's organizational chart, Kasowitz skipped all the usual steps and went straight to the top. During the meeting, he reportedly raised no new arguments to Vance, beyond those already advanced by the lawyers for Don Jr. and Ivanka to the prosecutors on the case.

Three months after the meeting with Kasowitz, Vance decided to drop the case. There would be no indictments against Don Jr. and Ivanka. Vance overruled his own line-level prosecutors, some of whom had pushed for charges.

Well, you might ask, what's the big deal, if Vance had already returned Kasowitz's campaign donation? Turns out, in September 2012—just weeks *after* he decided to drop the case—Vance accepted a brand-new, even larger campaign contribution from Kasowitz, who personally donated almost $32,000 and raised at least $18,000 more from his law firm partners and employees, among others. When the *New Yorker* article ran years later, in 2017, Vance again returned Kasowitz's money, explaining that "I don't want the money to be a millstone around anybody's neck, including the office's." Of course, Vance himself had placed that millstone around his office's neck (and his own) when he accepted the $50,000-plus worth of donations from Kasowitz in the first place.

..

Turned out, the Trump case wasn't the first time Vance made a decision favorable to a heavy hitter after accepting campaign donations from that person's lawyer. In 2015 Vance declined to bring sexual assault charges against the Hollywood mogul Harvey Weinstein, even though the New York Police Department had a credible victim who was willing to testify and a smoking-gun recording of Weinstein himself admitting his crime.

In 2015, the model Ambra Battilana Gutierrez reported to the NYPD that Weinstein had groped her during a meeting at his office in Manhattan. At the NYPD's urging, Gutierrez wore a recording device to a meeting the next day with Weinstein, during which he begged her to come into his hotel room. On the recording, Gutierrez protests—"I don't want to," "I want to leave"—and then confronts Weinstein directly about why he groped her breasts the prior day. "Oh, please, I'm sorry, just come on in," he pleads on the recording. "I'm used to that. Come on. Please." Gutierrez, sounding surprised, asks, "You're used to that?" Weinstein responds, "Yes. I won't do it again."

For a prosecutor, it doesn't get much better than a recording of a target admitting that he committed the suspected crime, and that it was a habit ("I'm used to that"). Yet despite this evidence, Vance declined to prosecute. "After analyzing the available evidence, including multiple interviews with both parties, a criminal charge is not supported," Vance announced—without addressing why Gutierrez's testimony and the recording of Weinstein admitting a crime didn't suffice.

Weinstein was represented in the matter before the Manhattan DA's office by Elkan Abramowitz, a former law partner of Vance's, who had donated over $24,000 to Vance's campaign, most of it before he took on the Weinstein representation. Another Weinstein lawyer, David Boies (who did not directly deal with the Manhattan DA's investigation), contributed over $55,000 to Vance's campaign over several years, including $10,000 shortly after Vance gave Weinstein a pass.

There is, perhaps, a debate to be had about who got it wrong and right on the prosecutorial merits of the Trump case and the Weinstein case. The Weinstein case rode largely on the testimony of one witness and one incriminating recording, though that evidence is commonly seen by prosecutors as enough to support a charge. The evidence in the Trump case, including emails, seems to establish that Don Jr. and Ivanka lied to real estate investors, knowingly and purposefully. A member of the prosecution team confirmed to me that the evidence was sufficient to indict, but not quite a no-brainer. In response to the *New Yorker*'s reporting, Vance declared in conclusory, self-exonerating fashion, "I did not at the time believe beyond a reasonable doubt that a crime had been committed. I had to make a call and I made the call, and I think I made the right call."

If Vance had simply disagreed with his prosecutors and the police and decided not to file charges against the Trump adult children or Weinstein, the stories would have been notable, but not explosive. Reasonable people can differ about the relative strength of a case, and senior prosecutors can and sometimes do overrule their subordinates.

But the money made all the difference here. There's no way to know for sure whether the campaign contributions influenced Vance's decision-making. Both he and the defense lawyers who donated denied that the money was intended to, or did, influence the outcome of any case. There's nothing to suggest that Vance gave away the case *because of* the donations; that would be bribery, a serious crime, and there's nothing to suggest Vance was a criminal. Things get a bit murkier, however, when we ask whether the donations might have influenced Vance in some subtle or incremental manner, and when we consider what the defense lawyers hoped to achieve by donating tens of thousands of dollars to the prosecutor's re-election campaign.

This much is beyond dispute: the sequence here looked terrible, and damaged public faith in the integrity of Vance and the DA's office. Kasowitz donates generously to Vance; Vance grants a meeting to Kasowitz but returns the money first; Vance accedes to Kasowitz's wishes, dumping the case and overruling the recommendations of prosecutors who had worked the case; Kasowitz donates again to Vance, who accepts the money but then returns it (again) only after a media exposé, years later. And in the Weinstein case, his lawyers made generous campaign donations to Vance both before and after he chose not to bring charges. Any reasonable person would be justified in questioning whether the campaign donations made any impact—even slight, or subconscious—on Vance's exercise of prosecutorial authority.

At a minimum, both transactions raised serious questions about Vance's impartiality. That in itself is problematic. Public perception absolutely matters, and ought to matter, to prosecutors. This concern for perception is why we have rigorous codes of conduct and ethical rules. For example, DOJ's *Justice Manual*—its formal written guidance to federal prosecutors across the country—requires that prosecutors not participate in any case "that would cause a reasonable person with knowledge of the facts to question an employee's [the prosecutor's] impartiality." Paul Grand, a former partner of Vance's in private practice who later was part of the defense team for the Trump adult children, contended in the *New Yorker* article that Vance's decision to drop the case was "reasonable." But he conceded that "the manner in which it was accomplished is curious" and "didn't have an air you'd like." That "air" matters when it comes to prosecutors. If the public even suspects that money can buy special access, then the prosecutor has damaged his credibility and lost public faith.

In this sense, the impact of big money on the criminal justice system is twofold. Rich defendants can pay for more lawyers and more lawyering, gaining high-level access (as in the Vance case) and at times overpowering a weak prosecutor (like Acosta). And even if money has no actual impact on any case, it surely undermines the institutional standing of a prosecutor's office when the boss accepts donations and then takes action favorable to the donor or the donor's client. Prosecution and money are a dangerous mix.

Chapter 5

INSULATION

The Hierarchical Pyramid

The Geas brothers were almost always ready, even eager, to kill. *Almost* always.

But when it came time to go after Adolfo Bruno—"Big Al," as he was known within the Genovese family—even the two vicious Geas boys, Fred and Ty, got cold feet. Bruno was a powerful captain, a swaggering, cigar-chomping mob veteran who ran the Genovese family's lucrative rackets in Springfield, Massachusetts. But Bruno had committed two cardinal sins. He was skimming "tribute" money that he should have been sending down to the family's top brass in New York. And the Genovese family suspected Bruno was talking to the FBI.

The order to kill Bruno came down as all mob hits must (or are supposed to, under standard operating procedure): from the top. At the time, the Genovese family's acting boss—they use "acting" titles much as the US government does, to denote a temporary placeholder until a formal full-time replacement can be appointed—was Artie Nigro, an old-school, Bronx-based mob fixture, short in stature but hard-edged. In keeping with organizational protocol, orders flowed downstream. Nigro gave the command to eliminate Bruno to a young, recently made guy, Anthony Arillotta. Traditionally the recipient of the order then has some leeway to put together a hit team: a triggerman, perhaps somebody to steal a car to use in the hit, maybe a driver, sometimes a backup shooter, potentially a getaway or crash car driver, occasionally somebody to assist with disposal of the body. Each hit is unique; whatever the occasion requires.

So Arillotta went to the Geas brothers, who we can fairly call "bloodthirsty." Put it this way: I've prosecuted plenty of murderers, but the Geases were the only ones who killed for sport, for the reputational enhancement and the pure thrill of it. For example, just three weeks before the Bruno hit, the Geas brothers (and others, including Arillotta) lured one of their own friends, Gary Westerman—who they suspected was talking to the police—into a remote area of Massachusetts, turned their guns on him, shot him, beat him over the head with a shovel, and then buried him in the woods. The FBI would dig up the decomposed body seven years later, as part of our investigation and prosecution. And in 2019, while he was in prison serving a life sentence, Fred Geas bludgeoned to death the notorious Boston mob boss James "Whitey" Bulger, who was then eighty-nine years old. Law enforcement officials confirmed that Bulger was beaten with a padlock stuffed inside a sock. "Mr. Bulger's eyes appeared to have been dislodged from his head, although it was unclear whether his attackers gouged them out or if they were knocked out because he was beaten so severely in the attack," the *New York Times* reported. Fred Geas was *that* kind of killer.

But when Arillotta approached the Geas brothers about the Bruno hit, even they were hesitant. Perhaps they feared that they might eventually suffer fatal consequences of their own if they went after a powerful made guy like Bruno. (The Geases were Greek, so could never get made, which requires Italian ancestry, though there's a highly intellectual dispute within the mob about whether both parents must be Italian or whether only one parent—the father, of course—is sufficient.) Maybe they worried that Bruno was too difficult a target, or that he might have bodyguards around him who would shoot back. Whatever the reason, the Geases (with permission from Arillotta) enlisted a local enforcer, Frankie Roche, to do the dirty work. They saw Roche as a "crash test dummy"—as they put it—who would mindlessly shoot anybody, for any reason, or no reason at all. The Geases gave Roche a few thousand dollars in cash and a gun, and let him do the rest.

Ultimately, Roche chose a direct approach. He knew that Bruno regularly held court and played cards at a downtown social club that functioned as a local Mafia headquarters. So one Sunday night Roche loaded his .45 Magnum, hid behind a soda machine outside the club, and waited. When Bruno finally emerged from the building at around 9:00 p.m., Roche—an imposing six-foot-four specimen with tattoos covering most of his torso, including one that read simply "GOD"—yelled Bruno's name, ran up to him, and emptied five shots into his face, torso, and groin. There was a dispute at trial about whether Roche shot Bruno below the belt intentionally, just to be extra cruel; Roche denied it, and it didn't really matter, legally.

When Roche unloaded his clip into Bruno, it was the last step in a chain reaction. Roche fired those bullets, but the ammunition came from other people far above Roche's Mafia pay grade.

Let's put aside the gore for a moment and focus on the cold math. There were five primary people involved: the instruction to kill Bruno went from (1) Nigro to (2) Arillotta to (3 and 4) Fred and Ty Geas to (5) Roche. That's a straight downhill trajectory, in terms of the power hierarchy, from a boss all the way down to an institutionally powerless enforcer.

All five players were criminally liable for the murder. But when it came to potential legal *risk*, the parties were not all equally situated. When prosecutors and the FBI came knocking, Nigro, as acting boss, enjoyed far more protection than the others. As the top guy, he had the luxury of being able to communicate the order directly to only one other person, Arillotta. He didn't have to say or do anything else. Thus, among all the key players, only one could squarely implicate Nigro in the murder. That's typically how it works; a boss speaks directly with as few people as necessary, and often a quick whisper to just one trusted subordinate is enough to get the job done.

Picture the barbeque scene in *Goodfellas* where a crew member comes over to the boss, Paulie Cicero (played by Paul Sorvino), and whispers something quickly in his ear. Paulie gives a simple nod, and that's that, the crew springs into action. As Ray Liotta's character says in narration, "For a guy who moved all day long, Paulie didn't talk to six people." That scene is entirely consistent with how real-world criminal leaders do business—at least the smart ones. It would be foolish, and reckless, for a boss to talk to more people than necessary. To quote a powerful mobster as he colorfully put it while unwittingly being recorded by an informant in another case of mine, "If you step on a cockroach, you gonna tell the whole world about it?"

Communications with leadership are both scarce and strictly regulated. Only players of a certain rank are permitted to speak directly with the boss. For example, Arillotta, as a made guy, could meet with a boss like Nigro (only upon Nigro's request, of course). But it would have been unthinkable, a grave breach of protocol, for lower-ranking associates like Fred or Ty Geas or Frankie Roche to discuss a murder—or any crime—face-to-face with a boss. Nigro never even met in person or spoke directly with the triggerman, Roche. He didn't need to. The same holds true of other organizations. Bosses often communicate on important matters only with trusted top brass, and the orders flow downhill from there. The rank-and-file who execute (literally, in the mob's case) based on those instructions typically have little or no direct contact with the boss who set the action in motion.

So while only one person could possibly directly implicate Nigro in the murder, the other four lower-ranking players—Arillotta, Fred Geas, Ty Geas, and Roche—all worked together on the hit, and thus all had the ability to turn on and incriminate one another. And that number could have been even higher if, for example, Roche had decided to enlist a getaway driver or a second shooter.

It's way more dangerous to be the guy at the bottom of the ladder. That disparity exists by design, because of the hierarchical structure of the mob, and it's the same in other organizations. Bosses across all industries have the power and the luxury to limit their communications, and hence their criminal exposure. The smartest bosses say as little as necessary to as few people as possible. But lower-ranking operators who carry out the commands usually have no choice but to deal with one another.

Bottom line: Nigro stood a far better chance of evading murder charges than his lower-ranking enforcers did. As it turned out, Arillotta—the one person who could testify directly against Nigro—did flip (as did Roche), enabling us to charge everybody, all the way up to the top. But the odds were stacked in Nigro's favor, solely because he was the most powerful player in the group. If anyone other than Arillotta had flipped, then the four lower-ranking guys who carried out the hit together would have been charged with murder, but Nigro likely would have skated.

Indeed, in the criminal world—and not only the Mafia—nothing protects power like power itself.

· ·

There are plenty of advantages to sitting at the top of any criminal hierarchy. Bosses carry the most power, they make the big decisions, and they make the most money. And then there's one lesser-known but potentially life-altering benefit: it's inherently tougher for prosecutors and cops to put together a case against the guys at the top.

We're used to seeing the image in movies and television of the criminal "org chart," the pyramid-shaped diagram depicting the structure of an illegal enterprise, with each headshot connected to the others by twine or hastily drawn arrows to show lines of command. Prosecutors and law enforcement agents do in fact create and use this type of chart not only for the Mafia—which, thanks to its rigid structure, complete with formal ranks, is particularly amenable to graphic representation—but for other kinds of criminal operations: drug trafficking groups, gangs, fraud syndicates, corrupt corporate and political networks. I'd keep these pyramidal representations of the five Mafia families pinned up on my office corkboard, the largest group (associates) on the bottom, soldiers above them, captains one more layer on top, and then up into management: the consiglieri, the underboss, and finally, at the point of the pyramid, the boss. Whenever a guy got "promoted"—they'd use that terminology in the mob, just like in any other business—I'd cross him off and scribble him in at the new, higher level. If somebody got killed, I'd just scratch him off permanently. Occasionally things changed enough that an FBI agent would drop off a freshly updated graphic: "New Gambino chart came out."

Often (but not always) a criminal case starts at or near the bottom of the organizational flowchart. The prosecutor's hope is that as the case progresses, you'll be able to climb up the pyramid. But often when you reach a certain level, you hit a dead end. In the narcotics business, for example, many cases start when the police or federal agents catch a street-level dealer with some product in his pocket or in his car, or when an undercover agent makes a few buys. The strategy is to arrest that low-level dealer and then try to flip him against his suppliers, on up the chain, hopefully to the kingpins.

Sometimes you get lucky and start in the middle. In one case of mine, for example, an Illinois state trooper made a traffic stop on the half-asleep driver of a swerving SUV and found two hundred kilos of cocaine (worth about $5 million total) in the trunk, destined for New York; apparently the drowsy driver wasn't dipping into his own supply. We flipped the driver, and then used his information to nab his immediate supplier and the mid-level players who were supposed to receive his delivery. But none of those people cooperated, and the case hit a dead end. Those two hundred kilos belonged to somebody, much higher up the chain, who stood to make the most money off the deal—but we never could figure out who.

At the SDNY, we would joke that every time a DEA agent arrested some street-level pitcher in the Bronx selling $20 bags of heroin, the agent would invariably promise, "This case is going to take us all the way up to El Chapo"—Joaquin Guzman, the legendary narcotics kingpin, who was finally brought to justice in the United States in 2019. Federal agents and cops occasionally made that exact promise to me. Each time we worked our way up a level or two, but got nowhere remotely within sight of El Chapo, or any other legitimate powerhouse. I admired the lofty investigative aspirations, but they often went unfulfilled.

It's just the nature of the business and a function of the hierarchical structure. As a prosecutor, you need to get lucky to move up the chain of command once, or a couple times. And the higher up you go, the tougher it is to flip people, and the more breaks you'll need to keep climbing. As a result, many cases end up with the riffraff and the mid-tier players in handcuffs but the bosses untouched.

• •

In both his political and business careers, Donald Trump sat alone atop the organizational pyramid. He didn't exactly work his way up to either position. He was essentially born into what would become the family-controlled Trump Organization, and he's only ever run for one political office, the presidency. The man was never cut out to be a middle manager.

The list of Trump's political allies and advisors—those who fall somewhere beneath him on one or both of his business and political hierarchy charts—who have been criminally charged is staggering. Here's a quick walk through the gallery of Trump-adjacent rogues who at some point felt the cold steel of handcuffs on their wrists:

MICHAEL FLYNN. Trump's campaign cheerleader (he once led a "Lock her up!" chant at the 2016 Republican National Convention) and first national security advisor, Flynn pled guilty (twice) to making false statements to the FBI about his contacts with Russia during the Trump presidential transition. Flynn originally cooperated with Mueller, but then turned full-blown conspiracy theorist and extremist cause célèbre. Before a federal judge imposed a final sentence, Trump rescued Flynn with a pardon.

ROGER STONE. Trump's longtime political advisor was convicted by a jury of lying to Congress and witness tampering. Among other bizarre rantings, Stone threatened to kill a key witness's therapy dog. (Note: juries hate this.) Stone was sentenced to forty months by a federal judge who specifically noted that he had lied to protect Trump's political interests. Like Flynn, he received a commutation and then a pardon from Trump before ever serving a day behind bars.

GEORGE PAPADOPOULOS. The Trump campaign advisor pled guilty in 2017 for lying to the FBI about his campaign-related contacts with Russian officials who offered dirt on Trump's campaign opponent, Hillary Clinton. (Awful lot of lying to the authorities going on around Trump, you may have noticed.) Papadopoulos served about two weeks in prison, and Trump later pardoned him.

PAUL MANAFORT. Trump's campaign chair pled guilty to conspiracy and obstruction of justice after being convicted by a jury of fraud and tax offenses. Through a tangled web of illegal business operations, Manafort became wealthy enough to buy a mansion in the Hamptons and, memorably, a wardrobe that included a $15,000 ostrich coat and an $18,500 python-skin jacket. (Now you know that python is slightly more expensive than ostrich, in case that ever comes up.) He was sentenced to seven-plus years behind bars but released early during the Covid-19 outbreak, after serving less than two years. He eventually became yet another Trump pardon recipient.

STEVE BANNON. Trump's onetime chief political strategist and White House senior counselor was federally indicted by the SDNY for scamming Trump supporters to donate to a private "We Build the Wall" fund. Unsurprisingly, Bannon pocketed much of the money for his own use. But before he faced the music, Trump issued a pardon, on his final night as president. In September 2022, however, the Manhattan district attorney brought state-level charges against Bannon for the same "We Build the Wall" scheme; Trump's pardon did not preclude state-level prosecutors from bringing subsequent charges. And in 2021, Bannon refused to comply with a subpoena from the House of Representatives' January 6 Select Committee, which sought information relating to his interactions with Trump in the run-up to the Capitol attack, among other issues. Bannon claimed Trump had instructed him not to testify based on a legally suspect claim of executive privilege. The Justice Department indicted Bannon for criminal contempt of Congress, a jury convicted him, and he was sentenced to four months behind bars.

RICK GATES. Trump's former campaign aide and deputy chair of the inauguration committee pled guilty to conspiring to defraud the United States and making false statements to the FBI. Unlike his fellow Mueller defendants, Gates cooperated with prosecutors. Also unlike the others, Gates received no pardon from Trump. Those two things seem to be connected.

MICHAEL COHEN. Trump's longtime personal attorney pled guilty to campaign finance violations (the aforementioned hush money payments to Karen McDougal and Stormy Daniels), lying to Congress about Trump's business development deals, and other crimes. He ended up serving just over a year in federal prison before he was released early to home confinement as the Bureau of Prisons reduced its inmate population during the Covid-19 pandemic. Cohen, like Gates, cooperated with investigators; Cohen, like Gates, did not receive a pardon.

PETER NAVARRO. The former White House trade advisor to Trump, Navarro (like Bannon) refused to comply with a subpoena from the January 6 Committee and was indicted by the Justice Department for criminal contempt of Congress. Navarro calmly called the members of the Committee "domestic terrorists" and claimed he was remaining silent to protect Trump's potential executive privilege claim.

THOMAS BARRACK. Trump's billionaire pal and chair of his inaugural committee was indicted for illegal foreign lobbying and lying to the FBI. Barrack allegedly secretly lobbied US government officials, including Trump, on behalf of the United Arab Emirates, successfully persuading Trump—who was either a willing party or woefully naive—to add language favorable to his secret foreign clients to official policy speeches. In 2022, Barrack went to trial and was acquitted by a federal jury of the most serious charges against him.

ELLIOTT BROIDY. A top Trump fundraiser who also pled guilty to foreign lobbying crimes, declined to cooperate, and—you guessed it—ultimately received a pardon.

LEV PARNAS AND IGOR FRUMAN. After his arrest, Parnas gained national attention for speaking out against Trump, but he was once an avid Trump sycophant. Before his public turnabout, Parnas (and Fruman) served as conduits for hundreds of thousands of dollars in illegal foreign campaign contributions to pro-Trump political committees. Parnas was indicted and convicted at trial in the SDNY for campaign finance violations, fraud, and other crimes; he later pled guilty to additional conspiracy charges and was sentenced to twenty months behind bars. Fruman pled guilty to soliciting foreign campaign contributions for pro-Trump political groups, and was sentenced to a year and a day in federal prison. (Federal judges give this unusual sentence sometimes as a benefit to defendants, who can receive a 15 percent reduction in time for good behavior, but only if the sentence exceeds one year—hence the one extra day. It's actually better for a defendant to get sentenced to a year and a day than to eleven months.)

SAM PATTEN. Another crooked conduit for foreign cash, Patten pled guilty to steering illegal contributions from a Ukrainian oligarch to the Trump inaugural committee. Patten cooperated with prosecutors, was sentenced to three years' probation, and, unsurprisingly, received no pardon from Trump.

GEORGE NADER. An informal policy advisor who met with Bannon, Flynn, and Jared Kushner about foreign policy issues during Trump's presidential transition, Nader pled guilty in 2020 to federal crimes involving sexual abuse of minors, and was sentenced to ten years in prison. (Nader also pled guilty to funneling millions in illegal foreign donations to Hillary Clinton's 2016 campaign.)

THE TRUMP ORGANIZATION AND ALLEN WEISSELBERG. In July 2021, the Manhattan district attorney charged the Trump Organization as a corporate entity and its longtime CFO, Weisselberg, with a long-running tax fraud scheme. Certain company employees, including Weisselberg, allegedly received valuable benefits—rent, tuition, car payments—as indirect compensation, to avoid paying taxes on that income. Weisselberg pled guilty to a deal that called for him to serve five months in prison. The charge against the corporation was mostly symbolic; such a charge can result only in monetary penalties, not imprisonment of any individual.

No president since Nixon has seen so many of his associates and advisors indicted. Methods of calculation vary—who exactly qualifies as an "associate" of a president, and what conduct should count against a president?—but all in all, it's not close. Even if we exclude the indictments of Weisselberg and the Trump Organization, which relate to conduct before Trump ran for office, the list of Trump associates above runs fifteen deep. (And we're not counting other fringy defendants charged and convicted by Mueller, like Alex van der Zwaan and Richard Pinedo.)

Working back in time, no significant Obama official or advisor was indicted for anything relating to the campaign or administration. The George W. Bush administration saw the conviction of Lewis "Scooter" Libby, a senior advisor to Vice President Dick Cheney (Bush commuted Libby's sentence, and then Trump issued a full pardon in 2018), plus about a half dozen others, depending how and who you count, most of whom were agency-level officials and not advisors or associates of Bush himself. Two Clinton administration officials were indicted: secretary of agriculture Mike Espy (charged for accepting improper gifts from lobbyists, but acquitted) and secretary of housing and urban development Henry Cisneros (convicted for lying to law enforcement agents about hush money payments to a former mistress, but ultimately pardoned by Clinton). None of the other presidents between Nixon and Trump came close to the bar set by our two most corrupt (or corrupt-adjacent) commanders in chief.

Maybe Trump just had bad luck and unwittingly chose to surround himself with an awful lot of crooks and liars. Or maybe Trump was drawn to people who were willing to break the rules, and vice versa.

Through it all, as his associates went down in droves, Trump remained elusive. Whether intentionally or by happenstance, he adopted habits that rendered him particularly difficult to pin down. He famously did not email or text. I can attest that prosecutors love electronic communications; there's no better evidence than a message typed by the subject himself. Whether Trump refrained because of his own limited technological capacity (not uncommon among his generation) or because he was wary of creating an evidentiary trail, the end result was that he'd never be tied directly to a smoking-gun email or text of his own creation.

Compounding the degree of difficulty for prosecutors, Trump, as the boss, had the luxury of restricting his contacts with those around him. Like Artie Nigro in the Bruno murder, Trump limited his direct interaction with his criminal associates, so that only a select few—often the most loyal—had direct knowledge sufficient to support criminal charges against him. And many of those who might have flipped and implicated Trump either stayed silent (at times enticed by the potential for a pardon or other political benefits) or, owing to their organizational distance from him, just didn't have the goods.

· ·

Bosses benefit from distance not only conceptually but also physically. The closer a person is to a crime scene, the more evidence that person leaves behind. In a mob hit, for example, the shooter has the most direct physical involvement; think of Roche waiting to pop out and blast Bruno outside that Springfield social club. A shooter might leave behind shell casings, or a gun, or fingerprints, or a DNA sample (a single hair, for example, or saliva on a discarded cigarette or drink). He could have been spotted at the scene by eyewitnesses, or captured on video by surveillance cameras.

But as you move up the chain of command, the evidentiary trail grows thinner. Eventually, by the time you reach the boss, his entire involvement, though crucial and often necessary, could amount to a single sentence, perhaps whispered into the ear of a lower-ranking mobster. For example, Nigro, the Genovese acting boss, green-lit the Bruno murder with a single sentence to a mob underling, well before and far away from the actual crime scene. The recipient of that order, Arillotta, testified years later at trial that Nigro simply told him to do "a piece of work . . . the thing with Bruno." That's all it took.

Or, for a less bloody example, take Trump's effort to get rid of Mueller in 2017. Trump could have done it himself, but that would have left an undeniable evidentiary trail. Instead, Trump engineered multiple games of whisper-down-the-lane in an effort to get the job done through others, and under cloudier pretexts.

Trump began the effort to dispatch Mueller by complaining to his then White House counsel Don McGahn and two other top advisors that Mueller had purported "conflicts of interest." Never a stickler for the subtleties of legal ethics around conflicts of interest, Trump made his intentions plain without quite saying them out loud: Mueller posed a threat, and he needed to go. Trump eventually instructed McGahn, "Call Rod [Rosenstein, then the deputy attorney general overseeing the Mueller investigation], tell Rod that Mueller has conflicts and can't be the Special Counsel." Note here how Trump structured the intended firing of Mueller: he insulated himself by placing two intermediaries—McGahn and Rosenstein—between the order and its execution. McGahn, it turned out, showed a modicum of common sense and waited out the storm without acting on Trump's direction.

A few days after he spoke to McGahn, Trump instructed his former campaign manager Corey Lewandowski to try to get then–attorney general Jeff Sessions to unrecuse himself from the Russia investigation and retake control from Mueller. Lewandowski stalled and then passed along the message to Rick Dearborn, a White House advisor, who ultimately declined to follow through. Again, Trump created a multilink chain that eventually placed two people, Lewandowski and Dearborn, between Trump and his target, Mueller. As Trump intuitively understood, it's a tougher case for prosecutors to make if other people do the dirty work.

Chapter 6

SAY IT WITHOUT SAYING IT

Some bosses become so powerful that subordinate players need not be given specific marching orders—they just come to know, through organizational culture and tradition, what is expected of them. In the process, bosses reap the benefits of crime, financial and otherwise, with minimal exposure to arrest and indictment.

Take, for example, Daniel Marino, the Gambino family powerhouse who green-lit the murder of his nephew Frank Hydell, as discussed in chapter 1. When the Gambino family's chosen intermediary met with Marino in prison to tell him that Hydell was talking to the police, Marino said all of nine words: "Are you sure?" and then, after the intermediary responded affirmatively, "Do what you have to do." Marino never said that Hydell should be killed, or even harmed, specifically. His lawyers could have argued at trial, had the case gone that far, that "Do what you have to do" is not an order to kill, or to do anything in particular. Maybe "Do what you have to do" means "Talk to him," or "Beat him up," or "Get concrete confirmation that he's cooperating before you do anything else." We would have argued in response that it was understood within the Mafia that when a boss says "Do what you have to do" about a person who is talking to the cops, that is universally intended and taken as an order to kill—as proven in part by the fact that Marino's words did result in Hydell's murder. But it would have been a tough case to make, and it was part of the reason we ultimately gave Marino a (perhaps unduly lenient) five-year plea deal.

Trump showed a similar ability to convey his criminal instructions without quite saying the words out loud. As we just saw, when Trump wanted to get rid of Mueller in 2017, he made his meaning clear to his underlings (get rid of Mueller), but he also built in just enough ambiguity to support a cover story (that the removal was based on purported "conflicts of interest" rather than Trump's desire to knee-cap the investigation).

Or consider another example: in November 2018, Michael Cohen pled guilty to lying to Congress during his testimony the prior year about Trump's efforts to build a Trump Tower in Moscow. Cohen had testified falsely to Congress that Trump's efforts to build the skyscraper had mostly ended by January 2016, and that the project was not discussed extensively with others in the Trump Organization. In fact, as Cohen admitted when he later pled guilty, negotiations about the Trump Tower Moscow project continued until at least June 2016, and he discussed the deal in detail with several other Trump Organization employees, including Trump and two of his adult children, Ivanka and Don Jr. Cohen lied to Congress because he wanted to minimize the links between Trump and Russia during the crucial months when the presidential campaign heated up in 2016. The (false) party line was that the Moscow deal was already dead before the Iowa caucus in February 2016. In reality, Trump continued to do business in Russia for months during the heart of the presidential campaign, even into the summer.

Cohen was once Trump's personal attorney and rabid enabler, but by the time of his guilty plea, he had completely turned. Yet despite his visceral hatred for Trump, Cohen simply could not directly implicate Trump in his false testimony to Congress about the Moscow project. In later congressional testimony—given in May 2019, after he had turned against Trump—Cohen conceded that "Mr. Trump did not directly tell me to lie to Congress." "That is not how he operates," he explained; rather, "I lied about it too because Mr. Trump had made clear to me, through his personal statements to me that we both knew to be false and through his lies to the country, that he wanted me to lie."

Cohen said that before he testified in Congress about the Moscow project, Trump called him in for a meeting. "He also wanted just to ensure," Cohen testified later, "I'm making the statement and I said it in my testimony, there is no Russia, there is no collusion, there is no—there is no deal. He goes, it's all a witch hunt and it's—he goes, this stuff has to end." When a member of Congress asked whether Trump had coached him to lie, Cohen responded, "Again, it's a difficult answer, because he doesn't tell you what he wants. What he does is, again, 'Michael, there's no Russia, there's no collusion, there's no involvement, there's no interference.'"

In other words, Trump never said to Cohen, "I need you to lie for me," much as Marino never told anybody, "I need you to kill Hydell." Rather, Trump (1) openly lied to the public about the timing of the Russia deal, for all to see—including Cohen and others in the Trump orbit; (2) explained the end goal to Cohen ("There is no Russia"); and (3) repeated the lie directly to Cohen, who drew the obvious conclusion that he, too, was expected to adhere to the party line (or party lie, such as it was). Just to make sure, Cohen explained, Trump's personal attorneys carefully crafted and reviewed Cohen's false testimony before he gave it. (It's not clear whether those attorneys knew the testimony was false, but they certainly understood that it did no harm to Trump.)

Therein lies the beauty of being a boss. Trump never said the magic words that would have obviously given rise to criminal liability. Instead he sent a subtle if unmistakable message—through his own pattern of lies, through long-established organizational culture, through his lightly coded hints to Cohen before the testimony, and through the involvement and supervision of intermediaries (here, the lawyers). Ultimately, Trump received the benefit of Cohen's original false testimony, but none of the legal risk.

Take Roger Stone as another example. A jury found that Stone lied repeatedly during his 2017 testimony before the House Intelligence Committee. Among other things, Stone falsely claimed he had not discussed with Trump his efforts to coordinate with Wikileaks over the public release of hacked DNC emails damaging to Hillary Clinton's 2016 presidential campaign. At sentencing, federal district court judge Amy Berman Jackson pronounced that Stone "was not prosecuted, as some have complained, for standing up for the president. He was prosecuted for covering up for the president."

As in the Cohen case, there was never any smoking-gun evidence that Trump had explicitly instructed or asked Stone to lie to Congress. Only Stone likely could have provided testimony on whether such a conversation had occurred; he remained mum, and ultimately was rewarded by Trump with clemency. Even if no such explicit conversation ever happened, Stone fully understood—and even helped author—the long-standing Trump playbook: "Admit nothing, deny everything, launch counterattack," to quote Stone on his own personal philosophy, which he plainly shared with Trump, his longtime political ally. There was never any doubt that Stone would lie to protect his boss. They had established their credo over many years. Similarly, Cohen testified to Congress in 2019 that "everybody's job at the Trump Organization was to protect Trump. Every day, we knew we were going to lie for him. That became the norm."

Mob bosses operate in much the same fashion as Trump. I never saw a case in which a mob boss had to directly instruct any other person to lie. Rather, bosses know that it's fully understood within the mob culture that you never implicate others—particularly the boss. At most, a mobster might mention to somebody, "I heard you got arrested," or "I heard you got a subpoena." The rest—"And you better not say anything, or else"—need not be said out loud. Trump may have never directly told Cohen and Stone to lie for him, and he didn't need to. They just knew what to do.

In a perverse way, this method of communication brings to mind the connection between the great NFL quarterback Patrick Mahomes and his star tight end, Travis Kelce. Kelce once described how the pair had mastered the art of nonverbal communication and could instinctively get on the same wavelength: "Right before the play, I'll look at Pat and give him the eyes like, 'yeah I'm about to make some shit up right here.'" No words exchanged, just two wily veterans who understand what to expect from one another. (Apologies to Mahomes and Kelce, both great players and model citizens, for the comparison; you get the point, I'm sure.)

••

Bosses enjoy the same advantages of distance and insulation when it comes to finances. In the Manhattan district attorney's investigation of the Trump Organization, prosecutors uncovered a million-dollar-plus tax fraud scheme that spanned fifteen years. Trump responded to the DA's indictment by calling the charges "a disgrace," "shameful," and, of course, a "witch hunt." "Disgrace, disgrace, disgrace," he added, just to be clear. The DA indicted the chief financial officer, Allen Weisselberg, and the Trump Organization as a corporate entity. But of course prosecutors never got to Trump himself.

An observer might wonder, quite rationally, how the Trump Organization and its CFO could run a systematic tax fraud scam for more than a decade without the knowledge or participation of the very person who owned the company. It could be that Trump wasn't actually involved in the tax scheme, and that Weisselberg did it himself, under Trump's nose and without his knowledge. Or it could be, on the other extreme, that Trump knew all about the tax fraud scam, developed it himself, and directly guided it. Indeed, a 2016 article in the *Guardian* concluded, based on interviews with twelve former Trump employees, that a "consensus emerged of a business-man obsessed with minute detail, prone to micromanagement."

But there's also a third, middle possibility: that it was widely understood within the company that it was fine to cut corners or fudge things a bit (or more than a bit) to feed the bottom line. There was just no need to say it out loud or write it up in a document or openly acknowledge it as a criminal fraud, in any format. Indeed, Cohen has claimed publicly that it was generally understood in the Trump Organization that it was fine—encouraged, even—to cook the books, and that Trump himself created and stoked this culture.

At the same time, Cohen was never able to point to one specific transaction and state definitively that Trump had directed a fraud in that particular case. In 2022, when pressed by CNN's Alisyn Camerota on this lack of specificity, Cohen acknowledged, "The problem is I can't tell you how it worked. Because the only person that actually knows how it worked is Donald Trump. It's whatever he thinks that the value of the asset is." Camerota followed up: "Were you in the room as he was sort of spitballing these different figures?" Cohen responded, "Ok so the answer is, it wasn't on a particular one-off basis." Cohen then described how Trump often made it known that he wanted to rank higher on the Forbes list of wealthiest individuals, and to appear rich in other media stories, at times gradually increasing his own assessment of his total net worth as the conversation progressed. Cohen added, "Our job—and when I say 'our,' I'm referring to mine and Allen Weisselberg—was to go back with those documents, figure out how to increase the net worth, go back to Donald in order to show him for his approval."

From a prosecutor's perspective, this rendered Cohen a marginally useful witness, at best (and that's before you account for his other credibility and partiality problems). There's a reason that no prosecutor ever brought a case against Trump that rested on Cohen's word. His potential testimony is fine and interesting in establishing general atmospherics at the Trump Organization, but it's also not enough to charge (never mind convict) a person on criminal fraud or conspiracy charges relating to a specific transaction. The same pattern emerges here as we've seen before: Trump makes his wishes broadly known, while others go out and do the dirty work for him. In the process, those subordinates incur the greatest criminal exposure. Ultimately, Weisselberg and the Trump Organization itself, as a corporate entity, were indicted for fraud. But Trump—the guy whose name was on the building—dodged the bullet.

It's nothing new for a corporate boss to raise the so-called know-nothing or delegation defense: "I'm not a micromanager, I let my people do their work, and I don't and can't know everything that happens in my company below me." Prominent financial and industrial titans commonly use variations of the see-no-evil, hear-no-evil defense, claiming they didn't know what their underlings were doing inside the businesses they ran. That's not to suggest the so-called delegation defense is necessarily false; results have varied over the years, as we'll see in a moment. But it's inarguably a defense available only to powerful players at the top of the organizational hierarchy.

Enron founder Kenneth Lay tried the delegation defense, ultimately without success, at his 2006 trial on a slate of charges relating to massive corporate criminality, including securities fraud, wire fraud, and conspiracy. Shortly after his indictment, Lay declared at a press conference that essentially everybody but he knew about the fraud: "I knew nothing at the time that would even get any suspicion of what was going on. I was not Chief Financial Officer. I was not Chief Accounting Officer. I'm not Chief Risk Officer. I was not General Counsel. There are a lot of things I was not." Lay eventually used a similar claim—colorfully dubbed the "idiot defense" by the media—at his trial. The jury didn't buy it and found Lay guilty on all counts. He died shortly after his conviction, just months before sentencing.

Worldcom CEO Bernard Ebbers tried a similar tack. Charged

by the SDNY with what was then the largest accounting fraud in US history, Ebbers testified at his trial in 2005, "I don't know about technology, and I don't know about finance and accounting," telling the jury that "I know what I don't know" and that he did poorly in college, where his "marks weren't too good."

"I never thought anything like that had gone on," Ebbers testified. "I put those people in place, and I trusted those people. I had no earthly idea that that would occur." The jury found Ebbers guilty on all charges. He was sentenced to twenty-five years behind bars.

Other corporate titans have used the know-nothing defense more successfully. CUC Corporation CEO Walter Forbes blamed a multibillion-dollar corporate fraud on his underlings. He testified at trial, "We were a public company with thousands of employees, divisions all over the country and all over the world. I don't think they would have expected me to be reading 10-Q's [forms required by the Securities and Exchange Commission]." The defense worked at Forbes's first two trials, both of which ended with hung juries— but he was finally convicted at his third trial in 2006. HealthSouth CEO Richard Scrushy also deployed the delegation defense to his advantage. He was acquitted on all counts at his trial in 2005, after his defense team blamed a massive corporate fraud on the "rats in the accounting department." (Scrushy was later tried and convicted on an unrelated bribery case.)

Ultimately, the delegation defense has met with varied results. Win or lose, however, it's a defense that can be made only by bosses, due to their placement atop the organizational chart. The very people who stand to benefit most from a crime are often the most difficult to prosecute.

••

Trump helped to propel the January 6 assault on the US Capitol in much the same manner as he ran his business and his presidential administration. He never explicitly instructed his supporters to storm the Capitol. But he set the charge, lit the spark, poured on accelerant while the fire raged, and hoped and intended to reap the benefits. The Capitol insurrectionists acted for Trump, in his name, and at his encouragement. And when they were finished, he praised them lavishly for what they had done.

Let's walk through the steps. First Trump made his views known publicly, often and loudly. He started attacking the integrity of the 2020 election far in advance, dating back to April 2020. He tweeted to his 80 million-plus followers about election fraud relentlessly, including over three hundred times in the two weeks following election day in November 2020. This was a well-worn playbook, familiar to Trump and his supporters alike. He had previously claimed voter fraud after losing the 2016 Iowa Republican caucus to Ted Cruz, and before the 2016 presidential election, in anticipation of a loss to Hillary Clinton that never came to be.

As the November 2020 election drew close, Trump kept up the drumbeat of rhetoric and began to set the fuse in earnest. At a presidential debate watched by tens of millions of viewers in September 2020, he was asked if he would denounce far-right extremist groups, including the Proud Boys. Trump responded, "Proud Boys, stand back and stand by"—much to the delight of the organization, which celebrated his comments, using them to promote their organization and recruit new members. Eventually over two dozen members and associates of the Proud Boys would be indicted by the Justice Department for coordinating and participating in the January 6 Capitol attack.

After the 2020 election, as Trump lost scores of lawsuits around the country challenging the results, and as any sentient being with even a tangential hold on reality (including political and legal advisors in his own administration) debunked his election fraud lies, he amped up the desperation and the rhetoric. Trump zeroed in on his last stand: he tweeted at least ten times to hype up a rally to be held in Washington, DC, on January 6, the day on which Congress would count the electoral votes. Like a promoter for a monster truck rally, Trump whipped up his followers, tweeting: "Statistically impossible to have lost the 2020 election. Big protest in D.C. on January 6. Be there, will be wild!" He retweeted one follower who wrote, "The calvary is coming, Mr. President! January 6, Washington DC." (Trump's lawyer would later claim at his second impeachment, implausibly, that "calvary" referred to a religious display, and was not a misspelled version of the military term *cavalry.*) Trump's marching orders spread outward to his followers with remarkable but predictable online efficiency. "Stop the Steal!" and "Save America" became popular rallying cries, echoed and recirculated endlessly through social media. Finally, on January 6, a crowd of thousands, many decked out in paramilitary gear, gathered by the White House Ellipse, a short walk from the Capitol. The crowd waved Trump flags and Confederate flags while chanting, "Fight for Trump!" Then the stage show began.

Trump's lunatic fringe worshippers got the crowd hyped up. Representative Mo Brooks exhorted the crowd to "start taking down names and kicking ass." Donald Trump Jr. declared, "You can be a hero or you can be a zero." Giuliani screeched about "trial by combat." Finally, Trump—knowing the crowd was armed—took the mic and lit the fuse. "We're gonna walk down to the Capitol," he began, literally pointing the way for his frenzied followers. "And we're gonna cheer on our brave senators and congressmen and women. And we're probably not gonna be cheering so much for some of them. Because you'll never take back our country with weakness. You have to show strength and you have to be strong." At that point it would've been a miracle if no violence occurred.

But Trump wasn't done yet. At 2:24 p.m.—about an hour after rioters breached police barriers at the Capitol, while the riot was underway—he sent a tweet attacking Vice President Mike Pence, who Trump had publicly faulted for declining to unilaterally reject electoral votes from certain states that Trump wrongly claimed he had won: "Mike Pence didn't have the courage to do what should have been done to protect our Country and our Constitution, giving States a chance to certify a corrected set of facts, not the fraudulent or inaccurate ones which they were asked to previously certify. USA demands the truth!" Video played by the January 6 Committee showed rioters at the Capitol reading Trump's tweet aloud and immediately breaking into chants of "Hang Mike Pence!"

Did Trump ever formally, explicitly tell his followers to violently attack the Capitol? Not in so many words. But did he manage to communicate his intent and his wishes to them? The January 6 riot itself answers that question in large part. And just to confirm that his message had been received and well executed, at 6:01 p.m.— moments after the violence had ended—Trump tweeted his appreciation for his supporters who had just torn apart the US Capitol: "These are the things and events that happen when a sacred landslide election victory is so unceremoniously & viciously stripped away from great patriots who have been badly & unfairly treated for so long. Go home with love & in peace. Remember this day forever!"

In the end, because of the way Trump communicates with his followers, because of his just-short-of-explicit language and technique, he never gave prosecutors an easy charge. Don't get me wrong. I'm not saying Trump couldn't, or shouldn't, have been charged for his role in inciting the insurrectionist mob on January 6 (as we'll discuss later). But no prosecutor—and most conspicuously not attorney general Merrick Garland—was ultimately willing to take on a charge that was anything other than a slam dunk. Combine Trump, who expertly senses how to leave himself just enough wiggle room, with a timid prosecutor like Garland, and the result is, well, nothing.

Chapter 7

IT TAKES A CRIMINAL
TO CATCH A CRIMINAL

The television cop shows—*CSI* and *Criminal Minds* and the like—would have us believe that criminal cases get made mostly by futuristic lab forensics or blood spatter analysis or psychological profiling. But the reality is that the vast majority of major criminal cases are built on the backs of people who were, not long before, criminals themselves.

It's a persistent catch-22 for prosecutors: the best way to nail a powerful leader is to flip one of his underlings. But then the prosecution rides on the inherently untrustworthy word of a criminal. That's another structural advantage that bosses commonly exploit: even if somebody in a position to implicate a powerful player does cooperate, that person is inherently flawed as a witness precisely *because he is a criminal.*

There's no magical way for prosecutors to undo or completely neutralize a cooperating witness's criminal past. That's why prosecutors, perhaps counterintuitively, openly embrace the cooperator's own sordid personal history. Watch any cooperator testify at trial, and you'll see the prosecutor spend hours, sometimes days, eliciting direct testimony from his own witness about every crime or other bad act he has ever committed. The idea, from the prosecutor's perspective, is that the cooperator is an open book, with nothing to hide and no agenda other than telling the jury the whole, unvarnished truth. And any prosecutor knows you have to front the bad facts yourself—otherwise revelations about the cooperator's criminal past will hit the jury even harder if the defense lawyer elicits them for the first time on cross-examination. (Keep in mind that prosecutors have a legal and ethical obligation to turn over all potentially damaging information about a witness to the defense, so prosecutors know that the defense has all the dirt in advance.) This is why prosecutors often call this tactic "pulling the sting"—it hurts for a moment, but it's better to get the pain over with quickly than to leave it in there for later, when it'll be even more painful. A prosecutor doesn't want the jury thinking during cross-examination of a cooperator, "Wow, this guy is really awful, and the prosecutor tried to hide it from us." The prosecutor wants the jury thinking, "Yeah, yeah, we already know about all this bad stuff, the cooperator already told the prosecutor about it before."

So prosecutors learn quickly that it's vital to embrace the cooperator's history, for better and for worse (and it's usually for worse). But the real trick, in the end, is convincing the jury to credit the cooperator's testimony. "This isn't about whether you like the cooperator," we'd often argue. "It's about whether you believe him." The key, it almost always turns out, is to find enough independent, corroborating evidence so the jury can comfortably rely on the cooperator's word.

This prosecutorial quest for corroboration can become a borderline obsession. One SDNY supervisor of mine who was particularly meticulous would say half-jokingly, "If a cooperator tells you there was an oak tree by the murder scene, have an FBI agent go take photos of the oak tree." The hypothetical oak tree would lend no particular support to the relevant aspects of the cooperator's testimony—who killed who, why, in what manner—but it would provide a sliver of peripheral support for the cooperator's overall testimony.

Sometimes you hit the jackpot. For example, when Anthony Arillotta flipped after we charged him and other Genovese family gangsters for the aforementioned murder of Al Bruno, he also led us to two other grisly murder plots.

At his very first proffer—the formal interview where prosecutors question the prospective cooperator—Arillotta casually mentioned that he knew where Gary Westerman was. The name didn't mean much to the New York prosecutors and cops in the room, but the Massachusetts-based FBI agents' eyes lit up; Westerman had been missing for nearly seven years. He was a rough-and-tumble kid who hung around the periphery of Arillotta's crew, so it was widely assumed he'd met an unfortunate end of some type. Arillotta definitively solved the mystery.

Arillotta explained that he, the Geas brothers, and another made guy, Emilio Fusco, suspected that Westerman was talking to the cops. So they decided he had to go. Arillotta and his cohorts came up with a devious plan: they told Westerman they wanted his help robbing the home of a local marijuana dealer in Agawam, Massachusetts. Westerman agreed, and on the appointed night he met his criminal compatriots in the woods behind the purported victim's home. He came dressed for the occasion, wearing dark clothes and a black ski mask, and carrying a Taser in his pocket (the plan, Westerman believed, was to subdue and tie up the drug dealer).

As they walked through the wooded area behind the house, the Geas brothers suddenly turned their guns on Westerman and started firing. But Westerman somehow survived the initial volley of .22-caliber gunshots (later forensic work would show a series of low-caliber gunshot indentations that didn't quite penetrate his skull). So to finish the job, Arillotta and Fusco grabbed heavy shovels and bashed him over the head, cracking his skull nearly right down the middle. After they had beaten Westerman to the point of what appeared to be his death, Fred Geas finished the job with a point-blank .38-caliber gunshot to the head. The team then dragged Westerman's body to a grave they had already dug nearby and pushed him in. Arillotta told us the body flopped clumsily into the hole, head down, feet up.

Seven years later, armed with Arillotta's information, we sent an FBI excavation team to the Agawam murder site. We had gotten permission from a judge for the FBI to take Arillotta out of prison for a day, on a macabre field trip of sorts, so he could show them precisely where to dig. FBI agents quickly found a series of .22-caliber shells on the ground, right where Arillotta had indicated—powerful corroboration in its own right, but merely a warm-up act for what happened next. The FBI team then used a front loader to skim thin layers of dirt, an inch or two at a time, from the spot where Arillotta claimed that Westerman's body would be found. The FBI sifted carefully through each bucketload of dirt, first by hand and then by using a straining device that looked like a massive colander. After the first few scoops yielded nothing, the FBI's front loader hit something hard—the soles of a pair of Nikes. It was Westerman's body, head down, feet up, just as Arillotta had told us. The team spent the next several days, aided by an archaeologist, carefully excavating the site. They ultimately recovered Westerman's decomposed remains—still with a ski mask over his head and a Taser in his jacket pocket, just as Arillotta had described. And inside the grave the team found the .38-caliber shell from that final close-range gunshot that Fred Geas put in Westerman's head.

There has never been better corroboration than this. Here's what I said to the jury during my closing argument at trial: "There's an expression that people use in regular everyday life: 'does he know where the bodies are buried?' It means, does this guy know what he's talking about? Is this guy for real? Well, here, you see that expression literally applied. Anthony Arillotta knew exactly where the body was buried."

And, believe it or not, Arillotta had yet another murder plot to confess. (This was a truly prodigious crew.) Nigro, the Genovese family's acting boss, who had sanctioned the aforementioned murder of Bruno, had a beef with a cement workers' union official named

Frank Dadabo. The dispute culminated around—I'm not making this up, I promise, though I acknowledge it sounds so ridiculous it could've come right out of a movie—tickets to a Tony Bennett concert. Dadabo had four tickets, he asked Nigro to go to the show with him and both their wives, there was some miscommunication, Dadabo ended up seeing the Bennett concert with another couple, word got back to Nigro about this unforgivable betrayal, and, well, feelings were hurt.

So Nigro gave the intended target's name and address in the Bronx to Arillotta, and assigned him to the hit. Arillotta recruited the Geas brothers, of course, to help him out. So, Arillotta told us, Fred Geas drove down from Massachusetts the day before the hit with the guns and stayed overnight at a hotel a bit outside New York City. Ty Geas and Arillotta drove down together the next morning, met Fred at the hotel, and then drove to the scene of the planned hit. They then watched from across the street as Dadabo left his home and got into his car. As Dadabo turned the ignition, Arillotta and Ty Geas walked up to the car and opened fire, blasting out the windows and hitting Dadabo with nine shots, all from point-blank range. (Fred Geas waited up the street in the getaway car.) Dadabo survived, somehow. He told the police at the time that all he knew was that two white guys in baseball hats shot him, but he didn't know who they were. (That was true; Dadabo had never met Arillotta or the Geases and would not have known or recognized them. Again we see the benefit to the boss, Nigro, who ordered the hit but was not present at the physical scene.)

Years later, when we prepped Dadabo for trial, he showed us the bullet wounds scattered across his torso and back and told us, with a hint of pride, that fragments of four bullets remained inside his body. I couldn't help but ask if he set off metal detectors at the airport. (He seemed confused; it was a dumb question, I can now acknowledge.)

Here's where corroboration comes in. Remember, Arillotta told us that Fred Geas had stayed at that hotel the night before the shooting, which we knew had happened on May 19. Arillotta didn't remember the exact hotel or location, but he knew it was a large chain hotel somewhere in the suburban area north of New York. The FBI agent on the case blanketed subpoenas on virtually every hotel within a twenty-five-mile radius. And there, on one page out of hundreds, was the needle in the haystack: a booking document from the Marriott Hotel in Rye, New York, showing that on May 18—the night before the shooting of Dadabo, about eighteen miles away from the scene of the crime—a room had been reserved in the name of "Freddy Geas." Bingo. And just to make it even more incriminating, not only had Geas reserved a room in his own name but he also used his own credit card to pay for it. The Marriott Hotel records were perhaps not quite as sensational as the recovered corpse of Gary Westerman, but as corroboration goes, they were every bit as persuasive. Arillotta pled guilty to the Dadabo shooting—all SDNY cooperators must plead guilty to their own criminal conduct—and the jury convicted Nigro and both Geas brothers, too.

..

Even where a prosecutor can establish sufficient backing for a cooperating witness, it still can be difficult to convince a jury to rely on testimony from a confessed criminal. We'd often say to juries, "Sure, we'd love to be able to call good people, nurses or schoolteachers, to come up here and testify to you about the mob. But nurses and schoolteachers can't do that. They're not part of the criminal underworld, and they don't know about it. Only a real mobster can do that." The same argument applies to any criminal organization, mob or other variety.

Sometimes cooperating witnesses can have so much criminal baggage that, even if the jury tends to believe their testimony, it just becomes too much to bear. It's a balancing act for prosecutors: we want the jury to credit the cooperator, to believe that he is withholding nothing—but we also don't want the jury to turn against a cooperator who is simply too horrible to accept. And sometimes the balance just tips too far.

Consider Arillotta, for example. How would you feel about basing a verdict on his testimony? You now know that he played an instrumental role in three murder plots: he coordinated the Al Bruno hit in downtown Springfield, he lured Westerman into the woods and bashed his head in with a shovel before dumping him in a wooded grave, and he stalked Dadabo and fired a volley of shots into him at point-blank range. Would you trust Arillotta? Would you find it difficult—or prohibitively distasteful—to rely on his word? Our jury ultimately believed Arillotta, finding Nigro and the Geases guilty on the murders and other crimes. But he had exceptional corroborative support from the other evidence around his crimes. And I'm sure it wasn't easy for that jury to get past their natural, visceral disgust for Arillotta's actions and to convict others based largely on his testimony.

Indeed, it doesn't always end well for prosecutors. For example, I tried a case against the notorious Gambino family boss John A. Gotti (the son of the legendary Mafia icon John J. Gotti, who rose to fame in the 1980s as a front-page fixture in the New York tabloids). Our star cooperating witness was John Alite, the Gotti family's longtime loyalist and enforcer. Alite, like any cooperator, had met with prosecutors dozens of times and understood that he had to admit every crime he had ever committed. So at trial Alite testified that he had punched out and baseball-batted (he casually used this phrase as a verb: *baseball-batted*) more people than he could count. And he openly admitted that during his mob career, he had shot something like thirty victims, most of them non-lethally; Alite developed a trademark of shooting his victims in the legs and butt to send a message—though he also did kill or plot to kill about a half dozen victims. So, yeah: bad guy.

None of that is what pushed the jury over the edge, however. It was the story of the contractor who did work on Alite's house while he was away on vacation. A neighbor later told Alite that one night he'd looked through an upstairs window and seen the contractor having sex with a woman on Alite's bed. Alite—well, he didn't appreciate that.

So, Alite explained matter-of-factly to the jury, he tied up his attack dog on a leash in his garage. He then lured the contractor into the garage and, at gunpoint, zip-tied him to a chair that was just barely beyond the leashed dog's reach. Alite then left the contractor there, bound and sitting within breathing distance of the frenzied dog, for hours. Alite eventually untied the contractor and marched him, still at gunpoint, to a small pond behind the house. He made the contractor walk into the frigid, waist-deep water, and fired shots as he flailed and splashed for his life. Alite didn't hit the contractor with any bullets—he never meant to—but this was inventive, sadistic torture (for the contractor and for the dog, really).

If your stomach is turning, so too was the jury's. It was just too much. They had listened carefully to Alite throughout his testimony up to that point. I'm not saying they loved him, but they were attentive. But as he told this sordid tale of the dog and the pond, I could feel the jury turn off. I saw at least one juror simply stop taking notes. They likely didn't disbelieve Alite—why would he make up such horrible stories *about himself?*—but it just got to a point where it was more than they could bear.

Gotti ultimately beat the charges in our case. The jury hung (meaning they could not reach a unanimous verdict), and we dismissed the case. When we talked to the jurors after the trial ended, some said that Alite was just such a bad guy that they couldn't bring themselves to base a guilty verdict on his testimony. Alite was our star witness, our most direct shot at the boss, but he was also deeply flawed, precisely *because* he had been an enforcer for Gotti, the boss, for so long.

..

The people around Donald Trump who could have flipped and implicated him were no John Alites or Anthony Arillottas. But they all had their deeply unseemly traits.

Michael Cohen is a convicted felon, several times over. He has, by his own admission in court, committed numerous frauds and other crimes. No matter what kind of personal turnaround he has engineered—and he has seemingly made a clean break from his former corrupt lifestyle—he is now a self-admitted perjurer with a white-hot, very public personal hatred for Trump, which would undermine his impartiality at trial. Indeed, as we discussed earlier, the SDNY concluded that Cohen's credibility was so badly damaged that they could not enlist him as a cooperating witness, despite his eagerness to testify against Trump. The Manhattan DA apparently reached a similar conclusion in its criminal investigation of the Trump Organization's finances.

Lev Parnas, too, got arrested and then did a national media tour to badmouth Trump. He likened Trump to a "cult leader" and claimed that "I wouldn't do anything without the consent of Rudy Giuliani, or the president . . . I was on the ground doing their work." Parnas's lawyer publicly begged prosecutors to let his client cooperate. He announced, "We very much want to provide substantial assistance to the government," and promised (with a smidge of hyperbole) that Parnas would be "perhaps the most pivotal witness that could be offered in a trial." But nobody bit. Prosecutors had no interest in enlisting Parnas, with all his baggage, as a witness. Like Cohen, Parnas was a convicted serial fraudster with deep credibility and impartiality issues. It's one thing for a former associate to want to testify against a boss; it's quite another for prosecutors to deem that person credible enough to merit a cooperation deal.

Had Michael Flynn or Paul Manafort followed through with their cooperation, they too would have been branded as habitual liars and crooks trying to save themselves while settling personal beefs against the boss. Same for Roger Stone or Allen Weisselberg, had they flipped.

The point is, if a boss surrounds himself with lying crooks, then only lying crooks can ever turn against him. Anytime a criminal cooperates up the chain of command, the boss has the luxury of painting the underling as a bad guy, a convicted felon, a proven liar or thief or worse, with an ax to grind and a personal incentive to help himself. As prosecutors often remind juries, nurses and schoolteachers could never take down Donald Trump, or any crooked boss. Only other criminals can do that.

Or consider the Justice Department's investigation of Congressman Matt Gaetz of Florida. Gaetz, one of Trump's most enthusiastic boot-lickers, became the subject of a federal investigation in 2020—notably initiated during the Trump administration, by Trump's sycophantic attorney general, William Barr—for a litany of potential federal crimes, including sex trafficking of a minor. The skies darkened considerably for Gaetz in May 2020 when his close political ally and Florida party pal Joel Greenberg cooperated with the Justice Department and pled guilty to a stomach-churning array of crimes, including sex trafficking of a minor, stalking, identity theft, and wire fraud. Even Gaetz sensed what was in the air, as he reportedly sought a pre-emptive pardon (without success) during Trump's final days in office.

Allow me to pause for a moment to explain just how vile a human being Greenberg is. As you're well aware from this book, I have enlisted some really, really bad guys—killers, even—as cooperating witnesses: Michael DiLeonardo, Arillotta, Alite, and plenty of others. Now, Greenberg never killed anyone but, in my view, his crimes made him a worse cooperator than any of my mob henchmen. As we know, there are ways for prosecutors to credibly present trial testimony from a confessed murderer without completely alienating the jury. You fully vet the cooperator, you back him up with as much corroborating evidence as possible, and you tell the jury straight up: *You may not like this guy, but you can believe him.* I did just that many times over, and it almost always worked out fine (almost; recall Alite).

But Greenberg, to me, is simply too grotesque to bear. I'd readily flip a murderer and give him a sentencing break if he helped us catch other killers. But a child molester—that's simply out of the question. That's partially an issue of visceral disgust and personal conscience; it's also that I simply don't believe most juries could bear to return a guilty verdict based on the word of Greenberg, or any admitted child sex abuser. To make matters worse, Greenberg admitted to a litany of other crimes, including—wait for it—falsely branding a political opponent of his as . . . a child molester. A jury is going to convict, unanimously and beyond a reasonable doubt, based even in part on the word of this guy? I doubt it.

Federal prosecutors in Florida apparently saw it differently from me, at least for a time, and they gave Greenberg a cooperation agreement. But in September 2022, multiple media outlets reported that the prosecutors handling the case had determined that their central witnesses were not credible enough to charge Gaetz. Understand how backward the Justice Department got this. Good prosecutors know that you do your diligence and determine that a witness is credible and corroborated *before* you give him a cooperation deal; yet these federal prosecutors apparently gave Greenberg a break first, and only later decided he was unusable.

In the end, as DOJ belatedly realized, Greenberg was just too vile to use. And as a result, a far more powerful person, Gaetz, walked away scot-free.

Chapter 8

FEAR IN THE JURY BOX

"We have a note from the jury," the judge said from the bench.

I could never help myself. Anytime we learned that a jury had sent a note, my heart jumped a bit, even after I had become a grizzled trial veteran. Jury notes—handwritten by the foreperson, folded up and put into an envelope, handed to the court security officer who guarded the jury room, and then walked over to the judge—were always moments of anticipation and drama. Notes can bring promising news, or terrible news, or confusing news landing somewhere in the middle.

At times, jury notes pose incisive and telling questions about the law: "Are we permitted to convict on one count but acquit on another?" or "Can we consider a co-conspirator's statement against the defendant?" Sometimes jurors ask to inspect certain pieces of evidence or to hear readbacks of specific passages from transcripts of witness testimony. Sometimes notes are just housekeeping requests— "We need more notepads" or "Please lower the temperature on the thermostat." But ultimately, when the jury is done deliberating, it sends the most dramatic note of all: "We have reached a verdict." (Juries are specifically instructed to send a note when they are ready to announce a unanimous verdict, but not to reveal what the verdict is; the actual "Guilty" or "Not guilty" is then read aloud in court, dramatically, like you'd see in a movie.)

Right away, we could tell this particular note was unusual. The judge looked puzzled as she read it. "Okay folks, we have a situation here," she said. Never good news for prosecutors. "The note says,

'Dear judge, I need to speak with you privately. Signed, Juror #5.'"
Already we could tell this would get messy. Jury notes almost always
come through the foreperson and are agreed on by the entire jury.
But this one came from an individual juror, who wasn't the foreperson. Juror #5's request to speak to the judge could only mean something had gone wrong.

"Let's talk to him and see what's going on," the judge said. The
judge had the court security officer get Juror #5 from the deliberation room and walk him into a small private anteroom, where the
judge, the defense lawyer, my trial partner, and I waited. When the
juror, slightly built and in his twenties, took one step into the room,
he saw the arrayed lawyers and immediately said, "No, Judge, I just
want to talk to you." The judge explained that the lawyers had to
be present, to protect their clients' legal interests. The juror, visibly
rattled, looked down. "Tell us what's going on," the judge said in a
calming manner. The juror blurted: "We're about to find him guilty,
but I'm scared what'll happen if we do."

This was a good news / bad news scenario. On one hand, the
jurors were apparently about to convict our defendant—a powerful,
coldhearted Genovese family captain, Angelo Prisco, who we had
charged with racketeering, murder, and other crimes. On the other
hand, Juror #5's reticence was a problem. If he could not continue
to serve, which now seemed in doubt, we'd either have a mistrial or
the jury would have to restart deliberations, with a new alternate
juror brought back in (this is one reason judges have alternate jurors
sit through the trial—just in case a juror has to leave the case during
deliberations). The judge asked Juror #5 to elaborate. "Why would
you be scared?" she asked. Juror #5 looked incredulous. "Because
he's charged with murder, and he's with the mob," he retorted. Fair
point.

The judge tried to bring him back: "Well, I can assure you there's
no reason to suspect this defendant would do anything, and there's

no known threat against you or anybody else here." The juror seemed ready for this and shot back, "Well then, why are you making us use numbers instead of our real names?" Again, fair point. Because this case involved a particularly dangerous defendant, we had requested, and the judge had granted, a pretrial motion for an anonymous jury. Hence this juror was known to the judge, lawyers, and his fellow jurors not by his name but simply as Juror #5.

The judge decided to play a bit of hardball. "Look," she said. "If I let you off this jury, either we're going to have to start this whole trial all over again with a brand new jury, or I'll have to bring in another person to take your place now, and this jury will have to start back from square one. But either way, this case will result in a verdict. So can you pull through, or do we need to let you go?" Something about the judge's direct approach seemed to bring Juror #5 back, a sobering slap to the face. "Okay, I'll stay," he replied.

As the prosecutor, I was relieved. We had salvaged our jury, which apparently was on the brink of a conviction. The defense lawyer nearly had a coronary while objecting, but he had nowhere to go, legally. Juror #5 went back to the jury room, and about ten minutes later, another note came out: "We have a verdict." We all had a pretty good sense of what it would be, and indeed, the jury found Prisco guilty on all counts. Prisco got a life sentence and died in prison a few years later. Nothing ever happened to Juror #5 or any others, and the verdict stood up on appeal.

· ·

Jury service can be a scary experience.

Even in a routine criminal case, it's quite natural for any juror to be fearful. You randomly get a summons in the mail, and on the appointed day, you're herded into a large waiting room with a few hundred others. Eventually your number gets called, and you're walked into a packed courtroom where lawyers and a judge ask a series of invasive questions, on the record, about your life: family, employment, political and other personal beliefs. If chosen, you're thrown together with eleven strangers to decide the fate of another stranger who has been accused of illegal acts—sometimes violent crimes, including murder, as in our case. You spend days or weeks listening to impassioned but squarely conflicting arguments from talented lawyers for competing parties. The judge looks down from the bench, makes rulings you may not understand, and at the end of the presentation of evidence, gives complicated legal instructions about how you are to decide the case. Armed security officers and other law enforcement officials stand guard in the courtroom. Trial is open to the public, so the defendants' friends and family might be in the gallery watching the proceedings. Sometimes the media scrutinizes the case, and even the jury itself. The weight of the verdict ultimately falls on you and your fellow jurors, who must deliberate in a closed room for as long as it takes until you arrive at a unanimous decision.

Big picture, precious little is known about juror behavior; jurors deliberate in secret, and judges often take steps to shield them from the parties, the media, and other outsiders, even after deliberations conclude. But the National Center for State Courts published a revealing broad-based study in 1998 by a panel of experts including lawyers, judges, court administrators, and experts in psychology, psychiatry, and analytics. The group's final report made big-picture findings consistent with my own courtroom experience. Based on interviews with over thirteen hundred judges, jurors, and potential jurors who were not chosen to serve, the study found that "individuals who have been through the [jury] process have lamented that they felt as if *they* were on trial. Many fear being embarrassed or humiliated. In addition, individuals are often unfamiliar with the process and unaware of how lengthy it can be. They are apprehensive about a process that requires a loss of privacy and wonder what the extent of that loss will be."

Jurors fear not only the trial process itself, but also potential retribution. "Even in less serious cases," the study concluded, "jurors may be worried about their safety if the charge involved the use of force or if the parties and/or spectators in the courtroom seem hostile. Fear of retaliation can continue long after the proceeding is completed." That fear can be particularly pronounced in cases like the Prisco trial, where the judge decides to take safety precautions (such as jury anonymity): "Jurors are usually sufficiently attuned to their environment to realize when the situation warrants extra security. Thus failing to inform them about steps taken may actually have the opposite effect of heightening jurors' fears." This is a double-edged sword, of course. A judge can either directly inform a jury about safety precautions or try to keep them hidden. But either way, as with our Juror #5, jurors have a way of sensing that something's happening.

Savvy criminals learn to exploit jurors' fears inside the courtroom. Trials are public proceedings, open to anyone who cares to attend. Often, in my experience, mobsters would pack the gallery with family members and certain carefully selected friends and sympathizers who, shall we say, looked the part. Sometimes during a trial I'd glance back at the courtroom seating area and see what looked like a casting call for *The Sopranos*. You can bet the jurors were able to see the same thing. And the truly experienced players took it to another level. Whenever the jury left the courtroom on a break or at the end of the day, they'd be lined up by a court clerk, led out of the jury box, and then walked through the public seating area into the jury room at the back of the courtroom. I've seen defense teams carefully place menacing-looking characters on the aisle, just inches away from the jury's path, so they could stare quietly in the faces of the passing jurors.

Now, imagine the pressure that a juror would feel in a criminal trial of Donald Trump. Forget about a few physically imposing figures standing on the aisle of the courtroom gallery—imagine tens of millions of fervent supporters, whipped up by Trump himself, who has openly called on his followers to engage in civic unrest in the event of a criminal prosecution: "If these radical, vicious, racist prosecutors do anything wrong or illegal, I hope we are going to have in this country the biggest protests we have ever had in Washington, D.C., in New York, in Atlanta and elsewhere, because our country and our elections are corrupt." Senator Lindsey Graham echoed Trump's thinly veiled call to action, vowing publicly that "there literally will be riots in the street" if Trump were to be indicted. Trump reiterated in September 2022 that if he were indicted, "I think you'd have problems in this country the likes of which perhaps we've never seen before. I don't think the people of the United States would stand for it. . . . I think they'd have big problems, big problems."

Indeed, fanatic Trump backers repeatedly have harassed and threatened people who have opposed or crossed him. District attorney Fani Willis in Fulton County, Georgia—referenced by Trump in his rant about prosecutors in "Atlanta" and elsewhere—became a target for threats and racist slurs as she conducted her criminal investigation. Willis ordered enhanced security, including bulletproof vests, for her team. Georgia secretary of state Brad Raffensperger—a key witness in Willis's probe—and his family received explicit death threats from Trump backers for months after he refused to help Trump steal the election in Georgia, at one point forcing Raffensperger's family into hiding; "We plan for the death of you and your family every day," read one text.

Virtually any person of any station who has crossed him has felt the vindictive wrath of Trump and his supporters, sometimes to life-altering effect. After he came forward as a witness in Trump's first impeachment in 2019, Lt. Col. Alexander Vindman and his family faced an unceasing spate of death threats and harassment, prompting Vindman to file a lawsuit alleging that Trump and his allies intentionally inflamed their followers to harass and intimidate him. Dozens of state and local election officials received death threats from Trump supporters after the 2020 election; "It's been a barrage every day," noted Arizona secretary of state Katie Hobbs. And during the January 6 Committee investigation, committee members received all manner of harrowing death threats. Representative Adam Kinzinger, for example, publicly released a three-minute-long montage of harrowing voice mails he had received: "Hey you little cocksucker, going to come protest in front of your house this weekend. We know where your family is and we're gonna get you," one deranged lunatic threatened.

In particular, Trump has shown a pointed tendency to inflame his supporters against the legal system and the people who work within it. He tweeted and retweeted direct personal attacks against Mueller's team (constant tweets blasting "Angry Democrats" and "corrupt FBI agents") and members of Congress leading investigations ("Do Nothing Democrat Savages" including "LYIN' SHIFTY SCHIFF," and "Nervous Nancy Pelosi"). He went after judges, from Amy Berman Jackson, the federal judge on the Roger Stone case ("rogue" and "totally biased"), to Justice Ruth Bader Ginsburg ("an incompetent judge" whose "mind is shot") to the entire US Supreme Court ("totally incompetent and weak").

Trump even attacked a juror—an ordinary civilian who simply did her public duty. After a jury in Washington, DC, convicted his longtime political henchman Stone, Trump tweeted, "There has rarely been a juror so tainted as the forewoman in the Roger Stone case. Look at her background." During the Stone trial, Alex Jones, the lunatic conspiracy theorist, defied the judge's warning against revealing the jurors' identities when he broadcast the name and photo of a person he believed to be on the jury, calling that juror an anti-Trump "minion." In 2020, a year after the trial, a group of Stone jurors pleaded with the judge not to release their names to a different extremist right-wing blogger. The jurors wrote, "It does not require guesswork or speculation to see that the jurors would face unreasonable infringements of their privacy and security if the court's protections were relaxed." They noted that "certain jurors have been subjected to harassment already, and there is every reason to believe that others likely will as well, unless their questionnaires remain private." Remember: this happened around the trial not of Trump but of Stone. Any rational juror in a trial of Trump himself would rightly worry: What will happen to me if I decide to convict? What will happen to the country?

. .

Jurors who do fear a particular defendant can do one of two things. Either the juror can put that fear aside and decide the case solely on its merits, as instructed by the judge at the outset of any trial. Or the frightened juror can stay quiet and let it influence him toward a not-guilty vote. As a prosecutor, anytime we'd hear about a jury that deadlocked with eleven jurors favoring conviction but one favoring acquittal, we'd have to wonder: Was that one holdout juror just too scared to vote guilty?

The more common prosecutorial problem in my experience was that we lost countless *potential* jurors during the jury selection process ("voir dire," if you prefer the Latin). A veteran defense lawyer once told me that jury selection isn't just a big moment in any trial—it's the whole ball game. That was borne out in my own experience. In bigger cases, including the Prisco trial, prospective jurors are given a broad overview of the charges and then must fill out a written questionnaire. In response to the standard question "Is there anything about this case that could prevent you from being an impartial juror?" we'd constantly see responses like "I'd be too scared to sit on a Mafia case" or "I'm worried they might come after me."

Whether that fear was genuine or faked, it was an easy out for any-body who wanted to avoid jury service. We'd often be disappointed when this happened, because jurors who feared the mob were al-ready predisposed in our favor. We wanted jurors who believed the mob existed and saw it as a threat. But ultimately, if a juror claimed he was too scared to serve, the judge would usually let him go with-out much resistance. Naturally, by eliminating potential jurors who are inclined toward the prosecution, this phenomenon creates an ad-vantage not only for mob bosses but also for any imposing, powerful criminal defendant.

Now imagine how jury selection might play out in a trial of Trump. Even putting aside the remarkably complex politics of trying a for-mer president (who might by then also be the presumptive Republi-can nominee for the 2024 election)—which we'll discuss more later in this book—let's consider for now just the most basic fear factor. Undoubtedly many potential jurors would fear some sort of retribu-tion, given Trump's well-established history of riling up his support-ers. So who would those potential jurors be—the ones who might fear the fallout of serving on a Trump jury? Logically, they would tend to be people who thought poorly of Trump in the first place; his supporters, it seems reasonable to conclude, would be less likely to fear retribution from other pro-Trump forces. So a prosecutor would immediately lose a broad swath of the jury pool that was naturally inclined in her favor, and the defense would thin out the herd by eliminating right off the bat jurors who saw Trump and his support-ers as a potential menace.

It's a math game, really. If you start with a hundred people in the jury pool, but you instantly lose, say, twenty who are inclined toward the prosecution, then you bend the odds in favor of the powerful defendant. And few if any putative defendants would tilt the scales like Trump.

Chapter 9

OMERTÀ

Enforcing Silence

We like to think of the criminal justice process as mechanical and dispassionate, beyond the reach of human frailty and error. But at its core, the legal system is run by human beings who are inherently susceptible to the entire range of emotion, instinct, and motivation. Under the black judicial robe is a person—a smart and accomplished one, but just a person. Go beyond the suits, the briefs, and the Latin phrases, and prosecutors and defense lawyers are just men and women, trying to do their jobs without falling on their faces. We tend to think of the jury as some monolithic soothsayer, but in fact it's just twelve strangers thrown together by chance, trying to render a verdict and get on with their lives.

Fear is, of course, among the most powerful human motivators. We understand that as children, before we can even speak. While the things we fear change as we get older, the impulse remains powerful in our everyday lives and in our legal system. Fear works.

Powerful people benefit within the criminal justice system from their ability to instill fear not only in jurors but also in potential witnesses. Mafia bosses by necessity move up the ranks only if they cultivate fear of violent retribution against anyone who crosses them. It's almost part of the job description; I've never heard of a powerful mobster who didn't have at least a reputation on the streets as a "capable" guy—"capable" of committing, or at least ordering, violence.

Of all the mob murders I prosecuted, by far the most common motive was to eliminate a suspected cooperator. We've already discussed three such killings in this book: the shooting of Frank Hydell outside Scarlet's strip club in Staten Island, the ambush of Al Bruno outside a social club in downtown Springfield, Massachusetts, and the murder of Gary Westerman, who was buried by his killers and later dug up by the FBI in the woods of Agawam, Massachusetts. Each of these murders eliminated a potential witness who had broken the mob's central tenet of *omertà* (silence)—and sent a broader message to anybody who might contemplate coming forward with information that could harm a boss or other powerful player.

Trump never sought bloody retribution, of course, but he acutely understood and brandished the power of fear to enforce silence and punish dissent. He and his supporters have relentlessly pursued payback against anyone who dared turn on him, as detailed in the prior chapter. Perhaps he consciously sought retribution to punish witnesses to his political and criminal misdeeds, and to deter others from coming forward. Or maybe he simply acted on base impulse, lashing out without thought as to consequence. Either way, Trump has tried to destroy anyone who posed a threat, and he's often done it right in the public square, for all to see.

It's easy now to roll our eyes at Trump's weaponization of social media—*big deal, so he sent a snippy tweet*—but his online presence absolutely mattered, and matters still, and is capable of inflicting devastating consequences on its targets. Before and at the time of his permanent suspension from Twitter in January 2021, Trump was the most powerful man in the world, as president of the United States, with an enormously influential social media account—more than 88 million Twitter followers and 35 million on Facebook, with uncommon (and at times unthinking) devotion. Even now, Trump's every utterance gains traction on social media and in the news. It can be easy to say dismissively, "Why does anybody even cover this guy?" But he's a former president who might well run again for the nation's highest office in 2024. His words and actions are newsworthy, and we ignore them at our peril.

Trump's social media posts could make or break a political career, a reputation, a person's spirit. The same holds true now, even post-suspension and post-presidency. He wields that power aggressively, gleefully even, leaving little to the imagination in his effort to intimidate investigators and would-be witnesses. He brings all the subtlety of a mob boss to his anti-witness tirades—or, if anything, less; mob bosses don't generally tweet or appear on extremist media outlets to speak for wide public consumption.

For example, Trump, channeling a low-rent caricature of an old-fashioned mafioso, used Twitter to attack Michael Cohen as "a 'Rat'" (the capital R is Trump's) and Don McGahn as a "John Dean type 'RAT'" (all caps Trump's) after they provided damaging information to Mueller and to Congress. He went after key impeachment witnesses Alexander Vindman ("was given a horrendous report by his superior, the man he reported to, who publicly stated that Vindman had problems with judgement, adhering to the chain of command and leaking information") and former ambassador to Ukraine Marie Yovanovitch ("Everywhere Marie Yovanovitch went turned bad. She started off in Somalia, how did that go?"). Trump eventually demoted Vindman, Vindman's uninvolved twin brother, Yovanovitch, and former ambassador to the European Union Gordon Sondland in a public retributive display. After Trump's former national security advisor John Bolton outed him for trying to shake down the Ukrainian president, Trump attacked Bolton as "wacko," a "Creepster," and a "lowlife." And when Cyberstructure and Infrastructure Security Agency director Chris Krebs and FBI director Christopher Wray confirmed publicly that the 2020 election had not been marred by massive voter fraud, Trump publicly bludgeoned them both, hurling accusations of incompetence and fraud. Trump didn't stop at witnesses, of course; he publicly flayed prosecutors, judges, and even jurors as they tended to the business of the justice system, as we saw in the previous chapter. The lesson to all: cross me at your own risk.

Trump also used fear tactics to exercise particular sway over Republican politicians, for whom a disapproving tweet or other public statement could pose an existential political threat. He attacked any elected GOP official who cast a vote against him or cooperated with an investigation.

Consider the ten Republican House members who voted to impeach Trump the second time, after the January 6 Capitol attack. When one of the ten, Representative Adam Kinzinger, announced in October 2021 that he would not seek another term in Congress— joining Representative Anthony Gonzalez, who also had voted for Trump's second impeachment—Trump issued a gleeful public statement: "2 down, 8 to go!" Trump eventually made good on his vow to exact vengeance against those Republicans who dared cross him. Ultimately, only two of the ten survived politically; four lost in 2022 Republican primaries to Trump-endorsed opponents, while another four, including Kinzinger, retired rather than face the grim political reality they had wrought by standing up against Trump.

Representative Liz Cheney, the highest-profile Republican who voted to impeach Trump after the January 6 attack, presents a revealing case study. After she took a powerful internecine stance against Trump, he lashed out in a public statement: "Liz Cheney is polling sooo low in Wyoming, and has sooo little support, even from the Wyoming Republican Party, that she is looking for a way out of her Congressional race." He called her a "warmongering fool" and predicted that "[s]he'll either be yet another lobbyist or maybe embarrass her family by running for President, in order to save face." Cheney, uncowed, struck back every bit as hard, and more coherently: "Today, we face a threat America has never seen before. A former president who provoked a violent attack on this Capitol, in an effort to steal the election, has resumed his aggressive effort to convince Americans that the election was stolen from him. He risks inciting further violence."

But few politicians have the fortitude and institutional backing of Cheney, and virtually all Republicans fell in line rather than risk taking on the party's most popular and powerful figure. Cheney showed no fear, telling her fellow congressional Republicans, "If you want leaders who will enable and spread his destructive lies, I'm not your person, you have plenty of others to choose from." Trump's minions did just that, voting Cheney out of her leadership position with the House Republican caucus and replacing her with a flame-throwing Trump apologist, Representative Elise Stefanik. In 2022, as she gained national prominence as vice chair of the House January 6 Committee, Cheney—who had won her prior congressional election in Wyoming in 2020 by over forty points—lost by over 30 percentage points to a Trump-endorsed Republican primary challenger, Harriet Hageman, who, despite having opposed Trump's candidacy in 2016, later turned around and called him "the greatest president of my lifetime."

Ultimately, many Republican politicians faced this take-the-silver-or-take-the-lead dilemma: either pose for the smiling, thumbs-up photo with the former president, or risk political ruin through public attacks from the party's leader.

Why does this matter? Of course Trump attacked any politician (or media figure, or judge, or prosecutor, or human being of any station) who posed any kind of resistance or threat. It's as much a part of Trump's brand as bronze makeup and extra-long red ties. But Trump's public attacks on other political figures also made it more difficult to fully investigate and potentially prosecute him.

Take Kevin McCarthy, for example. After the January 6 Capitol attack, McCarthy had a momentary encounter with moral clarity.

On January 13 he solemnly declared from the House floor that "the president bears responsibility for Wednesday's attack on Congress by mob rioters. He should have immediately denounced the mob when he saw what was unfolding." McCarthy even let slip that Trump himself had squarely acknowledged personal culpability for the January 6 attack: "He told me personally that he does have some responsibility," McCarthy said on a radio show recorded six days after the insurrection attempt. And it emerged during impeachment proceedings that McCarthy had spoken directly with Trump as the January 6 attack unfolded. As McCarthy described the call to other Republican lawmakers, he begged Trump to call off the rioters, who were Trump's supporters. Trump lashed back, "Well, Kevin, I guess these people are more upset about the election than you are." McCarthy, who was then inside the Capitol as rioters smashed windows and tried to break into locked offices, shot back at Trump, "Who the fuck do you think you are talking to?"

Now: any prosecutor investigating Trump in relation to the January 6 insurrection—for obstruction of Congress, sedition, incitement of a riot, or other potential federal crimes that we'll discuss later—would immediately recognize McCarthy as a crucial witness. Trump had acknowledged his own fault directly to McCarthy, and based on his widely reported conversation with Trump on January 6, McCarthy knew that the rioters were acting on Trump's behalf and at his behest, and understood that Trump had the unique ability to call them off. McCarthy's contemporaneous call with Trump also established that Trump was, if anything, pleased by the actions of the rioters, which could prove his criminal intent in calling them to Washington, DC, and then exhorting them at the rally to go down to the Capitol and "fight like hell." Trump's statements to McCarthy help prove that the rioters did precisely what Trump had hoped they would do.

But once the initial rush of candor subsided after the January 6 attack, political reality set in for McCarthy. Then the Republican House minority leader, he had set his sights on becoming Speaker of the House. To get there, two things had to happen: (1) Republicans had to win the House in 2022, and (2) McCarthy had to remain the party's chosen leader in the House. Trump's political support was instrumental to both.

So just two weeks after he boldly called out Trump for his complicity in causing the January 6 attack, McCarthy stashed away his integrity and flew down to Mar-a-Lago to kiss Trump's ring. They posed for an awkward photo together, and then issued a gauzy proclamation about how "a united conservative movement will strengthen the bonds of our citizens and uphold the freedoms our country was founded on."

Meanwhile, McCarthy fought like mad to prevent Congress from undertaking any meaningful investigation of the root causes behind the January 6 attack. He opposed efforts to establish a bipartisan investigative commission, and then relentlessly attacked and undermined the January 6 Select Committee. He threatened phone service providers who received subpoenas from the committee, vowing that House Republicans "will not forget" and would "hold them fully accountable under the law" for complying with perfectly lawful, routine subpoenas—which raised questions about what in those records so gravely worried him. And he publicly undermined the committee, mimicking Trump's (rather uncreative) denigration of the "Unselect Committee."

As this all played out, McCarthy's memory of the key events in question grew mysteriously fuzzy and far less damaging to Trump. Whenever he was asked about his conversation with Trump on January 6, he'd pivot to political talking points and nonresponsive answers about police preparedness. He did a 180 on his original statement that Trump "bears responsibility" for the attack; just four months later, McCarthy claimed that Trump "didn't see it [the riot].

What he ended the call with saying was telling me, he'll put something out to make sure to stop this. And that's what he did. He put a video out later." As the committee noted in a January 2022 letter seeking McCarthy's testimony (which he ultimately refused to provide), "Your public statements regarding January 6th have changed markedly since you met with Trump." Markedly, indeed.

McCarthy intentionally poisoned himself as a witness. By following his own initial statements implicating Trump in the attack with hazy, self-contradictory blather, he turned himself from a potentially damning witness against Trump in an impeachment or a potential prosecution into an essentially unusable witness whose account would be fatally riddled with inconsistencies and straight-up falsehoods.

Another powerful Trump loyalist, White House chief of staff Mark Meadows, went through a similar process of re-education. The committee sensibly included Meadows in its first batch of subpoenas, issued in September 2021. Who better to question than Meadows, who was in the White House by Trump's side as the Capitol attack unfolded?

After weeks of negotiation—and threats by committee members to hold Meadows in contempt and to refer him to the DOJ for potential prosecution—the parties reached an agreement calling for Meadows to provide some information, while potentially preserving his right not to answer certain questions that might have raised privilege concerns. Meadows, accordingly, gave the committee an explosive batch of documents. Those records included thousands of damning text messages, among them dozens in which prominent Republicans begged Trump to call off his supporters who were storming the Capitol as the January 6 attack unfolded. (One Republican congressman, Will Timmons, wrote, "The president needs to stop this ASAP"; Donald Trump Jr. texted, "He's got to condem this shit. Asap. The captiol police tweet is not enough" [*sic*]; Fox News host

Laura Ingraham wrote, "The president needs to tell people in the Capitol to go home. This is hurting all of us.") Meadows also produced for the committee a thirty-eight-page PowerPoint detailing a plan to overturn the 2020 election and texts and emails in which Meadows discussed options for a "direct and collateral attack" on the election results. In one text exchange, when Meadows learned of plans to appoint alternate slates of electors in states Trump had lost, he responded, "I love it."

Meadows also wrote in his book, which was published just weeks after he struck his cooperation deal with the committee in December 2021, about Trump's conduct on January 6 and other unflattering anecdotes about Trump's time in office.

Trump was, to put it mildly, displeased. He was reportedly furious at Meadows over the book, and deemed it "fake news," "garbage," and "fucking stupid." (He had previously praised the book as "fantastic.") Almost immediately following Trump's attacks, Meadows, like McCarthy, fell right back in line. Hours after Trump blasted the book, Meadows went on Newsmax and agreed with Trump that the reporting that quoted his own book was fake news. Just days later, the other shoe fell. Meadows backed out of his cooperation with the committee and, in a public demonstration of fealty to Trump, sued the committee, seeking to block its investigative efforts.

Turned out, Trump had used not just the stick but also the carrot. In early 2022, Trump's Save America political action committee disclosed to the Federal Election Commission that nearly six months before, in July 2021—weeks after the January 6 Committee was formally created—it had donated $1 million to the Conservative Partnership Institute, a conservative nonprofit that counted among its partners none other than . . . Mark Meadows. By the time of the public disclosure, Meadows had already reneged on his initial cooperation with the committee.

In the process of defying the committee, Meadows earned himself a contempt citation from the House and a referral to the Justice Department for potential criminal prosecution for contempt of Congress. But DOJ announced late on a Friday night in June 2022 that it would not file charges against Meadows or former White House deputy chief of staff Dan Scavino—even though the department did bring contempt prosecutions against Steve Bannon and Peter Navarro, who also had defied congressional subpoenas. In the end, Meadows clammed up and faced no meaningful consequences, while Trump escaped untouched by anything Meadows might have had to say.

· ·

The parallel sagas of McCarthy and Meadows bring to mind an actual witness-gone-bad in a Mafia prosecution of mine. The gangsters called him Gene the Carpet—his first name was Gene, and he ran a carpet store. (Not every mob nickname is creative, or even accurate; yes, Gene sold carpeting, but no, he was not an actual carpet.) Gene the Carpet was a longtime victim of extortion by Genovese family powerhouse Ciro Perrone, who presided quietly but menacingly from his Queens social club while his crew of loyal enforcers collected regular shakedown payments from sad-sack, terrified local merchants.

When our prosecution team first approached Gene to enlist his testimony in the case we were building against Perrone, he refused to talk. Only after we issued him a subpoena and sent out a couple federal agents to ensure his appearance at trial did he admit, reluctantly, that he had paid extortion money to Perrone for years.

But when it came time to implicate the powerful Perrone at trial, Gene the Carpet turned into a puddle. I still remember him fighting back tears in the witness room before he took the stand, gasping for breath. At first Gene tried to claim on the stand that he couldn't remember whether he ever paid Perrone anything—pure nonsense, of course, and also notably similar to McCarthy's convenient failures of recollection. Eventually we pried out of Gene a reluctant admission that, yes, he paid Perrone a few hundred dollars every week. But, Gene testified, with a healthy bit of self-protective revisionism, I paid Perrone not because I feared him—I paid because I liked him, respected him, and saw him as a friend.

Taken at face value, that testimony from Gene the Carpet could have tanked our extortion charge. Fortunately, we were able to recover from this bit of fear-induced sabotage. Of course Gene didn't pay Perrone hundreds of dollars every week as a friend, we argued to the jury; do you have any friends who pay you every week out of love and respect? Of course Gene the Carpet knew who Perrone was, knew Perrone was a mobster, knew he'd be helpless to defend himself if he crossed Perrone.

The jury convicted Perrone of extortion (and other offenses), despite Gene's semi-cooked, Perrone-friendly testimony. The judge astutely noted at Perrone's sentencing that "it is hard to get witnesses. People are afraid of retaliation against them and their families."

Kevin McCarthy and Mark Meadows are better coiffed and more glib than poor old Gene the Carpet. But they're really not all that different. They all stood up—at least for a moment—to terrifyingly powerful men, but then thought better of it, played dumb, and curled up into scared little balls.

· ·

Not everybody took the coward's road. When Cassidy Hutchinson, a former White House aide to Meadows, gave earth-shattering public testimony to the January 6 Committee in June 2022, Cheney revealed that two witnesses—one of whom, unsurprisingly, turned out to be Hutchinson herself—had received messages, through intermediaries, intended to intimidate them or, at a minimum, influence their testimony. One witness described the barely veiled message this way: "What they said to me is as long as I continue to be a team player, they know I'm on the right team. I'm doing the right thing. I'm protecting who I need to protect, you know, I'll continue to stay in good graces in Trump World. And they have reminded me a couple of times that Trump does read transcripts." Hutchinson received a similar message: "[A person] let me know you have your deposition tomorrow. He wants me to let you know that he's thinking about you. He knows you're loyal, and you're going to do the right thing when you go in for your deposition." Various media outlets later reported that the redacted "[A person]" was none other than Mark Meadows.

Hutchinson did eventually testify publicly before the committee, to devastating effect (even as prosecutors lagged inexcusably behind, reportedly just as "astonished" by her account as any common civilian). But to get to the witness table, she had to overcome all manner of obstacles. First, she shed her Trump-chosen (and Trump-funded) lawyer, as we discussed in chapter 3. Then people around Trump tried to silence her, or at least shape her testimony in a favorable manner; recall our discussion in chapter 5 about the benefits of the hierarchical pyramid, and Trump's tendency to have his associates, or associates of his associates, do the dirty work. And Trump's people tried to enforce her compliance not with overt threats but with coded language that stopped just short of an explicit call to criminality but nonetheless was unmistakable in intent, as we saw in chapter 6.

We know that, ultimately, Hutchinson broke through. But it took a rare mix of courage and defiance that few Trump supporters ever displayed—particularly those seeking elective office. We'll never know how many others lacked that determination, buckled to the pressure, and stayed silent.

Chapter 10

"WITHOUT FEAR OR FAVOR"

The Truth about How Prosecutors Treat the Powerful

During his twenty-plus years as a federal district court judge in the Southern District of New York, Judge William H. Pauley III presided over thousands of cases. He made decisions with broad political and economic consequences in cases involving government surveillance of citizens, fair housing, and regulation of large financial institutions, among other weighty issues.

But when Pauley died in July 2021, the *New York Times* obituary, in the very first sentence, cut almost immediately to the single case for which Pauley will always, fairly or not, be most remembered: "Judge William H. Pauley III, the Manhattan federal judge who sentenced Michael D. Cohen, Donald J. Trump's lawyer . . ." The obituary then took an eight-sentence detour to address other aspects of Pauley's life and distinguished service—hometown, cause of death, judicial appointment, a couple other important but less prominent cases—before returning to the true object of its fascination, Cohen, for the next six paragraphs. It's a close call as to who is actually the primary focus of the obituary—Cohen or the deceased himself. A Control-F word search gives it to Pauley by a narrow 11 to 10 margin, though three of the "Pauley" hits refer to his surviving family members.

I appeared in front of Judge Pauley dozens of times. He was old-fashioned, serious, and stern on the bench—intimidating, even. He insisted that lawyers use their full first names; if an attorney introduced himself as "Jim Rodgers for the United States," Pauley would interrupt from the bench, "I think you mean *James* Rodgers for the United States." (Pauley never quite knew what to do with my unusual first name, so he stayed quiet.) He studied every case carefully—not every judge did, candidly—and he was meticulously prepared.

Knowing Pauley, I'm certain he would have been exasperated (maybe worse) that the *Times* and other media outlets reduced his career, with all its breadth and significance, mostly to a recap of the Cohen-facilitated hush money payments to a porn actress and a *Playboy* model. I also recognized firsthand the strangeness, the incongruity, the disproportionality, of so much focus landing on this one case. It wasn't even much of a case, either, from a judicial perspective. Cohen never went to trial. He pled guilty right away, and Pauley's only substantive task, given the case's procedural posture, was to impose a sentence. He gave Cohen thirty-six months, which seemed about right and was fairly uncontroversial.

Pauley's obituary stands as a reminder of this cold fact: even the most prominent prosecutor, defense lawyer, or judge will be remembered publicly only for a handful of cases, or perhaps just one. It's not fair, it's not an accurate reflection of a career, but it's reality. Sometimes one case can cover a lawyer in glory for all time: "The prosecutor who took down [fill in your favorite villain here]." But every prosecutor who takes on a megapowerful defendant also understands the inevitable flip side: if you take a shot at a boss and fail, you take it to your grave (and, perhaps more importantly, to your Google search results while you're still alive and practicing).

People sometimes ask me if it was scary to take on murderous Mafia bosses. The answer, truthfully, is no. In a sense, it was easy. As the prosecutor, you're the good guy, the hero, Captain America. But I'll tell you what is scary: going after a powerful politician or a CEO or a wealthy celebrity who will battle you every millimeter of the way, claim he's been falsely accused, and do a public relations tour to discredit your entire case, and likely you personally. That's scary.

..

Here's an ugly but undeniable truth: prosecutors generally think harder, and require more proof, before they'll bring a charge against a boss than against a common defendant. It's not comfortable to acknowledge. The standard boilerplate prosecutor talking point goes something like: *We consider every case with precisely equal care and apply the same standards across the board, regardless of the defendant's station in life.* But that's simply not true.

Exhibit A: the *Justice Manual*, DOJ's own formal written guidance to all federal prosecutors across the country. The manual specifically requires higher levels of internal review and approval before charges can be filed against powerful people.

For example, while a US attorney typically has final authority to sign off on most charges, she must notify top Justice Department officials about "major developments" (including initiation of investigation, filing of charges, arrest, plea, trial, and sentencing) in "significant investigations and litigation." The *Justice Manual* defines those "significant" matters largely based on the identity and status of the subject, including any "national or statewide public official, public entity, or prominent public figure as a party, subject, target, or significant witness." So if the case involves a powerful politician or a famous person (a "prominent public figure") as a potential defendant or even merely as a witness, then Justice Department bosses must get involved and sign off. The manual also requires notice to the attorney general if the case involves a "high likelihood of coverage in national news media," which would apply to a prosecution of a celebrity or other influential target, but not to an ordinary case.

Take the aforementioned SDNY prosecution of Michael Cohen,

for example. If the case had merely involved a no-name local attorney who fudged his taxes and made some shady payoffs, it likely would've been handled by the frontline prosecutors on the case, perhaps with some guidance and input from a unit chief or deputy chief. But as we've seen, because the case involved Michael Cohen—and by extension Donald Trump—every minute decision went all the way up the chain of command, both within the SDNY and down in DC at Main Justice.

Even beyond written DOJ policy, any sensible prosecutor knows that if a potential defendant is a prominent person, he'd better run it up the flagpole first. Likewise, supervisors typically make clear to subordinates that they need to be kept updated about cases involving powerful or high-profile defendants. It's a refrain that I heard countless times when I was a newbie, and later repeated myself when I was a chief: "Don't let me learn about one of our cases from the newspaper."

There are legitimate justifications for these requirements. It's not just a matter of guts or cowardice. These extra layers of internal review are designed to protect against a high-profile mistake that could damage the reputation of the prosecutor and the prosecutor's office itself. But the effect, intended or not, benefits bosses and other powerhouses. Each layer of review means one more prosecutor, at one higher level, must agree before charges can be filed. Purely as a mathematical proposition, more layers of review mean more chances for a higher-ranking prosecutor to veto a charge and for a powerful defendant to escape indictment.

Anecdotal evidence is plentiful. For example, in 2006 I charged a case against thirty-one defendants who ran a sex trafficking ring throughout the northeastern United States. The defendants, all Korean nationals, smuggled young Korean women into the United States, often under false pretenses, and then put them to work as, essentially, sex slaves. The defendants kept the victims in horrific conditions, often locked inside brothels—sometimes thinly disguised as "massage parlors"—for weeks at a time. The women were made to have sex with as many as ten customers per night. We ended up taking guilty pleas from twenty-six of the defendants and then trying and convicting the remaining five. It was a big case, and an important case, but no big names were involved. As a result, I made almost all of the major decisions by myself, as a third-year prosecutor, in loose consultation with my unit chiefs from time to time, as needed. The SDNY bosses had essentially nothing to do with the case, and there was no need for them to be involved.

Fast-forward a couple years, to early 2008. I got a call one day from one of the top officials at the SDNY. He asked me a pointed question about my sex trafficking case, which had concluded by then. "Did you charge the johns in your case?" he asked, referring to the customers who paid for sex. I told him that because we raided the brothels at 6:00 a.m., we didn't actually come across any johns. I couldn't help but snoop a bit, so I asked why he wanted to know. He responded that he was trying to figure out what to do on a similar case. I didn't press any further, but it struck me as odd that one of the SDNY's bosses would be involved in a sex trafficking case that would ordinarily be far below his pay grade (and much closer to mine).

Everything snapped into focus one morning a few weeks later. The SDNY announced a series of arrests in a sex trafficking case that was similar to mine in many respects, except one: one of the johns in that case was the sitting governor of New York, Eliot Spitzer, famously branded in the criminal complaint as "Client-9." Suddenly it all made sense. The SDNY's bosses were handling this case because it involved a powerful, boldface name. Had the sitting governor not been involved, the case never would have gone much above the line-level prosecutor for approval on a charging decision. But in the Spitzer case, the decision whether to charge (or, as it turned out, not to charge) went all the way up the chain and was subject to far more rigorous scrutiny than any ordinary case involving non-gubernatorial subjects.

I had another case at the SDNY in which a well-known major league baseball player (I won't give his name here because he was never publicly charged, but he made a few all-star teams) was caught up in a gambling ring with a mob family. An ordinary gambling case would've never risen above my fairly low level. But because this case involved a celebrity, we sent word up the chain to the head of the office's criminal division. If this player had never made it to the majors, and was not well known, the decision about how to handle him would've been mine alone. But because the case implicated a boldface name, it went higher up the supervisory chain. (We ultimately decided not to charge, but we turned the subject into a confidential informant who quietly fed us information leading to other cases.)

Later, when I was a supervisor at the New Jersey attorney general's office, we prosecuted over a hundred defendants who had defrauded a fund for people who had lost their primary residences during Superstorm Sandy. Most of the defendants had sustained damage to vacation houses down the shore, but falsely claimed they lived there year-round. We churned these cases out by the dozens—until we came to one defendant who had worked in the office of the then-governor, Chris Christie. We knew this case would capture local headlines and cast the governor's office in a bad light. (Further complicating matters, Christie was gearing up to run for president at the time, and his response to Sandy was a key selling point in his campaign pitch.)

So we pulled this one case off the assembly line and sent word up to the state attorney general, who ended up scrutinizing every nuance of the case, over several months, before he approved the charge. The governor's office employee eventually did get charged, but it took far longer and was subject to magnitudes greater prosecutorial scrutiny than the normal Sandy fraud case.

Any US attorney, or state attorney general, or county-level district attorney, supervises dozens or hundreds of prosecutors who bring hundreds or thousands of cases every year. The US attorney in the SDNY oversees about 150 prosecutors at a time, and the office typically charges about 1,000 to 1,500 defendants per year. When I was in charge of the New Jersey Division of Criminal Justice, I supervised over 500 people total, including about 120 prosecutors, and we charged about 1,000 cases annually. I know this: there's simply no way that every case, or even more than a select handful, can land on the boss's desk. Yet it's essentially unthinkable, either as a matter of formal written policy or just plain common sense, that an office would bring any charge against a famous or powerful defendant without running it up the line, regardless of the severity of charges. As a line prosecutor, I didn't give briefings to the US attorney (or even my own unit chief, who was my direct supervisor) on every mob extortion or street robbery—but you can bet I briefed the higher-ups on the lowly gambling case involving the professional baseball player. And when I was in charge in New Jersey, I wouldn't sign off on every retail theft case or every drug seizure. But the attorney general and I spent hours scrutinizing the low-level fraud case involving the governor's office employee.

It's perfectly reasonable and even appropriate for prosecutors to give extra scrutiny to high-profile cases before filing charges. Failure in one headline case can undermine public confidence in the prosecutor's office and the criminal justice system in a way that can't be offset even by years of good work on routine matters. Think of Cy Vance, for example. He'll be remembered, rightly, for his failures on the high-profile cases discussed in this book—the Trump adult children, Harvey Weinstein—much more than for the thousands of successful routine prosecutions he oversaw during his twelve years in office. Or take Alexander Acosta, who gave away the original Jeffrey Epstein case in Florida. Who remembers anything else about his tenure as US attorney, no matter what else he might have accomplished? So it is indeed natural and understandable that prominent names get more intense internal scrutiny.

But it also leads inevitably to this outcome: the bar is higher for rich people, powerful people, and celebrities. Prosecutors require more proof, more certainty, and more layers of review and approval before they'll charge a boss. Prosecutors love to remind the world that we do our jobs "without fear or favor." But the fact is, we do approach certain subjects with more fear than others.

Chapter 11

PREY ON THE VULNERABLE

It started in 2005, when the Palm Beach Police Department received a complaint from the stepmother of a fourteen-year-old girl who had been sexually abused by Jeffrey Epstein, a well-connected but mysterious billionaire.

Epstein then counted among his friends presidents past (Bill Clinton) and future (Donald Trump), and he possessed a literal black book filled with the names of celebrities and titans of politics and industry. *New York* magazine ran an article in 2002 titled "Jeffrey Epstein: International Moneyman of Mystery," which in retrospect is equal parts foreboding and creepy in its glamorization of Epstein's predatory lifestyle. The piece opens: "He comes with cash to burn, a fleet of airplanes, and a keen eye for the ladies . . ." (Yes, "a keen eye for the ladies.") Trump chortled in the piece, with palpable admiration, "I've known Jeff for fifteen years. Terrific guy. He's a lot of fun to be with. It is even said that he likes beautiful women as much as I do, and many of them are on the younger side. No doubt about it—Jeffrey enjoys his social life." Clinton also weighed in, through a spokesperson, though he turned the focus away from those "younger side" women: "Jeffrey is both a highly successful financier and a committed philanthropist with a keen sense of global markets and an in-depth knowledge of twenty-first-century science."

Undaunted by Epstein's deep connections to the most powerful people on the planet, the Palm Beach police did their jobs and identified about twenty victims who had been sexually abused by Epstein when they were teenagers. The FBI also got involved, and began to unravel a complex network in which Epstein would induce vulnerable young girls into a sex trafficking ring, using them, as a federal judge later found, "not only for his own sexual gratification, but also for the sexual gratification of others." It is impossible to say for certain precisely how many young women ultimately fell victim to Epstein. The federal government at one point identified 36 victims, and a federal judge found that Epstein had "sexually abused more than 30 minor girls." About 150 people eventually made successful claims from a fund established to compensate his victims.

Looking back now, there's no question: the prosecutors in Florida who gave Epstein a pass during his first run-in with the law for sexual abuse of underage girls knew they were letting him walk with a preposterously light plea deal. And to cover it up—they nearly succeeded—those prosecutors mistreated Epstein's young female victims, lied to them, and broke the law. Alexander Acosta—then the US attorney for the Southern District of Florida, who later (briefly) became secretary of the US Department of Labor in the Trump administration—made an indefensible, unjust deal with Epstein, a serial child rapist. Acosta permitted Epstein, who could have faced decades behind bars had he been prosecuted federally, instead to plead guilty to low-level state offenses carrying minimal jail time.

Epstein is dead now, of course. He spent his final days in federal prison after he was charged years later by the Southern District of New York, and then only after bold journalism and public outrage forced the issue. His top confederate, Ghislaine Maxwell, was tried and convicted for sex trafficking crimes, and is now serving a twenty-year federal sentence.

Both of these irredeemable villains, Epstein and Maxwell, met with brutal, if just, fates. But it's important to remember: they both came awfully close to walking away virtually unscathed, even though dozens of young women came forward with evidence of sexual exploitation and abuse. Epstein and Maxwell might have escaped with little to no consequence, with Acosta holding the door wide open for them, but for the public furor that arose after a local reporter, Julie K. Brown, blew the lid off the special treatment that prosecutors afforded to a powerful serial sexual predator—at the expense of scores of young, vulnerable female victims.

..

The Epstein case landed in Acosta's office in 2006, when he was the US attorney for the Southern District of Florida, the top federal prosecutor in the Miami area. Acosta's prosecutors initially notified Epstein's victims about the case, as required by federal law. The law enforcement team informed the victims that the case was under investigation, that DOJ would make its "best efforts" to protect their rights, and that they had "the reasonable right to confer with the attorney for the United States in the case" and "to be reasonably heard at any public proceeding in the district court involving [a] . . . plea."

Meanwhile, having assured victims that they would be kept informed on the case, Acosta and his prosecutors engaged with Epstein's powerhouse celebrity legal team—Kenneth Starr, Alan Dershowitz, and the rest. As detailed earlier in chapter 4, Epstein's lawyers applied intense pressure on Acosta and the Justice Department to give their client a pass. Although the frontline prosecutor handling the case, Maria Villafaña, drafted a sixty-count indictment accompanied by a detailed evidentiary memo, Acosta ultimately declined to bring federal charges. Instead he gave Epstein a non-prosecution agreement (NPA), so long as Epstein pled guilty to low-level state offenses.

Villafaña put her dissent on the record. Before Acosta finalized the non-prosecution deal, she emailed her boss about the plight of Epstein's victims: "One girl broke down sobbing so that we had to stop the interview twice within a 20 minute span. She regained her composure enough to continue a short time, but she said that she was having nightmares about Epstein coming after her and she started to break down again, so we stopped the interview." Villafaña concluded, "These girls deserve so much better than they have received so far, and I hate feeling that there is nothing I can do to help them." (Hand it to Villafaña here; as a rank-and-file prosecutor, I never would've had the courage to send such a defiant, though righteous, email to my boss.)

Epstein's legal team, displaying gumption of their own, continued to fight for even more lenient treatment. But ultimately Epstein accepted Acosta's generous offer, and pled guilty to Florida state-level charges of solicitation of prostitution and procuring minors for prostitution. He received a sentence of eighteen months, but with time off for good behavior, he served thirteen months in a minimum-security Palm Beach County facility. He was allowed to leave for twelve hours per day to participate in a work-release program at a shadowy newly formed business called the Florida Science Foundation, located at the same address as one of his attorneys. (It remains unclear precisely what kind of "science" was being advanced.)

Epstein and his lawyers achieved a dream result, far better than any serial child rapist could ever hope for in front of any minimally competent federal prosecutors. But one problem remained: the victims.

Epstein's legal team wanted to keep the sweetheart deal with Acosta as quiet as possible, to minimize public scrutiny. It stood to reason that the victims might not take kindly to Acosta's generous NPA and might just raise a fuss about it. Epstein's lawyers implored Acosta's office to keep the NPA under wraps, writing at one point in an email, "Please do whatever you can to keep this [i.e., the NPA] from becoming public."

Acosta's office was generally on board with keeping things mum; after all, there wasn't much for the prosecutors to be proud of either.

Villafaña at one point emailed Epstein's lawyers about their mutual desire to "avoid the press," suggesting ways she might file an obstruction of justice charge in an adjacent federal district to "hopefully cut the press coverage significantly." Acosta's prosecutors also assured Epstein's lawyers that the federal NPA would not be filed publicly, and that they would only give it up if forced to do so by a court. Accordingly, the final document was filed under seal (secretly, not available to the public without a court order).

At one point a member of Epstein's legal team, Jay Lefkowitz, emailed Acosta's office and demanded that "neither federal agents nor anyone from your Office should contact the identified individuals [victims] to inform them of the resolution of the case." Despite the audacity of this request to keep the victims in the dark, Acosta had a private breakfast with Lefkowitz. Apparently it went well for Lefkowitz, who followed up by emailing to Acosta, "I also want to thank you for the commitment you made to me during our October 12 meeting in which you . . . assured me that your Office would not . . . contact any of the identified individuals, potential witnesses, or potential civil claimants and their respective counsel in this matter."

True to that agreement, as negotiations progressed, Acosta's office never notified any of the dozens of Epstein's victims that it was considering giving him a pass on federal charges. Prosecutors at one point asked for the victims to display "patience," without telling them it was in the process of negotiating an NPA. Worse, the government later assured victims that the matter was "ongoing," even after the federal NPA had already been executed and finalized.

A federal district court judge, Kenneth Marra, later blasted Acosta and his team for their mistreatment of Epstein's victims. Judge Marra found that Acosta had sought "to conceal the existence" of the generous non-prosecution deal with Epstein, and that he had misled "the victims to believe that federal prosecution was still a possibility" even after the NPA was final and he had already given away the case to the state authorities.

In November 2020, more than a year after Epstein's death, the Justice Department's Office of Professional Responsibility (OPR) issued a report on the handling of the Epstein matter by Acosta and others. The OPR report concluded, with a spoonful of in-house generosity, that Acosta exercised "poor judgment" but "was within the scope of his authority" to give Epstein a sweetheart plea deal. It also said it "did not find evidence that his decision was based on corruption or other impermissible considerations, such as Epstein's wealth, status, or associations." (It's unclear what might have met this absurdly high burden set out by OPR, short of some hypothetical internal email in which a prosecutor wrote "Hey, let's cut this guy a break because he's rich and powerful.")

The OPR report tap-danced around Judge Marra's conclusion that Acosta tried to hide Epstein's non-prosecution agreement from the victims and affirmatively misled them. OPR cleared Acosta and the other subjects on this count because they "did not have a clear and unambiguous duty under the CVRA [Crime Victims' Rights Act] to consult with victims before entering into the NPA because the USAO [US Attorney's Office] resolved the Epstein investigation without a federal criminal charge." Allow me to translate this nonsense. According to OPR, the victims had no right to be heard on this case because Acosta decided to give the case away without prosecuting it, thereby rendering it not technically a "case" in the first place. By that logic, if a prosecutor screws up or gives away a case badly enough to the point that he never charges it, he never has to notify the victims at all. Hey: no case, no victims.

The OPR report goes on to note that the misleading letters sent to victims (stating that the case, which had already been quietly resolved, was still "under investigation") couldn't be held against

Acosta or other leaders of the US Attorney's Office because they "were sent by an FBI administrative employee who was not directly involved in the investigation." OPR therefore blamed the ministerial FBI employee who sent the letters, and absolved the higher-ranking officials who were responsible for the letters' content and for complying with the law regarding communication with victims. (The Justice Department itself is not above a little insulation for the bosses.) The OPR report did concede that "the letters risked misleading the victims and contributed to victim frustration and confusion by failing to provide important information about the status of the investigation"—but to no consequence for Acosta, or anybody else.

In another burst of empty rhetoric, OPR proclaimed that Acosta's treatment of the victims "reflected poorly on the Department as a whole, and is contradictory to the Department's mission to 'minimize the frustration and confusion that victims of a crime endure'" and that "the victims were not treated with the forthrightness and sensitivity expected by the Department." Yet somehow, according to OPR, nobody really did anything too terribly wrong. Horrible outcome, sure. Mistreatment of victims, yes. Violation of law, perhaps. But ultimately: nothing to see here, folks.

One of Epstein's victims, Jena-Lisa Jones (who alleged that Epstein had sexually assaulted her when she was fourteen years old), said publicly that the OPR report "felt very much like another slap in the face." Another victim, Dainya Nida, noted with a palpable sense of recurring frustration, "Any time I am involved in any of this I never have any expectations anymore because I know I am never going to get the answer why."

Villafaña, the federal prosecutor who had prepared a draft indictment of Epstein, also took issue with OPR's tepid conclusion. The "injustice" of Epstein's lenient plea deal was, she said in a public statement, "the result of deep, implicit institutional biases that prevented me and the FBI agents who worked diligently on this case from holding Mr. Epstein accountable for his crimes." Villafaña added that "by not considering those implicit biases based on gender and socioeconomic status, OPR lost an opportunity to make recommendations for institutional changes that could prevent results like this one from occurring in the future."

Years later, in December 2021, an SDNY prosecutor, Maurene Comey, hit it on the head in her rebuttal argument to the jury in the trial of Epstein's primary accomplice, Maxwell. "The defendant never thought that those teenage girls would have the strength to report what happened. In her eyes, they were just trash beneath her," Comey argued. "Those girls would never stand up to a power couple like Jeffrey Epstein and Ghislaine Maxwell. And if they did, who would believe them?"

Epstein (and Acosta) almost got away with it. But Julie K. Brown, a tireless reporter for the *Miami Herald*, brought wide public attention to the injustice of Epstein's first prosecution. Ultimately, with renewed public focus—intensified by Trump's selection of Acosta as US secretary of labor in 2017—the SDNY in July 2019 brought federal charges against Epstein for sex trafficking of minors. Epstein faced up to forty-five years in prison, and a likely sentence of at least a decade. Four days after the SDNY filed charges against Epstein, Acosta resigned his cabinet post in disgrace.

It took over a decade before the SDNY brought the heavy federal charges that Epstein should have faced long before in Florida. But Epstein's lawyers quickly raised in his defense the specter of Acosta's original non-prosecution agreement, arguing that it bound the Justice Department as a whole and precluded the SDNY's subsequent prosecution. This motion had some merit and posed a potential threat to the SDNY case. But before the judge could rule, Epstein died by what was officially deemed suicide inside the Metropolitan Correctional Center in Manhattan in August 2019.

Undoubtedly, many factors contributed to Acosta's decision to go light on Epstein—cowardice, stupidity, arrogance. But it's also impossible to ignore what Villafaña and many victims have called out: the bias that Acosta and his staff displayed toward Epstein's victims, all of whom were young and female. The victims generally were scared, powerless, and inexperienced in the criminal justice system. Not only did Acosta strike a deal that trivialized the victims' plight—but he kept them in the dark to protect a wealthy, powerful man.

• •

Dramatic as it was, the Epstein case was no outlier. This pattern has played out with astonishing regularity: rich, powerful man is accused of multiple sexual assaults; prosecutor and police take a look, often belatedly or half-heartedly, and insufficient charges (if any) are filed; media digs in and exposes law enforcement incompetence or malfeasance; as public outrage builds, the original prosecutor (or another prosecutor) backtracks, takes another look, re-evaluates, and brings appropriate charges, if still legally and practically possible; and, occasionally some administrative body investigates, does a postmortem report, and concludes that, ahem, *mistakes were made*. Rinse and repeat.

Take, for example, Harvey Weinstein. Now that the disgraced movie producer has been convicted and will likely die behind bars, it's easy to forget that he, like Epstein, nearly slipped away from law enforcement despite straightforward evidence of his guilt.

Weinstein sexually assaulted dozens of women in and around Hollywood, over decades, including incidents involving forcible, nonconsensual oral sex and intercourse. As discussed earlier, Manhattan DA Cy Vance had a clean shot at Weinstein in 2015 but gave him an inexplicable pass—even though a credible witness, Ambra Gutierrez, had worked with the NYPD to capture him on a recording admitting that he had groped her, and others before.

Vance let Weinstein slip away temporarily, but he wasn't able to keep this one under wraps for long. In 2017 the *New Yorker* ran an exposé on Gutierrez's allegations and the incriminating recording. The then-governor of New York, Andrew Cuomo, jumped on the bandwagon after the story's publication and demanded a review of Vance's decision not to charge Weinstein. (Cuomo would resign in 2021 when *he* was accused of sexual misconduct.) Later in 2017, the *New York Times* published an investigative report detailing decades of sexual abuse by Weinstein, including allegations by actresses Rose McGowan and Ashley Judd. Another actress, Paz de la Huerta, told *Vanity Fair* in 2017 that Weinstein had raped her twice in New York City in 2010. The *Vanity Fair* piece explicitly called out prosecutors with the headline "Paz de la Huerta Says Harvey Weinstein Raped Her Twice. Will That Bring Him to Justice?"

Only after these journalistic revelations caused public pressure to boil over did Vance double back and take another look at Weinstein. This time, in 2018—three years after he originally declined to prosecute Weinstein—Vance announced a spate of serious charges relating to the sexual assaults of actresses Jessica Mann in 2013 and Lucia Evans in 2004 (the judge eventually dismissed the charge relating to Evans when prosecutors failed to disclose a witness who cast doubt on Evans's accusation). Vance would later add another charge, for forcing an alleged sex act on production assistant Miriam Haley in 2006.

In 2020 a trial jury heard testimony from six women who alleged that Weinstein had sexually assaulted them, including Mann and Haley. After four weeks of testimony, the jury found Weinstein guilty of a criminal sexual act in the first degree and rape in the third degree relating to Haley and Mann, respectively. After the jury rendered its verdict, Vance, seemingly banking on the public forgetting that he had given Weinstein an inexplicable free pass back in 2015, crowed, "This is the new landscape for survivors of sexual assault in America. This is a new day."

The judge sentenced Weinstein to twenty-three years in prison. He stated pointedly from the bench, in a comment seemingly aimed at Vance, "This is a first conviction, but it is not a first offense."

· ·

Bill Cosby was, for decades, a universally beloved comedian and actor. For all his national and international popularity, he was worshipped in the Philadelphia area, where he had attended Temple University. I remember going to Temple basketball games at the Palestra in the late 1980s and watching Cosby walk around courtside, beaming in his cherry-and-white Temple sweatshirt, playfully interacting with students and fans. The man seemingly had it all, and he was *real*, too. Nationally, he was a hero; in Philly, he was a god.

When Andrea Constand started working at Temple in their basketball program in 2002, she quickly came to know this local deity. But as their relationship developed, Cosby made several sexual advances, which Constand rebuffed. In 2004, Constand alleged, Cosby invited her to his home, drugged her, and sexually assaulted her. Constand kept the incident to herself until about a year later, when she told her mother and reported it to the police. The case wound up in the district attorney's office in Montgomery County, where Cosby lived, right outside Philadelphia, on the hometown turf where he was so admired.

Local authorities investigated, sort of. The Cheltenham, Pennsylvania, police interviewed Constand for the first time over the phone and concluded that she seemed "nervous." Any minimally competent sexual crimes prosecutor or investigator knows not to interview a potential victim for the first time over the phone; it's tough enough to establish the necessary trust and communication with a victim in person, and it's difficult or impossible remotely.

In contrast, the police traveled to Manhattan to interview Cosby in person, in the comfort of his lawyer's office. Cosby claimed he had merely given Constand one and a half Benadryl pills and that they then had consensual sexual contact, but not intercourse. One police official, perceptibly starstruck, later told *Vanity Fair* that Cosby was "cooperative, congenial. . . . He came in wearing the typical Cosby sweater. I was asking the question, and I thought [Cosby] was a gentleman. I didn't think he was evasive. He answered every question I put to him. He said it was a consensual sexual encounter. That summarizes it." (The relevance to law enforcement of the "typical Cosby sweater" is unclear; the official didn't say whether he got Cosby's autograph.)

In February 2005 the elected Montgomery County district attorney, Bruce Castor (who would in 2021 represent Donald Trump at his second impeachment trial) announced his conclusion: "There was insufficient credible and admissible evidence upon which any charge against Cosby related to the Constand incident could be proven beyond a reasonable doubt." Neither Castor nor anyone else in law enforcement notified Constand in advance of the decision not to charge. She learned of it only when a reporter appeared at her attorney's office later that evening.

Castor later testified that he took the step of publicly announcing that he would not charge Cosby in a roundabout effort to *help* Constand, who eventually filed a civil lawsuit seeking money damages against Cosby. According to Castor, if Cosby had a potential criminal charge hanging over him, he could invoke the Fifth Amendment and refuse to testify in a deposition in a civil suit. But in Castor's view, with criminal charges off the table, Cosby had no Fifth Amendment right and would have to testify under oath.

And testify he did. In his deposition, Cosby denied the gist of Constand's allegations but, unburdened by the prospect of a Pennsylvania criminal charge, held back little when discussing his prior predatory behavior. He admitted that he would give women quaaludes "the same as a person would say, 'Have a drink.'" Cosby said he knew it was illegal to hand out quaaludes. An attorney asked, "When you got the quaaludes, was it in your mind that you were going to use these quaaludes for young women that you wanted to have sex with?" Cosby replied, flatly, "Yes." When detailing one incident when he had drugged a woman in the 1970s, Cosby explained that "she became in those days what was called high," and "she meets me backstage. I give her quaaludes. We then have sex." Perhaps not surprisingly given his own damning admissions, Cosby eventually settled Constand's civil suit for $3.38 million.

More victims emerged. Thirteen other women claimed in formal statements submitted in Constand's civil suit that Cosby had sexually assaulted them. And the floodgates opened even wider in 2014 when, in a viral clip of a stand-up performance, the comedian Hannibal Buress went right at Cosby: "It's even worse because Bill Cosby has the fuckin' smuggest old black man public persona that I hate. He gets on TV, 'Pull your pants up black people, I was on TV in the '80s! I can talk down to you because I had a successful sitcom!' Yeah, but you rape women, Bill Cosby, so turn the crazy down a couple notches. 'I don't curse on stage!' But yeah you're a rapist, so . . . I'd take you saying lots of 'motherfuckers' on Bill Cosby himself if you weren't a rapist."

Soon after Buress's riff, in November 2014, Barbara Bowman, who had submitted a formal statement in Constand's civil case, wrote a *Washington Post* op-ed titled "Bill Cosby Raped Me. Why Did It Take 30 Years for People to Believe My Story?" The next month actress Judy Huth filed a civil lawsuit claiming Cosby had sexually molested her when she was a child in Los Angeles in 1974, but the district attorney declined to bring criminal charges because the statute of limitations (the amount of time after a crime occurs within which a prosecutor can bring charges) had expired. Eventually, more than fifty women publicly accused Cosby of sexual assault.

Public pressure mounted as the number of Cosby accusers ballooned while prosecutors passed on filing criminal charges. But in December 2015, just before the expiration of the statute of limitations, Montgomery County district attorney Kevin Steele—who had defeated Castor in an election weeks before while attacking Castor's original decision not to charge Cosby—announced that his office had charged Cosby with aggravated indecent assault relating to Constand's allegations. Steele's office tried Cosby in 2017, but the jury hung, resulting in a mistrial.

Steele's office retried the case in 2018, and this time the jury found Cosby guilty. At trial, prosecutors used Cosby's damaging admissions at his deposition about his use of quaaludes. That evidence, not surprisingly, made an impact on the criminal trial jury. One juror, when asked on *Good Morning America* what led him to find Cosby guilty, responded, "It was his deposition, really. Mr. Cosby admitted to giving these quaaludes to women, young women, in order to have sex with them." The judge sentenced Cosby to three to ten years in prison.

On appeal, Cosby's legal team argued that prosecutors had violated his rights by promising not to prosecute—thereby inducing him to waive his Fifth Amendment rights and give deposition testimony—and then later changing course, filing a new charge, and using Cosby's own damning testimony against him at trial. An intermediate appeals court rejected Cosby's argument and upheld his conviction. But in June 2021 the Pennsylvania Supreme Court issued a stunning reversal. The court found that Castor's decision not to prosecute was binding and that prosecutors' later use of Cosby's testimony against him at a criminal trial was improper.

Hours after the court's decision, Cosby walked out of maximum-security State Correctional Institute Phoenix in Montgomery County, Pennsylvania. Cosby, who was then eighty-three years old, had served three years of his three-to-ten-year sentence. In 2022 the US Supreme Court declined to take the case, leaving the Pennsylvania court's ruling intact and putting an end to the Cosby prosecution.

The reversal of Cosby's conviction caused widespread anger. There certainly was plenty of blame to go around, but it should start with the prosecutors. Local police and prosecutors ran a half-hearted, dubious investigation and ultimately passed on a criminal charge. Years later, Steele foolishly tried to go back on Castor's promise, and then recklessly introduced Cosby's deposition testimony against him at trial, despite the chance—which ultimately came to fruition—that that tactic could jeopardize a conviction. In the end, although over fifty women publicly accused Cosby of sexual assault, he was never finally and officially convicted of anything at all.

• •

Each of these high-profile cases involved a unique set of circumstances. But it's impossible to ignore the common thread running through them: police and prosecutors initially failed to take seriously and act decisively on credible allegations of serial sexual crimes made by young women against powerful men. Law enforcement authorities eventually doubled back and took corrective measures, or tried to, but only after media focus and public condemnation compelled action. And when prosecutors did bring criminal charges, they often did so belatedly and clumsily. While these high-profile cases followed similar trajectories, it turns out they also fairly represent broader trends in our justice system.

Chapter 12

BIASES, INDIVIDUAL
AND SYSTEMIC

The recent spate of high-profile serial sexual assault cases underscores that our criminal justice system is infected by bias against women, particularly young women and minorities, and in favor of men who are powerful, rich, and famous. This disparity in treatment is now widely recognized, and there's little dispute that other biases pervade our criminal justice system. But the extent to which the scales are tilted against women, girls, and racial minorities, specifically in sexual assault cases, is extraordinary. I was a prosecutor for over fourteen years, and I'll admit I was taken aback at the broad-lens data.

Sexual assault is, by a wide margin, the most underreported category of crime. Numbers vary depending on source and time period measured, but the data consistently establishes that only between 25 and 40 percent of all sexual assaults are reported to law enforcement. For example, a 2013 Justice Department study found that just 36 percent of rape and sexual assaults against women were reported to the police from 2005 through 2010. More recent DOJ data consistently lands in the same range; in 2017, 2018, and 2019, approximately 40, 25, and 34 percent of sexual assaults were reported, respectively. By comparison, Justice Department statistics typically show reporting rates of approximately 45 to 50 percent for burglary, 45 to 65 percent for robbery, and 50 to 60 percent for aggravated assault.

The bias at play here takes two forms: human bias and institutional bias embedded in our rules and procedures. Let's start with the human factors, those conscious or unconscious biases that lead us to value or devalue particular groups of people. Even among those sexual assault crimes that are reported to police, a disproportionate number do not result in referral to prosecutors for potential charges—a judgment call, at bottom, that requires a cop to decide, *Is this allegation serious and credible enough to justify arrest and potential prosecution?* Justice Department statistics show that only about one in six sexual assault cases that are reported to police result in arrest. This is far lower than the arrest rate for robberies (more than one in four reported cases result in arrest) and assault and battery (about two out of five). The difference is even more pronounced given that in sexual assault cases the suspect's identity is almost always known to the victim and police, whereas in robbery cases, for example, law enforcement may be unable to identify the suspect in the first place. Yet arrest rates are lower in sexual assault cases.

These disparities are even more striking based on the race of the victim or complainant. Several studies have proven that, even among those cases that are reported to law enforcement, prosecutors are more likely to charge a case involving a white victim than a black or other minority victim.

In 1983, a group of professors led by David Baldus conducted a groundbreaking study of over two thousand murder cases in Georgia in the 1970s. The study, published in the *Journal of Criminal Law and Criminology* and later cited by the US Supreme Court, reached a stunning conclusion: while black defendants were more likely to receive a death sentence than similarly situated white defendants—no major surprise there, sadly—an even wider disparity existed based on the race of the *victim*. As the Supreme Court explained it: "Even after taking account of 39 nonracial variables, defendants charged with killing white victims were 4.3 times as likely to receive a death sentence as defendants charged with killing blacks." So while black defendants got worse treatment than white defendants, people (of any race) who killed white victims were punished far more severely than people who killed black victims. A black life taken, it turned out, did not matter nearly as much as a white one.

Similar biases historically have infected decision-making by police and prosecutors in sexual assault cases. One 2016 study of prosecutorial charging decisions in sexual assault cases, published in the *American Journal of Community Psychology*, concluded that police were consistently more likely to deem a black or other minority victim "uncooperative," which decreased the likelihood that the police would refer the case to a prosecutor for potential charges. A 2001 study by a group of criminal justice professors of 140 sexual battery cases in Florida, led by Cassie Spohn, concluded that the victim's race was a strong factor in the prosecutorial charging decision and that "prosecutors rejected charges more often if the victim was a racial minority or if the suspect was black." Another study by Spohn and professor David Holleran of over 500 cases in Philadelphia and Kansas City revealed that prosecutors were four and a half times more likely to file charges in cases involving assaults by strangers if the victim was white than if the victim was black. Note the consistency with the aforementioned Georgia death penalty study, which found a similar four-plus-fold disparity based on the race of the victim.

• •

Beyond these human biases, we also need to consider structural biases. Most fundamentally, there is an inherent disconnect in our criminal justice system between what is generally known, on one hand, and what a prosecutor can use as evidence to support a criminal charge, on the other. My fellow prosecutors and I would sometimes check one another: "Of course you know it, but can you prove it?" And by "prove it," we meant "within the strictures of the law." What looks like a mountain of evidence in the public record can amount to much less after you filter it through the law and its many restrictions.

For example, it has been widely and credibly reported that Trump allegedly sexually assaulted twenty or more women, over many years. The numbers on Epstein, Weinstein, and Cosby run even higher. But that doesn't mean a prosecutor can stack all of those allegations on top of one another and present them to a jury, banking on the overwhelming force of numbers to ensure a conviction. In normal conversation, one might argue persuasively, "Come on, could twenty women *all* be lying about this one guy?" But it doesn't work that way in court.

In fact, our courts systemically limit what type of evidence a prosecutor can use to charge and prove a criminal case, often to the benefit of serial sexual offenders. These legal guardrails are centuries old, and they can be foundational protections of individual liberties for the accused. They weren't originally designed to stifle accusations or to protect the powerful—but they often have that practical effect.

Take, for example, the statute of limitations—the legal principle requiring a prosecutor to bring charges within a certain amount of time after commission of a crime. Statutes of limitations are as old as the law itself. They go back to ancient Rome, and have been built into our American legal system from the start. Statutes of limitations codify the notion that, at a certain point, a suspect should no longer live under a cloud of uncertainty about whether he will be charged. Limitations periods also reflect doubt about the reliability of evidence over time. It generally (but not always) becomes more difficult as time passes for a prosecutor to prove a case and for an accused to defend himself.

While statutes of limitations vary by offense and jurisdiction, we've recently seen broad movement toward expansion or even abolition of statutes of limitations in sexual assault cases. In 2018 and 2019, as the #MeToo movement gained public visibility and sway, fifteen states extended their criminal or civil statutes of limitations in sexual assault cases.

This trend arose from two root causes. First, widespread frustration about high-profile cases in which famous people could not be charged for offenses committed many years in the past has spurred lawmakers to take corrective measures. For example, in 2019—as the public learned about the initial failures of prosecutors to bring appropriate charges against Epstein, Weinstein, and others—New York State expanded its statutes of limitations for third-degree rape from five years to ten years, and for second-degree rape from five years to twenty years. Then-governor Andrew Cuomo (ironically, given his eventual political demise when numerous women accused him of sexual harassment and assault) signed the legislation at a ceremony, flanked by leaders of the Time's Up movement, including actresses Mira Sorvino and Michelle Hurd, who had made public allegations of sexual impropriety against Weinstein and Cosby, respectively.

Second, by expanding statutes of limitations, states have begun to recognize that victims of sexual assault often do not come forward immediately, if ever, for reasons that are intuitive and justifiable but were long misunderstood or ignored. Many victims are minors or young adults, and it can be particularly difficult for children to come forward with allegations against adults—especially those who are rich and powerful. Victims commonly face stigma, shame, and victim-blaming, which can deter reporting to law enforcement. And many victims experience another layer of trauma when they recount their experiences, particularly to the police or in a public setting like a trial.

As Virginia Giuffre, one of the women who accused Epstein of sexually assaulting her when she was a teenager, put it to *Glamour*: "It's just ridiculous. I mean, compare rape and murder, or being sexually abused and murder. There's no statute of limitations on murder, right? But [with sexual abuse] you've just basically taken a person's life away. And not only that, but it takes so many years to want to [come forward] because we carry that shame. We're told we're the bad ones; we're told we're the dirty ones, and it's our secret to hide. But that's what needs to change."

Even with states adopting longer and more victim-supportive statutes of limitations, these changes in the law only apply prospectively. They cannot legally be applied backward to revive criminal cases that already have expired. For example, E. Jean Carroll alleged publicly that Trump raped her in a New York department store in the late 1990s. (Many other sexual assault allegations against Trump date back to the 1980s and '90s.) But in the 1990s the statute of limitations for sexual assault in New York was five years—meaning that the statute of limitations expired, and prosecutors lost the ability to charge the Carroll case, in the early 2000s. Only later, in 2006, did New York abolish the statute of limitations for certain offenses, including forcible rape. But those changes did not (and legally could not) apply retroactively to revive potential criminal charges based on an incident, like the one alleged by Carroll, that happened in the late 1990s. Once the statute of limitations has run out, it's gone forever.

· ·

Jurisdiction and venue requirements, like statutes of limitations, are foundational to our justice system, and are designed to protect the liberties of the accused. We decided very early on (and quite reasonably) that it would be unfair for a person who commits a crime in Massachusetts to be charged and tried in Virginia, for example.

While the principles underlying jurisdictional and venue rules are generally benign and uncontroversial, they also have the practical effect of limiting the evidence that any one prosecutor can present against a serial sexual offender. Many such predators—particularly those with enough wealth and power to travel frequently—commit sexual assaults across a swath of the United States and overseas. This holds true of our high-profile subjects: Trump, Epstein, Weinstein, and Cosby were accused of committing sexual assaults across various counties, states, and countries. But a prosecutor likely could charge only the offenses that occurred within her particular jurisdiction, offering a jury less than the full picture of a subject's conduct.

In some instances, judges will permit prosecutors to present "other bad acts" evidence—also called 404(b) evidence, after the applicable federal rule—of offenses that occurred in another jurisdiction or so far in the past that the statute of limitations has expired. But there are limits on 404(b) evidence. It cannot form the basis of a criminal charge; it can only support other charges by establishing that the defendant had a particular mode of operation or displayed a specific pattern of conduct. It also cannot be introduced to prove generally that the defendant was a bad guy, or had a propensity to commit certain crimes. And judges typically limit the amount of testimony about other offenses that a jury can hear; they worry that at a certain point, evidence of uncharged acts will overwhelm the jury's ability to decide the case fairly and impartially. Appellate courts have reversed convictions where judges allowed prosecutors to introduce excessive evidence of other bad acts by the defendant.

When all these systemic factors come into play—statutes of limitations, jurisdictional and venue requirements, and limits on 404(b) evidence—the end result is that the pool of complainants against a serial sexual offender gets winnowed down, often dramatically. Take Weinstein, for example. Putting aside for the moment the prosecutorial ineptitude (or worse) that originally let him off the hook, of the more than eighty victims who came forward publicly, only six testified at his 2020 trial in New York. And in the Cosby trial in Pennsylvania, a total of six women testified, out of the over fifty victims who came forward publicly. Or consider Cuomo. In 2021, eleven complainants came forward to the New York attorney general's investigators with allegations of sexual harassment or assault—yet no district attorney found sufficient evidence, once the evidence was parceled out county by county, to file criminal charges.

Trump similarly benefited from the legal system's tendency to parse a mass of accusations. He allegedly assaulted about two dozen women, but many of the incidents, including those that occurred in the 1980s and '90s, have long been removed from consideration by the statute of limitations. He committed the assaults in various states, so it would be difficult or impossible to charge all of them together in one indictment. And because a judge likely would limit "other bad acts" evidence, no one prosecutor could line up the entirety of his conduct, or anything close, for a jury. Indeed, there's no publicly available evidence that any prosecutor ever came close to charging Trump with sexual assault, despite the dozens of women who came forward with credible allegations.

..

The recent high-profile cases involving celebrity subjects align neatly, and perhaps to a disturbing extent, with the broad-lens data. This simply can't be coincidence. It can't be just happenstance that time and again, police and prosecutors have discounted the significance of allegations made by women (many of them young, some minorities). It can't be mere accident that the FBI, police, and prosecutors have fawned over the celebrity accused, fudged the damning statements of victims, and later lied to investigators about what they had done. And it's difficult to fathom that hard-driving prosecutors, with their rhetoric about standing up for victims, have repeatedly declined to file timely and appropriate charges against powerful men based on statements by young women.

In the final calculation, some powerful serial sexual predators have faced full accountability—but only after media exposure and broad public condemnation spurred police and prosecutors to action. Epstein died behind bars. Weinstein seems certain to meet a similar fate as he serves out sentences that far exceed his remaining lifespan. Cosby caught a break with his release from prison after only three years, at age eighty-three. But remember: every one of them nearly got away with it entirely in the first place. And, true to form, Trump—despite facing dozens of public accusations—has never faced any criminal consequence at all.

ONE MAN,
ABOVE THE LAW

When the Boss
Is the President

Chapter 13

INDICTMENT-PROOF

He Who Shall Not Be Charged

It sounded, for a fleeting moment, as if Robert Mueller was taking a stand that could threaten Donald Trump's presidency—and that could all but ensure that Trump would be charged criminally when his term in office ended.

It was July 2019. Four months earlier, Mueller had issued his maddeningly inconclusive written report, which declared, despite ample evidence that Trump had obstructed justice many times over, "While this report does not conclude that the President committed a crime, it also does not exonerate him." The Mueller report continued, just as unhelpfully, "If we had confidence after a thorough investigation of the facts that the President clearly did not commit obstruction of justice, we would so state. Based on the facts and the applicable legal standards, however, we are unable to reach that judgment." So, essentially: *If we could clear him, we would, but we can't, so we won't, but if he did commit a crime, we wouldn't say so, and we're not saying anything here.* Not helpful.

To an extent, Mueller's bureaucratic double-speak (or perhaps non-speak) was the result of his own characteristic reticence. But as Mueller noted repeatedly in the report and in his testimony, his hands were tied by the long-standing DOJ policy, memorialized in an opinion memo by the Justice Department's Office of Legal Counsel (OLC)—a group of Justice Department lawyers who provide advice to the executive branch on thorny constitutional problems—recommending against indictment of a sitting president.

The report left unanswered this all-important question: Would Mueller have indicted Trump if he could have? If Trump, at that moment in 2019, had been anybody but the sitting president of the United States, would Mueller have charged him for obstruction of justice? In a sense, Mueller's answer to that question would be academic—but only temporarily, for as long as Trump held the White House. Because, despite the Justice Department's controversial no-indictment policy, two things remained clear: (1) Congress would soon have to decide whether to pursue impeachment; and (2) a former president certainly could be indicted once out of office. Mueller's answer would weigh heavily, and perhaps decisively, on both fronts.

Mueller's congressional testimony got off to a brutal start for Trump. Republican representative Ken Buck, trying to poke holes in the investigation, suggested that Mueller lacked the evidence necessary to indict Trump on obstruction: "When it came to obstruction, you threw a bunch of stuff up against the wall to see what would stick, and that is fundamentally unfair." Mueller pushed back: "I would not agree to that characterization at all." Buck then walked right into a trap of his own making. "OK, but the—could you charge the president with a crime after he left office?" Buck asked. "Yes," Mueller replied. Buck tried again: "You believe that he committed—you could charge the president of the United States with obstruction of justice after he left office." Again, Mueller offered a devastating one-word reply: "Yes." Moments later, Buck's time expired (mercifully, for him and for Trump).

It was a needle-scratch moment. Mueller appeared to testify not just that any hypothetical former president could be indicted after leaving office, but that Trump specifically could *and should* be indicted for obstruction once he was no longer president.

Later, Democratic representative Ted Lieu decided to put the big question directly to Mueller himself. Lieu began by laying out a hit list of the most damning pieces of evidence that Mueller had found relating to obstruction of justice (including Trump's most indefensible conduct: his instruction to Don McGahn to get rid of Mueller and then lie and create a false document about it). "I believe any reasonable person," Lieu declared, "looking at these facts, could conclude that all three elements of the crime of obstruction of justice have been met." He continued, "I'd like to ask you the reason, again, that you did not indict Donald Trump is because of the OLC opinion stating that you cannot indict a sitting president. Correct?" "That is correct," Mueller testified.

Lieu's question left a bit of ambiguity, but it sure sounded like Mueller meant that he would have indicted Trump if he could have—that is, if not for the OLC policy. "The reason," as Lieu phrased the question that Mueller affirmed, suggested that the no-indictment policy was *the* one and only reason.

Lieu, a former criminal lawyer in the military, then did what any savvy trial practitioner does when he gets a good answer: he left it alone. There's a natural temptation for a prosecutor or defense lawyer to reiterate or dwell on a favorable response, for the benefit of the jury or the viewing audience—but that often enables the witness to water down or retract his initial testimony the second time around. Smart litigators know that once you've got it on record, you move along and preserve the golden nugget to argue at closing. Lieu did just that.

The hearing eventually adjourned for lunch, and all hell broke loose. Experts and commentators wondered aloud: Had Mueller just said what it sounded like he said? My former boss at the SDNY, Preet Bharara, tweeted, "This is very very close to Mueller saying that but for the OLC memo, Trump would have been indicted." On CNN, Bharara said Mueller's testimony was "the closest thing to something that's a bombshell, both legally and politically" and that "the record as it stands now is the reason he [Trump] wasn't indicted, one reason: the OLC opinion." National security lawyer Bradley Moss tweeted that Buck "just gave Mueller a clear and concise moment to say the only reason Trump wasn't indicted is because DOJ policy prohibited it."

But during the break, either Mueller or somebody in his orbit must have realized that his testimony had caused a national spit-take. So Mueller opened the afternoon session with a firm walk-back. Before any House member even posed a formal question, Mueller testified: "I'd like to go back to one thing that was said this morning by Mr. Lieu who said, and I quote, 'You didn't charge the President because of the OLC opinion.' That is not the correct way to say it. As we say in the report and as I said at the opening, we did not reach a determination as to whether the President committed a crime." Mueller later reiterated, "What I wanted to clarify is the fact that we did not make any determination with regard to culpability in any way. We did not start that process down—down the road." Mueller had retreated right back into the ambiguous fog of the legal non-conclusions stated in his report.

There's no way to know whether Mueller's original, damning responses to Lieu and Buck were intentional, or were inadvertent but revealing slips of the tongue, or whether he simply misunderstood or misspoke. But given Mueller's actions up to that point—his report laid out a damning case against Trump and methodically explained how the evidence could satisfy each element of the federal obstruction statute, several times over—it was entirely understandable that some experts initially took Mueller's comments to mean that he did believe Trump should be charged, eventually.

Mueller ultimately ended up back where his report had left off: DOJ policy, as set forth in the OLC memo, prohibited him from indicting a sitting president, and as a result, he never even considered whether the evidence he had amassed during his two-year in-vestigation was sufficient to support a criminal charge. That DOJ policy—coupled with Mueller's cryptic conclusions and a tactical disinformation campaign by Attorney General William Barr and others to distort the report in Trump's favor—saved Trump's hide, both politically and criminally.

We like to believe the axiom "Nobody is above the law," but we ought to add a qualifier: "except the president." No person is as in-sulated from the criminal justice process as the sitting occupant of the Oval Office, and there is no close second place. Nobody ever exploited that protection, and other legal benefits unique to the pres-ident, quite like Trump.

. .

It's not quite right to say the Justice Department *can't* indict a sitting president. Rather, DOJ has, for decades, *voluntarily decided that it won't try* to indict a sitting president.

In 1973, as the Watergate scandal escalated, the OLC issued a formal opinion memo concluding that the president could not (or at least should not) be indicted while in office. The OLC reasoned that "a necessity to defend a criminal trial and to attend court . . . would interfere with the President's unique official duties" and that a presidential indictment "would be politically and constitutionally a traumatic event" for our government.

Given the timing, one might reasonably assume that the OLC drafted the 1973 memo because the burgeoning Watergate scan-dal raised questions about the future of President Richard Nixon. But while Watergate was certainly on the national radar at the time, it hadn't yet mushroomed into a politically existential threat to Nixon, and his fate was more of a secondary concern. In fact, as confirmed publicly by J. T. Smith, a DOJ official who helped draft the 1973 memo, the real impetus was a pending bribery investigation into Vice President Spiro Agnew, which was unconnected to Watergate and eventually led to Agnew's resignation. (The memo concluded, unhelpfully for Agnew, that a sitting vice president *can* be indicted.)

In 2000, in the wake of the impeachment of President Bill Clinton, the OLC revisited the issue, and came to the same conclusion as it had twenty-seven years earlier. The OLC confirmed its view that "the indictment and criminal prosecution of a sitting President would unduly interfere with the ability of the executive branch to perform its constitutionally assigned duties, and would thus violate the constitutional separation of powers."

At bottom, the OLC memos grapple less with pure constitutional analysis (does the law permit indictment of a sitting president?) and more with practical concerns (how on earth would our government function if the president was indicted?). The OLC memos contemplate a series of mind-boggling, Constitution-bending scenarios. For example:

Can the Justice Department indict a president while he's in office but then wait until he's out of office to hold the criminal trial? (No, according to the OLC memos; still too disruptive.)

Can federal prosecutors file an indictment against a sitting president "under seal"—secretly, on file with a court, to be unveiled only after the president leaves office? (OLC: Probably not. Recall that the SDNY wrestled with this one before coming to the same conclusion during its hush money prosecution of Michael Cohen.)

What if a president was indicted, tried, and convicted, but not impeached and removed from office—how would we function with a president exercising his powers from prison? (OLC: It would be a disaster, and hence something we should not countenance.)

Does the statute of limitations run while a president is in office, and if so, can a president simply run out the clock if he holds office long enough? (OLC: maybe and maybe, but we don't know for sure.)

The OLC memos are the best-known documents setting forth DOJ's position, but they're actually neither exclusive nor conclusive, as detailed by former acting US solicitor general Walter Dellinger in a 2018 *Lawfare* article titled "Indicting a President Is Not Foreclosed: The Complex History." In fact, the Justice Department has taken the position in other contexts that a sitting president *can* be indicted. For example, in a 1974 internal memo, DOJ attorneys on the Watergate special prosecutor's team concluded that there was no formal legal bar to indicting a sitting president, but that such an indictment would create practical and political issues and should be pursued, if at all, only with incontrovertible proof. So: it's okay to indict a sitting president, but only if there's a dead-bang case to be made. In a Supreme Court brief filed the same year, Watergate prosecutors argued that "it is an open and substantial question whether an incumbent President is subject to indictment." And in a murky opinion that independent counsel Kenneth Starr appears to have solicited from a little-known law professor in 1998, the professor concluded that then-president Bill Clinton "is subject to indictment and criminal prosecution," though he might not have to serve any prison term until after he left office.

Only one thing is sure: nobody's sure. The Justice Department has kicked it around internally for decades, but both the 1973 and 2000 OLC memos concede that we simply do not know conclusively whether the law permits indictment of a sitting president. Nobody has ever tried, the Constitution itself doesn't answer the question, there's no statute on the books, and no court has ever ruled squarely on the issue.

Despite the uncertainty, DOJ still abides today by the no-indictment policy that has been in place for nearly the past fifty years. During that time, no president has benefited more from that policy than Trump. Only Nixon is even close, but even he can't compare in the broad view.

Most pointedly, the DOJ policy against indicting the sitting president confounded Mueller and essentially stifled his investigation. He repeatedly cited the policy in his report, and he'd later assert at a press conference, "Under long-standing department policy, a president cannot be charged with a federal crime while he is in office. That is unconstitutional." Mueller got it half right here. True, the Justice Department has a long-standing internal no-indictment policy, and he was bound by it. But he was wrong to declare categorically that an indictment of a sitting president would be "unconstitutional." That's unknown, and ultimately a question for Congress or the courts, neither of whom have weighed in.

Mueller also was unnecessarily reticent when he declined even to state in his report or testimony whether his findings would support charges, but for Trump's status as president. The regulations under which Mueller served actually *required* him to issue a "report explaining the prosecution or declination decisions reached by the Special Counsel." Yet Mueller, citing the risk of reputational harm to Trump, declined to do so. That left the door open for Barr to publicly distort Mueller's findings (while withholding the report from the public for nearly a month) and to unilaterally declare Trump free and clear.

Beyond the Mueller investigation, the OLC memos also tied the SDNY's hands when it came to the hush money payoff scheme, as we saw in chapter 2 of this book. And DOJ's no-indictment policy protected Trump (while he held office) against any potential federal criminal consequence arising from either of the two acts for which he was impeached: his attempted shakedown of the Ukrainian president in 2019 and his monthslong effort to steal the 2020 presidential election, which culminated in the January 6 Capitol attack in 2021. All told, the OLC memo provided Trump an insurance policy that he cashed in on repeatedly, on unconnected matters, spanning most of his presidency. Even Nixon can't match that.

. .

On paper, the president's protection against federal indictment expires when he leaves office. But in practice, the OLC policy has a longer tail. While the policy certainly does not formally preclude indictment of a former president, it does make indictment more difficult and more unlikely in at least two respects.

First is the technical concern that, if prosecutors must wait for a president to leave office before he can be indicted, they could lose months or years waiting out the end of his term. The statute of limitations—five years for most federal crimes—could expire during that time, particularly if a sitting president wins reelection. (Note, however, that it's an open legal question whether the statute continues to run, or is paused, while a president holds office.) Even if the statute of limitations has not expired by the time a president leaves office, delay is costly to prosecutors. As time elapses between commission of a crime, indictment, and trial, witnesses' memories tend to fade, physical evidence can degrade or expire, documents might be lost or destroyed, emails and texts get deleted. The aphorism "Justice delayed is justice denied" applies not only to a defendant's right to speedy trial but also to the ability of prosecutors to bring a successful prosecution.

Second, the atmospherics around a case tend to change as time passes. The crime itself begins to feel more distant and less urgent. Consider, for example, the 2019 Ukraine scandal, triggered by Trump's effort to use hundreds of millions of dollars in foreign aid to strong-arm the Ukrainian president into announcing an investigation of the Bidens. At the time, it seemed earth-shaking. But when Trump's term expired in January 2021, it was already regarded mostly as a historical footnote, lost to time and the swirl of other controversies—even though, at this very moment, any crimes committed during that scandal remain within the five-year statute of limitations, and potentially chargeable. The same applies to Trump's obstruction of the Mueller investigation; it felt urgent and seismic back in 2018, but now it feels more like a chapter in a history book.

Technically, this type of atmospheric consideration—*Do people still care about this?*—shouldn't matter to a prosecutor. But it does. Take it from me: prosecutors read the press regularly and compulsively, with a special emphasis on their own clippings. (Ask any of your prosecutor friends if they have a Google alert set for their own names, and watch them squirm.) There's nothing wrong with that. Any prosecutor would be remiss not to consider the public perception of his actions, including the impact that public sentiment might have not only on the perceived legitimacy of a prosecution (particularly one that is politically sensitive) but also on a prospective jury pool. If a jury—or even a single juror—feels that a prosecutor is out chasing old ghosts, that's potentially disastrous for a case against a former president.

We do have a bit of a historical track record when it comes to indicting, prosecuting, and potentially imprisoning a former president or vice president. In modern American history before Trump, we've faced the realistic prospect of such criminal prosecution three times. All three times, through different legal mechanisms and in divergent political atmospheres, the outcome has been the same: no trial and no imprisonment.

Nixon is, of course, the most famous example. When he resigned on August 9, 1974, he faced the genuine prospect of federal criminal prosecution for obstruction of justice for his role in the Watergate scandal. Nixon had bugged his own White House, and those recordings threatened not only to end his presidency but also to land him in prison. In one recording widely known as the "smoking-gun tape," Nixon and his chief of staff H. R. Haldeman discussed having CIA officials shut down the FBI's investigation under the pretext that it posed a national security threat. In another tape—which in my prosecutorial view is even more damning—Nixon and his White House counsel, John Dean, discussed making illegal cash payments to Watergate burglars. When Dean said it would cost "a million dollars over the next two years" to ensure the silence of the burglars, Nixon responded, "We could get that. On the money, if you need the money you could get that. You could get a million dollars. You could get it in cash. I know where it could be gotten. It is not easy, but it could be done. But the question is who the hell would handle it? Any ideas on that?" This would've been what prosecutors call a "just press play" trial: just press play on the tape, sit back, and wait for the guilty verdict to roll in. (It's never quite that easy, of course, but you get the point.)

But only one month after Nixon's resignation, Ford issued a blanket preemptive pardon for all federal crimes that Nixon "committed or may have committed or taken part in" while in office. Up to that point, Nixon faced a real threat of criminal prosecution. As the *New York Times* noted in its coverage at the time, the pardon "exempts him from indictment and trial for, among other things, his role in the cover-up of the Watergate burglary." Ford's famous quote—"Our long national nightmare is over"—is sometimes associated with the pardon, but in fact he said that line upon taking the presidential oath of office, a month earlier. The same concern for finality motivated the pardon. As Ford testified in Congress in October 1974, shortly after the pardon: "I wanted to do all I could to shift our attentions from the pursuit of a fallen President to the pursuit of the urgent needs of a rising nation. . . . We would needlessly be diverted from meeting those challenges if we as a people were to remain sharply divided over whether to indict, bring to trial, and punish a former President, who already is condemned to suffer long and deeply in the shame and disgrace brought upon the office he held." The Ford-Nixon pardon remains perhaps the most infamous and controversial act of clemency in the nation's history.

Nixon's first vice president, Spiro Agnew, had an even more perilous brush with the law in 1973, unrelated to Watergate. Agnew, who had accepted tens of thousands of dollars in cash bribes and kickbacks when he was governor of Maryland in the 1960s, had the temerity to continue accepting envelopes of cash even while he held office as vice president. He took one bribe inside his federal office in the Old Executive Office Building. As a Justice Department investigation closed in on Agnew, he reached a deal with prosecutors: he would resign the vice presidency and plead no contest to charges that he evaded taxes on cash bribes that he had accepted in 1967. In return, prosecutors recommended and a federal judge imposed a non-incarceratory sentence of three years' probation. (Here's a little trivia for you. The Twenty-Fifth Amendment has been used to fill a vice presidential vacancy only twice in our nation's history: once in 1973, when Nixon chose and Congress confirmed Ford to replace the disgraced Agnew, and then again in 1974 when Nixon resigned, Ford became president, and Nelson Rockefeller became VP. The amendment was ratified in 1967, just in time to guide us through this cataclysmic chain reaction.)

A generation after Nixon and Agnew, Bill Clinton faced the prospect of criminal prosecution when his second term as president ended in January 2001. Clinton was impeached by the House in December 1998 and acquitted by the Senate in February 1999 for committing perjury in a civil deposition regarding his affair with White House intern Monica Lewinsky, and for obstruction of justice for attempting to influence witnesses. But during Clinton's final days in office in January 2001, his legal team worked out a deal with Robert Ray, who had taken over as independent counsel after Kenneth Starr. Clinton issued a public statement acknowledging that he had given false testimony under oath, paid a $25,000 fine, and agreed to a suspension of his law license in Arkansas. In return, Ray agreed not to pursue a federal indictment, sparing Clinton from potential criminal prosecution.

Nixon, Agnew, and Clinton posed unique scenarios but they all represented a common dilemma for prosecutors: What to do with a former president or vice president who appears to have committed crimes while in office? The cases took different paths to similar end results—no criminal prosecution for Nixon and Clinton, and an abbreviated prosecution resolved with a guarantee of no prison time for Agnew. In all three cases, prosecutors and other key decision makers recognized the difficulty of a full-bore prosecution, complete with potential incarceration, even of a *former* president or vice president: political resistance and backlash, the prospect of an all-consuming trial, the unimaginably high stakes of an uncertain outcome, and the passage of time and political attention since commission of the potential crimes. On paper, Justice Department policy permits such a criminal prosecution. But in practice, thus far in American history, we are zero for three.

Chapter 14

"WE'RE FIGHTING ALL THE SUBPOENAS"

Executive Privilege Gone Wild

Imagine, for a moment, being Richard Nixon's lawyer during the summer of 1974. You represent the president of the United States as a dogged special prosecutor bears down on him over an exploding, once-in-a-generation scandal. The world has learned that your client secretly bugged the White House, and you are one of very few people who knows that the resulting tapes will doom him.

The Watergate special prosecutor has demanded those tapes. You've resisted, but a federal district court judge has taken the other side and ordered you to turn them over. Now you've gone to the US Supreme Court, and you've made an argument that relies on a rarely used, little-understood concept known as "executive privilege." You know that if you lose, and those tapes go over to the prosecutor, your client almost certainly will be impeached and removed from office, and he might face criminal charges after that.

On July 24, 1974, the ruling comes down. This is before the internet, social media, cable news, or electronic case filing, so you've probably received a paper copy by courier, and the president himself, your client, doesn't know the outcome yet. You scan the opinion and realize it's a good news / bad news scenario—but the bad entirely swamps the good, for your client's immediate interests.

You enter the Oval Office and deliver the good news, not so much

for Nixon but for future presidents and the presidency itself: the Supreme Court has unanimously recognized that your legal theory on
executive privilege is real and legitimate. Executive privilege is officially a thing now, thanks to you. But the bad news, for your client:
he doesn't get to use this newly recognized executive privilege here.
The Nixon tapes are coming out. It's over.

Just over two weeks after the Supreme Court's ruling on executive
privilege, Nixon resigned. The tapes were too damaging, and Republican political support had eroded to the point where impeachment by the House and conviction by the Senate were inevitable.

Historically, the Supreme Court's decision lives on as the final straw
for Richard Nixon's presidency. Legally, it stands as a landmark in
a centuries-long battle that still carries on today: how much power
does the president have to keep secret his own communications, and
the communications of others within the executive branch?

Nixon and his legal team didn't invent the notion of executive privilege. It goes all the way back to George Washington himself, who in
1796 initially denied a request by the House of Representatives for
executive papers relating to a controversial treaty negotiated with
Britain by Supreme Court justice John Jay. Many other presidents
between Washington and Nixon cited some form of executive privilege in response to congressional or prosecutorial demands for information: John Adams, Thomas Jefferson, Teddy Roosevelt, Dwight
Eisenhower, and John Kennedy, to name a few.

Eisenhower's administration first brought the phrase "executive
privilege" into popular usage, and he still holds the record with approximately forty total invocations, some relating to congressional
requests during the McCarthy hearings. But it took until the 1974
Nixon ruling for the Supreme Court to formally acknowledge executive privilege as a valid legal doctrine for the first time, and to flesh
out some (but not nearly all) of its parameters.

Every president since Nixon has invoked executive privilege, some more often or more explicitly than others. In testimony to the US Senate in 2021, Dean Marc Rozell, a constitutional scholar at George Mason University, summarized the two decades that followed Nixon: "Due to its association with Nixonian abuses of power, Presidents Gerald R. Ford and Jimmy Carter avoided the use of the term *executive privilege* as much as possible. President Ronald Reagan backed off each of his several claims of that power, and President George H. W. Bush largely concealed its exercise to avoid controversy while still protecting secrecy."

But Bill Clinton reverted to a more aggressive, Nixonian use of the privilege, invoking it fourteen times during his eight years in office. Clinton at one point tried to use the privilege to block Starr's prosecutors from questioning senior White House aides in the Lewinsky investigation. A federal judge in 1998 rejected Clinton's claim, making him the first president since Nixon twenty-four years before to take an executive privilege claim to court and lose.

George W. Bush invoked executive privilege six times during his two terms as president. In one instance, he tried to use the privilege to block the testimony of former White House counsel Harriet Miers about the firing and forced resignations of nine US attorneys. A federal district court judge rejected Bush's claim, finding that the need for testimony from Miers outweighed the president's need for secrecy.

Before he became president, Barack Obama in 2007 publicly criticized Bush's use of executive privilege in the congressional probe of the US attorney firings: "You know, there's been a tendency on the part of this administration to try to hide behind executive privilege every time there's something a little shaky that's taking place, and I think the Administration would be best served by coming clean on this." But in 2012 Obama invoked the privilege when Congress demanded records relating to the Operation Fast and Furious scandal, in which the ATF allowed illegal gun sales in an effort to track the purchasers, including some tied to Mexican drug cartels; some of the guns could not be tracked, and one was linked to a murder of a US border patrol agent. Over three years later, in January 2016, a federal district court judge rejected Obama's claim of executive privilege. The administration eventually agreed to turn over thousands of disputed documents to Congress, rather than pursuing an appeal.

While presidents over US history have used executive privilege with varying frequency, they have almost always ended up either dropping the claims of privilege or reaching negotiated agreements with prosecutors or Congress. Only relatively rarely have executive privilege cases caused showdowns that spilled into the courts, and even those disputes have ultimately ended in negotiated resolutions between the parties.

But then along came Donald Trump.

In April 2019, as it became clear Congress would pick up the investigative baton after the release of the Mueller report, Trump defiantly declared from the lawn of the White House, "We're fighting all the subpoenas." ("These aren't, like, impartial people," he added.)

Anybody who took Trump's statement of his blanket intent to stonewall as hyperbole would end up mistaken. Over the remainder of Trump's presidency and beyond, he did fight just about "all the subpoenas." His weapon of choice: executive privilege (and its even more aggressive, unbound theoretical cousin, "absolute immunity"). Whereas prior presidents generally had used executive privilege like a scalpel to strategically carve out exceptions in carefully chosen subpoena battles, Trump wielded it like a machete, hacking away at everything in front of him.

Trump was able to invoke executive privilege so broadly largely because the precise contours of executive privilege remain somewhat fluid and elusive. The Supreme Court in *Nixon* did set some important fence posts. Executive privilege is not absolute. It is meant to keep confidential vital policy discussions including, most fundamentally, those relating to "military, diplomatic, or sensitive national security secrets." But the privilege does not guard against disclosure of official wrongdoing or abuse of power, and it's not a generalized shield for the president against potential criminal prosecution. Those bits of guidance from the court, though important, also left plenty of gray area.

While executive privilege has had its moments of expansion and retraction over the years since *Nixon*, this much is clear: Trump blew the lid off when he applied executive privilege across the board, regardless of content or context. He characteristically took the privilege to a new level when his legal team relied on an even broader concept known as "absolute immunity"—the notion that the president has the power to defy any congressional or prosecutorial request for information, for any reason or even for no reason whatsoever, and that the president can order any member of the executive branch to do the same.

Trump's lawyers didn't invent the concept of absolute immunity. It had been kicked around in prior administrations, and typically dismissed as a bridge too far. In the *Miers* case, for example, a federal court firmly rejected the Bush administration's absolute immunity claim: "The Executive cannot identify a single judicial opinion that recognizes absolute immunity for senior presidential advisors in this or any other context." (That'll leave a mark.)

But no prior president deployed the absolute immunity claim as aggressively as Trump. Suffice it to say: it didn't go well. One federal judge, Thomas Griffith (a George W. Bush appointee) asked a Trump lawyer in January 2020, with a palpable sense of incredulity, "Has there ever been an instance of such broad-scale defiance of a congressional request for information in the history of the Republic?" "Not to my knowledge," replied the unfortunate DOJ attorney who had to stand up and defend Trump's unprecedented stonewalling.

In 2019, then judge (later to become US Supreme Court Justice) Ketanji Brown Jackson excoriated Trump's absolute immunity claim as a "fiction" that gets constitutional separation-of-powers principles "exactly backwards." And in 2020 the Supreme Court, by a 7–2 majority, firmly rejected Trump's effort to use absolute immunity to dodge a subpoena from the Manhattan district attorney. The majority, which included both Trump-appointed justices then on the court (Neil Gorsuch and Brett Kavanaugh), ruled that "in our judicial system, 'the public has a right to every man's evidence.' Since the earliest days of the Republic, 'every man' has included the President of the United States."

Consider Trump's onetime national security advisor John Bolton, who emerged as a crucial witness in Trump's first impeachment. During the Ukraine scandal, Trump had told Bolton straight up that he was withholding $391 million in foreign aid until Ukrainian officials agreed to investigate the family of his likely Democratic challenger (and future president), Joe Biden.

Bolton's testimony went right to the heart of the pivotal disputed issue: whether there was some connection between the withheld foreign aid and the announcement of the Biden investigations. But Bolton hid behind the president's broad invocation of executive privilege and declined to testify until ordered to do so by a court. Impeachment investigators, lacking the luxury of time, could not spend months litigating the issue, and dropped the effort to secure his damning testimony. Bolton, not one to favor patriotic duty over cash, never testified in the impeachment proceeding, but he later spilled all in his bestselling book.

Or take Don McGahn, who stood to implicate Trump directly in the scheme to obstruct Mueller's investigation. McGahn took refuge behind Trump's claim of absolute immunity and contested the House's subpoena for his testimony—tossing the dispute into the federal courts and predictably causing paralyzing delay, as the Bolton case had threatened previously. By the time McGahn finally did testify in Congress in June 2021, after nearly two years of litigation and negotiation, Trump was out of office and nobody much cared.

Even from the post-presidency comfort of Mar-a-Lago, Trump continued to invoke executive privilege and other expansive immunities to try to silence witnesses who might have given damaging testimony about him, particularly relating to the January 6 Capitol attack. When Trump tried to use executive privilege to block the House of Representatives' January 6 Select Committee from obtaining documents from his administration stored at the National Archives, a federal district court judge slapped him down with a biting rejoinder: "Presidents are not kings, and Plaintiff is not President." A three-judge court of appeals panel unanimously upheld that ruling, and the Supreme Court concurred.

Trump lost that legal dispute, but he managed to drag it out for nearly three months in the courts. And he succeeded in keeping other key witnesses quiet. Steve Bannon hid behind Trump's executive privilege claim and found himself held in contempt of Congress; he was indicted federally for contempt of Congress, convicted by a jury, and sentenced to four months—but he never said a word under oath. Former Trump White House chief of staff Mark Meadows and two former senior White House advisors, Dan Scavino and Peter Navarro, similarly refused to provide certain evidence to the committee, citing Trump's invocation of executive privilege. The House voted to hold all three in contempt, and the Justice Department eventually charged Navarro but not Meadows or Scavino. None of them testified under oath.

In August 2022, after federal agents conducted a search warrant at Trump's Mar-a-Lago beach resort and recovered hundreds of highly classified documents, he once again reached into the legal toolkit and unsheathed executive privilege in an effort to delay the Justice Department's investigation. Behind hazy legal claims, Trump requested that a federal judge appoint a neutral third-party "special master" to review and filter out from prosecutors any document covered by executive privilege. The Justice Department protested that Trump had no legitimate claim and that appointment of a special master "would do little or nothing to protect any legitimate interests that Plaintiff may have while impeding the government's ongoing criminal investigation." The district court judge appointed a special master, over DOJ's objection, to review the approximately eleven thousand documents seized by the FBI at Mar-a-Lago. But a three-judge court of appeals panel, including two nominated to the bench by Trump himself, later rejected Trump's privilege claims as to a subset of about one hundred classified documents. The special master's review of the remaining documents nonetheless took more than three months to complete. Once again, Trump lost the legal battle over executive privilege, but he managed to create a substantial delay in the proceedings.

The luxury of invoking executive privilege is uniquely available to the president of the United States. Even other bosses—mobsters, CEOs, narcotics kingpins, other powerful politicians—must dream of having the power to invoke a hazy legal doctrine to silence those who might implicate them in wrongdoing or criminality, or to throw a procedural wrench into an ongoing prosecution.

Trump never won a final ruling on the merits in the courts on executive privilege or absolute immunity. Yet merely by saying the words out loud and invoking these legal doctrines, he managed to effectively neutralize or at least sideline potentially devastating witnesses to his misconduct relating to Mueller, the Ukraine scandal, and January 6. The self-professed master of *The Art of the Deal* learned to practice The Art of Delay.

Chapter 15

PARDONS FOR THE SILENT

Of all the constitutional imperatives granted to the president, the pardon power was among Trump's favorites. In 2018, Jonathan Swan and Mike Allen of Axios quoted an anonymous source close to Trump who explained, "What he enjoys most about this job is finding things he has absolute power over. He got a kick out of pardons, that he could pardon anybody he wants and people would come to him to court him and beg him."

Indeed, the brute simplicity of the federal pardon power, which is virtually unlimited by the Constitution, aligned nicely with Trump's view of his own presidential omnipotence. And its straightforward point-and-click application played perfectly with Trump's limited interest in procedural nuance.

It's nothing new for a president to use pardons disproportionately to rescue and reward the powerful, the rich, and the politically connected. Infamous examples abound. On his final day in office in 2001, Bill Clinton pardoned the fugitive billionaire financier Marc Rich, spurring a congressional inquiry and a criminal investigation by the SDNY, which did not result in charges. Seemingly for self-serving good measure, Clinton also pardoned his own half brother, Roger, who had been convicted on cocaine possession charges. In 1992, George H. W. Bush pardoned former secretary of defense Caspar Weinberger and five others who had been charged criminally in connection with the Iran-Contra scandal, pre-empting a trial that could have shone a damning light on Bush and his predecessor, Ronald Reagan. And of course, just weeks after he took office, Ford pardoned Nixon, sparing him from potentially becoming the first president in US history to be indicted after leaving office.

But even taking into consideration these historical blights, Trump took things to a new low—both to rescue his powerful friends and, inventively, to protect himself.

Trump actually used the pardon power far less frequently than most of his predecessors. He granted clemency—pardons (full forgiveness from a criminal charge, resulting in dismissal of the entire case) plus commutations (sentencing reductions)—a total of 237 times. Since 1900, only two presidents, George H. W. Bush and George W. Bush, have granted fewer acts of clemency. Barack Obama issued clemency to over 1,900 people (the majority of them low-level, nonviolent drug offenders), and every other non-Bush predecessor of Trump's dating back to William McKinley doled out at least 400 pardons plus commutations.

But relatively tight-fisted as he was on the whole, Trump set a new standard for using the pardon power to reward his own powerful, well-connected cronies. A November 2020 study published in the *New York Times* by noted conservative constitutional scholar Jack Goldsmith found that, of the forty-one acts of clemency Trump had granted by that point, thirty-six recipients had some personal or political connection to Trump himself. "No president has come close to using the pardon power in such persistently self-serving ways," Goldsmith concluded.

Trump issued most of his pardons and commutations during his final months in office, after the publication of Goldsmith's study. While many of those late-game acts of clemency went to people with no particular connection to Trump, including low-level drug offenders serving life or other draconian sentences, he also doled out free passes to powerful political allies and friends: Michael Flynn, Roger Stone, George Papadopoulos, Elliott Broidy, and Alex van der Zwaan (all convicted in the Mueller probe); Steve Bannon (a close Trump political advisor, indicted by the SDNY for fraud, as discussed in the prior chapter); Charles Kushner (father of Trump's son-in-law Jared Kushner, who had been convicted of various crimes after he set up his own brother-in-law with a prostitute, had the encounter filmed, and sent it to the brother-in-law's wife); and Republican congressmen-turned-federal convicts Duncan Hunter, Chris Collins, and Steve Stockman. During his final moments in office, Trump issued one last pardon, to Albert Pirro—the husband of Fox News host and vitriolic Trump cheerleader Jeanine Pirro.

The official White House press releases announcing Trump's pardons and commutations almost seem to assume that a person's wealth, status, or fame is a prerequisite to clemency or that, at a minimum, a recipient must have the endorsement of some celebrity backer. For example, the White House noted that pardon recipient Eddie DeBartolo Jr., convicted of bribery-related offenses, is a member of the Pro Football Hall of Fame and that "during the 23 years that he owned the San Francisco 49ers, the team won an unprecedented 13 division titles and 5 Super Bowl Championships"—as if football glory somehow justified criminal clemency. (What if he never had Jerry Rice and Ronnie Lott on the team? No leniency?) Trump seemed to base other pardons on the celebrity recipient's musical talents. He pardoned hip-hop stars Lil Wayne, Michael Harris (whose cause had been promoted by Snoop Dogg), and Kodak Black, pointing to their musical talents as part of the explanation for clemency.

Even if the person receiving a pardon or commutation was not likely to be featured on TMZ, the Trump White House press releases commonly listed other powerful people who had vouched for the recipient, ranging widely over the landscape of American celebrity: Rudy Giuliani, Jesse Jackson, Joe Montana, Chris Christie, Maria Bartiromo, Rick Santorum, and Geraldo Rivera, to name a few. In a neat act of celebrity begetting celebrity, in 2018

Trump commuted the sentence of Alice Johnson, who had been convicted of a nonviolent drug offense, based primarily on lobbying by Kim Kardashian. (Trump granted a full pardon to Johnson in 2020.) Largely because of Kardashian's advocacy, Johnson herself achieved a measure of fame. Trump, in turn, would later cite Johnson as the seemingly mandatory celebrity endorser for other clemency recipients.

Trump deployed the pardon power to benefit already powerful, well-connected recipients, and in that respect he trod a well-worn path. But Trump changed the game when he figured out how to use the pardon power to his *own* benefit. He never issued the country's first-ever self-pardon, despite his June 2018 tweet claiming, "As has been stated by numerous legal scholars, I have the absolute right to PARDON myself, but why would I do that when I have done nothing wrong?"

But Trump still found a way to use the pardon power to protect himself against potential prosecution. In what became a predictable pattern, whenever the possibility emerged that one of Trump's confidants might cooperate with prosecutors, he publicly floated the possibility of a pardon, as Mueller detailed in the section of his report covering potential obstruction of justice. In so doing, Trump appealed to the fundamental calculus of self-interest. Defendants cooperate with prosecutors not because they have suddenly turned from criminals into conscientious citizens bent on doing the right thing. Defendants almost always cooperate to help themselves, to minimize their own potential prison sentences. If, however, a defendant believes he will receive a presidential pardon—the ultimate sentencing benefit, a decisive end to any criminal case—then no incentive remains to cooperate with prosecutors and help them make cases against other people. Nobody who expects to be pardoned has any rational reason to cooperate.

Take Michael Flynn, for example. For over a year after he pled guilty to lying to the FBI, the former Trump campaign aide and national security advisor cooperated productively with Mueller's team. Mueller confirmed in a December 2018 court filing that Flynn had provided "particularly valuable" information relevant to "several ongoing investigations," including "the investigation concerning any links or coordination between the Russian government and individuals associated with the campaign of President Donald J. Trump." But just weeks after Flynn's guilty plea, Trump publicly floated the possibility of a pardon: "I don't want to talk about pardons for Michael Flynn yet. We'll see what happens. Let's see. I can say this: When you look at what's gone on with the FBI and with the Justice Department, people are very, very angry." Eventually Flynn had a change of heart and bailed out of his cooperation, putting himself in jeopardy of a prison sentence—until Trump rode to the rescue with a pardon in November 2020.

After a jury convicted Trump's former campaign chair Paul Manafort on bank fraud and tax fraud charges in August 2018, he too began to cooperate with Mueller. Trump reportedly broached the topic of a pardon with Manafort's lawyers, according to the *New York Times*. Later he said it right out loud for all to hear, telling the *New York Post* that a Manafort pardon "was never discussed, but I wouldn't take it off the table. Why would I take it off the table?" (Note how Trump managed to deny dangling a pardon, while dangling a pardon.) In November 2018, Manafort, like Flynn, thought better of it and scuttled his own cooperation with Mueller's team, subjecting himself to at least the seven-plus years to which he had been sentenced. Yet Manafort served just over a year of that sentence in prison before being released to home confinement in May 2020 when the federal Bureau of Prisons tried to reduce its inmate populations as Covid-19 spread. Trump then ensured that Manafort never served another day behind bars, or on home confinement, when he gifted a full pardon to Manafort two days before Christmas in 2020.

In 2019, Trump's longtime political advisor Roger Stone was convicted by a jury of lying to Congress (to protect Trump, as the judge noted) and witness tampering. Trump railed against the Stone prosecution, at one point tweeting, "This is a horrible and very unfair situation. The real crimes were on the other side, as nothing happens to them. Cannot allow this miscarriage of justice!" Trump openly tweeted praise for Stone for having the "guts" not to testify against him. After the conviction, a judge sentenced Stone to forty months in prison. Stone never attempted to cooperate with Mueller or anyone else, but he made his expectations known, declaring publicly that "I had 29 or 30 conversations with Trump during the campaign period. He knows I was under enormous pressure to turn on him. It would have eased my situation considerably. But I didn't." Sure enough, Trump rescued Stone with a sentencing commutation just four days before he was due to start serving his prison sentence and then followed up with a full pardon in late December 2020.

Or consider Bannon, one of four defendants charged by the SDNY in 2020 with stealing hundreds of thousands of dollars from unwitting donors to a "We Build the Wall" fundraising campaign. During his final hours in office, Trump pardoned Bannon—but, conspicuously, not the other three defendants in the case. If Trump believed the prosecution itself was somehow unjust, he would have pardoned everybody. Instead he singled out Bannon, his longtime political advisor, and the only of the four defendants who he knew personally. Bannon, it turned out, plotted with Trump and others to try to steal the 2020 election. But when a subpoena arrived from the House January 6 Committee, Bannon stayed mum. By refusing to testify, Bannon earned himself another indictment from the Justice Department, this one for contempt of Congress.

Flynn, Manafort, Stone, and Bannon were all close political advisors to Trump, and all of them could have helped themselves by giving prosecutors damaging information about him. Flynn and Manafort had actually started to cooperate with prosecutors but then abruptly stopped, at their own peril. But Trump pardoned them all—and nobody testified.

Chapter 16

"TAWDRY," "DISTASTEFUL"—
BUT PERFECTLY LEGAL

While no person in American life enjoys the legal protections afforded to a president—the DOJ no-indictment policy, executive privilege, and the pardon power—our laws are rife with other features that favor powerful people of all stripes. In particular, the Supreme Court has shown a recent penchant for gutting the ability of prosecutors to pursue elected officials, even beyond the president.

Take the Bob McDonnell case, for example.

It wasn't the dog vitamins that brought down the former Virginia governor. It wasn't the digestive system detox cleanse, the fresh-breath strips, or the sleep elixirs. Sure, the governor and his wife, Maureen, used taxpayer money to buy themselves all manner of potions and lotions. But following public revelations about the Virginia first family's liberal expenditure of public money for their own curious household goods, the McDonnells repaid the state for at least part of the money (there were no receipts for some items, so a full accounting was impossible). It seemed that the McDonnells would glide through the kerfuffle over toiletries and tonics, bruised but relatively unscathed.

Problem was, the home-goods spending scandal was just a brisk warm-up act of corruption for the governor and his wife. Turned out, the McDonnells were involved in a more lucrative and even shadier arrangement with a man named Jonnie Williams, who ran a company called Star Scientific. For years, Williams showered the first family of Virginia with gifts. He let the governor use the corporate plane for trips worth tens of thousands of dollars. He took Maureen on a $19,000 shopping spree for clothes and jewelry in New York City. He cut a check for $15,000 to cover catering at the wedding of one of the McDonnell daughters, and he gave a $10,000 engagement gift to another. He lent his vacation house and Ferrari and golf tab to the family. He bought an engraved Rolex for the governor. And he made $70,000 worth of "loans" to the McDonnells' real estate company. In total, prosecutors alleged that the McDonnells accepted $175,000 in gifts and benefits from Williams.

Williams was a generous fellow, but he wasn't simply making benevolent donations to needy friends. Alas, he had a few targeted asks for the governor in return for his largesse. Williams's company, Star Scientific, had developed a nutritional supplement called Anatabloc. Williams told the governor that Star Scientific needed his help. Specifically, Williams sought studies of Anatabloc at two leading public universities, the University of Virginia and Virginia Commonwealth University.

The McDonnells, in turn, used their official positions to help him out. Maureen emailed a senior staffer in the governor's office, "Gov wants to know why nothing has developed w studies after [Williams] gave $200,000." McDonnell himself emailed an aide, "Pls see me about anatabloc issues at VCU and UVA." The governor instructed his cabinet secretary responsible for state employee health plans to meet with Williams about Star Scientific's products. The McDonnells spoke publicly about the virtues of Star Scientific and its products, and hosted a luncheon at the executive mansion to help launch Anatabloc.

Eventually this cozy arrangement between the McDonnells and Williams unraveled and resulted in a federal indictment charging the governor and his wife with a spate of federal crimes including extortion (using official power to obtain payoffs) and "honest services" fraud (depriving the citizenry of an official's faithful representation by accepting bribes).

Williams flipped and testified against the McDonnells at trial, and the jury convicted both the governor and Maureen on various charges, premised on the prosecution's theory that Virginia's first couple had accepted benefits from Williams in exchange for "official acts." Prosecutors recommended six and a half years in prison for the governor, but the judge went light and gave him two years. The judge later sentenced Maureen to a year and a day in prison.

The judge permitted both McDonnells to stay out of prison pending completion of their appeals, which seemed unlikely to succeed. Governor McDonnell argued on appeal that even if he and his wife had accepted lavish gifts, he had not undertaken any "official act," as defined by federal statute. Seemed like a long-shot argument, though not lacking in chutzpah. It's fine for a governor to accept hundreds of thousands of dollars' worth of payoffs and, in return, to use his official position to arrange meetings with powerful policymakers in his administration and to host promotional corporate events at the executive mansion? A three-judge federal court of appeals panel unanimously rejected McDonnell's brassy claim.

But the US Supreme Court saw it differently. In a unanimous eight-to-zero decision handed down in June 2016, the court (which was one judge short following the death of Justice Antonin Scalia but before the confirmation of his successor, Neil Gorsuch) threw out Governor McDonnell's conviction. The justices noted that McDonnell's conduct was "tawdry" and "distasteful" and "it may be worse than that." But the court held that to qualify under the statutory definition of an "official act," a public official must take some specific, formal action—casting a vote, issuing an executive order, or vetoing legislation, for example. According to the court, other conduct, like instructing a subordinate agency head to take a meeting, making phone calls, or hosting events, didn't count as "official acts." Essentially, the Supreme Court green-lit influence peddling for cash, so long as the elected official worked behind the scenes and was discreet enough about it.

If you're miffed, and might like to blame the "other side," keep in mind: this was not some ideological or partisan outcome. This unanimous opinion united left with right, conservative with liberal, Justices Clarence Thomas and Samuel Alito with Ruth Bader Ginsburg and Stephen Breyer, in a kumbaya quest to water down the nation's federal corruption laws.

The fallout from the *McDonnell* decision was swift. Prosecutors dismissed all charges against McDonnell and his wife, both of whom walked free without ever serving a day behind bars. And the Supreme Court's ruling kneecapped other corruption cases then pending around the country. For example:

WILLIAM JEFFERSON. The former US representative from Louisiana was convicted by a jury in 2009 of bribery and other offenses. Memorably, FBI agents found in Jefferson's freezer $90,000 in cold, hard cash (literally), which he intended to deliver to the vice president of Nigeria. But when the *McDonnell* decision dropped, the judge who had presided over Jefferson's trial dismissed most of the counts of conviction and let Jefferson, who was five years into a thirteen-year sentence, out of prison. The judge noted that Jefferson's conduct was "venal" and that "public corruption is a cancer on this country and it needs to be revealed, prosecuted and punished," but nonetheless found that the *McDonnell* decision compelled dismissal of certain counts on which the jury had found Jefferson guilty. Prosecutors then dropped the remaining counts, and Jefferson went home.

SHELDON SILVER. In 2015, about seven months before the *McDonnell* ruling came down and narrowed the law governing corruption cases, a federal jury convicted Silver—the powerhouse Democratic Speaker of the New York State Assembly who had spent decades in back rooms building and presiding over a political empire—for taking bribes and kickbacks worth over $3.5 million. (McDonnell, who made a measly $175,000 for his abuse of power, could've learned a thing or two from Silver about monetizing his corruption.) But in 2017, a federal court of appeals threw out Silver's conviction, specifically citing the *McDonnell* decision. Prosecutors in my former office, the SDNY, retried Silver and convicted him again in 2018. Silver's corruption, it turned out, was so brazen and the evidence so strong that the case survived even under the scaled-back post-*McDonnell* version of the law. But the second prosecution took an additional year to complete, and Silver caught a break when his original twelve-year sentence was cut nearly in half, to seven years.

CHAKA FATTAH. Like Silver, Fattah—a former US congressman from Pennsylvania—was tried and convicted by a jury shortly before the Supreme Court issued the *McDonnell* decision. The jury found Fattah guilty of twenty-three federal corruption charges based on an audacious series of schemes that netted him hundreds of thousands of dollars. In one instance, Fattah accepted cash and gifts from a politically connected friend; in return, Fattah advocated (without success) for the friend to receive an ambassadorship in the Obama administration. Based on the *McDonnell* decision, a federal court of appeals vacated some but not all of Fattah's bribery-related convictions. Fattah was eventually sentenced to ten years in prison, but he was released in 2020 after serving less than five years, apparently as part of the federal effort to reduce inmate numbers during the Covid-19 pandemic.

Here's the bottom line: as of this writing, in the six-plus years since the Supreme Court decided *McDonnell* in 2016, no US representative, US senator, federal cabinet secretary or other senior executive branch official, federal judge, or state governor has been successfully prosecuted federally on a bribery theory under the narrowed-down law. Zero. Since then, only one such official has even been charged at all under the laws impacted by *McDonnell*: US senator Robert Menendez from New Jersey, in a spectacularly failed prosecution that began in 2015 (before the *McDonnell* decision) and ended in 2017, when a jury could not reach a unanimous verdict. The judge then dismissed some counts, and the Justice Department dropped all those that remained.

A handful of other members of Congress have been prosecuted federally during that time, but for other, non-bribery offenses unaffected by *McDonnell*. It bears repeating: since the Supreme Court in the *McDonnell* decision narrowed the scope of key federal corruption laws over six years ago, not a single powerful federal official or state governor has been convicted under those laws.

Nor did the Supreme Court stop at *McDonnell*. In 2020 the justices scaled back another law that prosecutors use to go after corrupt public officials. Following the Bridgegate scandal in New Jersey—in which top officials in the administration of then-governor Chris Christie reduced the number of traffic lanes going from Fort Lee, New Jersey, to New York City over the George Washington Bridge, causing gridlock, as political retribution after Fort Lee's mayor declined to politically endorse Christie—the US attorney for New Jersey charged three public officials with corruption-related offenses, including wire fraud and fraud against a federal program or entity. One defendant pled guilty, while two others went to trial and were convicted by a jury.

As with the *McDonnell* case, a three-judge federal court of appeals panel unanimously upheld the jury's corruption-related verdicts in Bridgegate (though it did throw out one charge for interference in civil rights by snarling traffic). And as with *McDonnell*, the Supreme Court unanimously disagreed and threw out those convictions. The court found in a 2020 ruling that the defendants engaged in "wrongdoing—deception, corruption, abuse of power" that "jeopardized the safety of the town's residents," entirely for "political payback." But, the court declared, the defendants' brazen misconduct didn't count under the charged federal laws because the defendants' primary motive, politically corrupt as it was, was not to obtain money or property. Once again, this was a cross-ideological, non-partisan outcome, with conservative justices Brett Kavanaugh and Neil Gorsuch harmonizing with liberal justices Elena Kagan and Sonia Sotomayor. The court's ideological wings disagree on much, but recently they've marched in lockstep when it comes to sanding down the edges of corruption laws.

The *McDonnell* decision and its progeny marked a whiplash-inducing turnabout for the Supreme Court with respect to its interpretation of corruption laws. Both cases narrowed key statutory terms to only the most flagrant acts of political corruption—cash for votes, and comparably brazen conduct. In contrast, back in 2003, in a case involving campaign finance law, the court rejected a "crabbed view of corruption, and particularly of the appearance of corruption, [that] ignores precedent, common sense and the realities of political fundraising." Indeed, common sense and reality dictate that *of course* a governor exercises official power when he instructs a cabinet member to meet with a specific private interest, as McDonnell did. But the Supreme Court saw it otherwise, to the benefit of all powerful elected officials with open palms and crooked intentions.

..

In its recent decisions narrowing the scope of federal corruption statutes, the Supreme Court did not change the law. Rather, the court did what it always does: it examined existing laws, as written and passed by Congress, and interpreted them. In these cases, the court construed federal anti-bribery and fraud statutes so narrowly as to render them effectively useless against power players and other elected officials.

However, Congress has the power to go back to the drawing board and craft new legislation that defines corruption offenses or their component parts more broadly. For example, in the *McDonnell* case, the court read the statutory definition of "official acts" to include formal, dispositive acts like voting on legislation but exclude influence peddling by setting up meetings or making behind-the-scenes phone calls. While the current definition of "official acts" is already quite expansive—"*Any* decision or action, on *any* question or matter, that may *at any time* be pending, or which may by law be brought before *any* public official, in such official's official capacity" (italics added here for emphasis)—it apparently wasn't broad enough to encompass certain forms of influence peddling, according to the court. So Congress could, for example, clarify that "official acts" include not only final, dispositive public actions (like casting a vote on a bill) but also other informal exercises of power (like setting up a meeting in exchange for some gift or payoff).

Congress can close the gaping loopholes that the Supreme Court has opened. But there's zero present indication that lawmakers have any intention of refortifying the anti-corruption statutes that the Supreme Court has effectively rendered impotent.

Through its recent decisions, coupled with congressional inaction, the Supreme Court has winnowed down the law to make it virtually impossible for prosecutors to pursue other public officials for bribery and other corruption offenses. A frustrated veteran federal corruption prosecutor put it to me this way in the immediate wake of the *McDonnell* and the Supreme Court's anti-anticorruption rulings: "Now, unless we catch a guy on videotape accepting a cash-filled envelope marked 'Bribe Money for Votes,' there's just no way to charge anyone with anything anymore."

PURSUING DONALD TRUMP

Chapter 17

UNITED STATES V. DONALD JOHN TRUMP

Donald Trump has, as of this writing, never been charged with a crime. He has been investigated criminally at the federal level and in several states for crimes ranging from endangering-the-republic serious to the technical and obscure. But he has never been criminally charged, ever, with anything.

That's a far cry, of course, from saying that Trump has never actually *committed* a crime. To the contrary, as I'll argue here, he has committed many crimes, dozens even (depending how thinly we slice each of his criminal episodes into component parts), often in open public view. He has simply gotten away with it.

Trump might still face charges at some point; it's possible he gets charged by somebody, somewhere, with something, between the writing of this book and publication. (The Fulton County district attorney in Georgia seems the most likely of anyone to file charges, as we'll discuss in chapter 19.) But given the time that has lapsed, and the complex legal, structural, and political obstacles that any prosecution is certain to encounter, Trump's ultimate conviction and imprisonment are now more the stuff of fantastical Twitter memes than reality.

So, looking back at Trump's history of criminality, we need to consider the counterfactual. What charges might Trump have faced, in a (hypothetical) world where he received no formal legal protection while he was president, and none of the other advantages that bosses commonly enjoy and exploit, both during and after his presidency? What if Trump had done all he did, but was just an ordinary guy?

And what if prosecutors had taken action quickly and decisively, without spinning their wheels for years and allowing the political landscape to shift under their feet?

Before we begin, I need to make this clear: I reject the casual assertion that a prosecution of Trump would be easy, or a given. I've worked long enough as a prosecutor to know that there's no such thing as an automatic conviction, and that a criminal case against a former president would be extraordinarily difficult, regardless of the strength of the evidence. But we also need to move beyond the defeatist shrug of the shoulders—"Well, it's complicated, he was the president, it's never been done before, it'll cause dissension, what are you gonna do?" There's a substantive discussion to be had between these poles.

We do not, of course, have all the facts that were available to prosecutors—or *would have been* available, had they opened criminal investigations and pursued them in a timely and aggressive manner. But we do know an awful lot, often more than enough to conclude with confidence that Trump did in fact commit a particular crime.

We know about Trump's conduct, first, because journalism about his misdeeds has been remarkable for its scope, depth, and accuracy. There have been sporadic misfires, but by and large, media reporting about Trump's conduct has been spot-on, and countless scoops have later been definitively confirmed. Of course we'll rely here only on those factual allegations that have now been established beyond serious dispute.

Over time, even more evidence has entered the public domain. Grand jury materials have now been publicly disclosed, as criminal cases against Trump's cohorts (and, at times, co-conspirators) have progressed and concluded. Judges have ordered the Justice Department to turn over internal documents to Congress, media outlets, and public transparency advocates. Congress, inspectors general, and others have uncovered new evidence through their investigative work; the House January 6 Select Committee has uncovered particularly damning evidence about Trump's quest to steal the 2020 election. People who were directly involved in Trump's crimes, or witnessed them, have come forward (at times, conveniently, just a bit too late for prosecutors or other investigators to make meaningful use of their information). Heck, Trump himself has openly admitted much of his wrongdoing—bragged about it, even—in his tweets (pre-ban) and other public statements. The amount and quality of evidence varies by crime, but we have an ample factual record to proceed here.

Also—and this is important but often overlooked—we can use common sense. As we've seen in earlier chapters, the jury process, and our legal system more broadly, is not mechanical. It's human, by design. That's why judges instruct juries that they are permitted, and indeed duty-bound, to use logical reasoning and judgment to reach their verdicts. This point was so important that we SDNY prosecutors typically would end our closing arguments by reminding jurors that they need not check their basic, everyday common sense at the courthouse door.

A party can deny an allegation, but the jury is free to reject that denial if it is unconvincing or unsupported by the facts. If a witness gives noncredible testimony, a juror can disregard it. Jurors also can and must draw reasonable inferences. To borrow an example commonly used by SDNY judges when instructing juries: if you're in a windowless room and a person walks in the door wearing wet boots and holding a dripping umbrella, then, yes, you may conclude that it's raining, even if you cannot actually look outside and see raindrops falling from the sky. It's an essential part of the jury's job, and our criminal process, to apply reason and intuition. So we'll do the same here.

Trump would, of course, mount a spirited defense to the charges discussed below, as any defendant is entitled to do, and we'll assess the viability of those arguments as we proceed. Certain proposed charges are stronger than others, and some but not all of Trump's defenses hold at least some water. In addition, the politics and atmospherics around the prosecution of a former president would be enormously complex and likely perilous to the prosecution. But all in all, based on my experience as a prosecutor, I'd have been confident charging the below-listed crimes and arguing them to a jury.

Now let's run down Trump's rap sheet. We'll arrange it roughly in chronological order, and at times we'll lump several distinct crimes under one header, where he committed bulk offenses relating to the same general set of facts. We'll include in the hypothetical indictment (the "counts") only those crimes for which, given the available facts and law, a prosecutor could comfortably bring charges. Then we'll turn to other acts, unrelated to his candidacy and presidency, for which we don't have quite enough evidence to be confident in a criminal charge, or where he would have a substantial enough legal defense to throw his guilt into meaningful question.

One final note before we dive in. As discussed earlier, the DOJ policy against indicting the sitting president certainly explains why Trump was not charged federally during his tenure in office. But it also is well settled that a president *can* be charged criminally after he leaves office. Trump has been out of office for two years. We now have ample information to envision what an indictment of Trump should have looked like—and (mostly) still could.

COUNT 1: OBSTRUCTION OF JUSTICE
(MUELLER INVESTIGATION)

The details are now familiar, if receding a bit in the collective memory, of Trump's efforts to derail Mueller's investigation of Russian interference in the 2016 presidential election. In his report, Mueller laid out the facts in compelling and largely uncontroverted detail. Some highlights:

- Trump tried to persuade FBI director James Comey, who was then investigating Trump's former national security advisor, Michael Flynn, to do Flynn (and by extension Trump) a special favor and drop the case. "I hope you can see your way clear to letting this go, to letting Flynn go. He is a good guy. I hope you can let this go," Trump infamously beseeched Comey in the Oval Office in February 2017. Comey, a former US attorney for the SDNY, did no such thing.
- In 2017 Trump tried to have other officials, including his White House counsel, Don McGahn, fire Mueller, through other intermediaries and using the thin pretext of Mueller's purported "conflicts of interest." When news broke in 2018 about Trump's effort to dispatch Mueller, Trump asked McGahn to lie and to write a memo falsely denying the story.
- Trump used lightly veiled threats delivered through an attorney to try to intimidate Flynn into not cooperating with Mueller. Later, Trump dangled (and eventually delivered, in 2021) pardons in an effort to persuade (and eventually reward) Flynn, Paul Manafort, and Roger Stone to keep quiet—as we discussed in chapter 15, on Trump's inventive use of the pardon power to protect himself.

The Mueller report details a half dozen more incidents of at least potential obstruction, though some of those are too close to the line to use in our hypothetical charge. But as to the specific conduct laid out above, suffice it to say: Trump obstructed justice and tried to obstruct justice, many times over, and rarely subtly.

For historical comparison, in the so-called smoking-gun tape that led to President Richard Nixon's resignation in 1974, Nixon took part in a conversation about pressuring the FBI to shut down the Watergate investigation. Here Trump did as much, and much more: he explicitly tried to get Comey and the FBI to shut down the Flynn case, he worked to get others to shut down Mueller's entire investigation, and he tried to cover those efforts up, after the fact.

Trump's obstruction was so blatant that over a thousand former federal prosecutors (including me) who had worked under the administrations of both political parties signed a statement concluding that, but for Trump's status as sitting president, his conduct would "result in multiple felony charges for obstruction of justice." By contrast, those who have been willing to go on record in Trump's defense are scarce and have little if any substantive backing. They raise two primary defenses, both of them unavailing.

We'll turn here to Trump's sycophantic attorney general, William Barr. Months before he became AG, Barr publicly prejudged Mueller's obstruction investigation to be "fatally misconceived" and "asinine." Trump caught wind of this, liked what he heard, and chose Barr as attorney general; Barr, in turn, delivered as advertised. In a widely panned and deeply dishonest four-page letter released just two days after he received the 448-page, single-spaced Mueller report, Barr declared in a conclusory tone that "the evidence developed during the Special Counsel's investigation is not sufficient to establish that the President committed an obstruction-of-justice offense." With a few casual keystrokes, Barr dismissed the mountain of evidence in Mueller's report.

But Barr offered next to nothing of substance to justify his astonishing (and astonishingly wrong) conclusion. He noted that Trump had not been charged with any underlying crime, and that "while not determinative, the absence of such evidence [of another, underlying crime] bears upon the President's intent with respect to obstruction." Barr failed to mention that DOJ routinely charges people with obstruction even without any underlying crime. Just weeks after Barr's letter, for example, his own Justice Department charged a man named Abdirizak Jaji Raghe Wehelie with obstructing an investigation by making false statements, but without any underlying crime. Or Barr could've just looked at his fellow Trump cheerleader, the aforementioned Stone, who was charged and convicted for false statements and witness tampering but, again, no underlying crime—in what Barr himself termed a "righteous" prosecution.

Second, Barr and others have argued publicly that the president generally cannot commit a crime when exercising a constitutional imperative of the office. But this argument collapses quickly upon scrutiny. Of course the president has broad discretion to exercise his constitutional duties. At the same time, he cannot deploy that constitutional authority *for criminal purposes*. For example, a president surely can issue pardons. Nobody disputes that. But is there any question whether it would be a crime if the president issued pardons in exchange for cash bribes? (Barr actually conceded when pressed during July 2020 congressional testimony that such an exchange would in fact be criminal.) By the same reasoning, sure, the president can fire the special counsel. He has that constitutional power. But if his motivation is to corruptly derail an investigation, then that would be criminal obstruction of justice. It wouldn't necessarily be easy to prove the president's criminal intent, but Trump has provided sufficient ammo here.

And even if Barr is right—even if some of Trump's conduct could be excused as falling within his constitutional purview—still, some of his actions exceeded the outermost boundaries of such protections. For example, even if a president has unlimited constitutional power to issue pardons or fire executive branch officials, he has no such authority to instruct another person to lie or to create a false document intended to mislead an investigation, as Trump did when he asked McGahn to cover up the effort to fire Mueller. Not even the craftiest constitutional doctrinaire can navigate around that.

Bottom line: Trump obstructed justice, and even his most ardent loyalists have failed to proffer any convincing defense. The evidence is strong, the law is on our side, and this charge is leading our indictment.

COUNT 2: CAMPAIGN FINANCE VIOLATIONS
(HUSH MONEY PAYMENTS)

In 2016, just weeks before the November presidential election, Trump (through various intermediaries including Michael Cohen) paid a total of $280,000 in hush money to silence Karen McDougal and Stephanie Clifford, both of whom had allegedly had extramarital sexual affairs with Trump.

We detailed the evidence in chapter 2, and there's no meaningful dispute now that (1) the payments were made, with Trump's knowledge, and (2) they were meant to silence Trump's alleged former mistresses. The only real question is whether the payments were intended, in some substantial part, to protect Trump's electoral interests—or if they were merely meant to protect him or his family from personal embarrassment, without regard to the presidential election. So let's focus on Trump's intent.

At first Trump flatly denied that he knew about the payments, but that lame defense collapsed quickly. Turned out, Trump had personally signed several of the hush money checks, and Cohen secretly recorded him talking about the payments. As discussed earlier, the SDNY formally stated in a court filing that Cohen "acted in coordination with and at the direction of Individual-1." So Trump knew, and his false public denials are evidence of what prosecutors (and the law) call "consciousness of guilt."

Trump and his defenders have argued publicly that perhaps the true intent behind the payments was simply to minimize public embarrassment to Trump and his family, unrelated to the election. (Trump's personal attorney Rudy Giuliani publicly claimed it was just a "crime of interpretation," whatever that means.)

But there are two main problems with this line of defense. First, it's still a campaign finance crime as long as some substantial part of the motivation was to protect Trump's electoral prospects; a person can, of course, have multiple motives for any action. Second, and relatedly, the timing is awfully difficult to explain away. McDougal alleged that she had an affair with Trump that lasted until 2007; the Trump campaign bought out her story (through AMI and the *National Enquirer*) nine years later, in August 2016, three months before the election. And Clifford claimed that she and Trump had a sexual encounter in 2006—yet Trump and his campaign paid her on October 26, 2016, ten years later and just one week before the 2016 election. Why, when both affairs allegedly had occurred nearly a decade prior, did Trump pay off both women right before the 2016 election?

Both the Justice Department and the federal judge who accepted Cohen's guilty plea formally determined that the hush money payments were indeed criminal. And SDNY prosecutors on the case felt confident that, if not for Trump's status as sitting president, they likely had sufficient evidence to charge him, too. I concur.

COUNT 3: BRIBERY, EXTORTION, FOREIGN ELECTION AID, AND WITNESS RETALIATION AND TAMPERING (UKRAINE)

You'll remember this one as the basis for Trump's first impeachment. As a quick refresher, in mid-2019, Trump tried to leverage

$391 million in US foreign aid to pressure Ukrainian president Volodymyr Zelensky to publicly announce an investigation of Joe Biden, Trump's likely (and eventual) opponent in the 2020 election.

Trump's misconduct was so flagrant that Chris Christie—former New Jersey governor and US attorney, and then one of Trump's most dogged political allies—inadvertently condemned it by describing what he thought was a hypothetical worst-case scenario. Just hours before the White House released the incriminating transcript of Trump's July 25, 2019, phone call with Zelensky, Christie said on ABC News that the transcript would be most damning "for instance, if he's saying, listen, do me a favor, go investigate Joe Biden." Turned out, likely to his own dismay, Christie was virtually spot-on. Trump—channeling Christie's fictional fellow New Jerseyite, Tony Soprano—actually said to Zelensky, "I would like you to do us a favor, though," before demanding an investigation of the Bidens and other conspiracy theories relating to the 2016 election.

Trump's own words, as recorded in the White House's official transcript, are the most powerful evidence against him. In characteristically blunt fashion, he proposed this deal to the Ukrainian president: you do what I want (announce a politically damaging investigation of the Bidens), and I'll do what you want (release hundreds of millions of dollars to Ukraine, then facing the prospect of war with Russia—which exploded into full-blown combat in 2022, underscoring the gravity of Trump's effort to use foreign aid, which was essential to Ukraine's ability to defend itself militarily, to coerce Zelensky).

On its face, that arrangement falls within the federal law against bribery: an exchange of "anything of value personally" to a public official (here, Zelensky's announcement of the Biden investigation, to Trump's political and electoral benefit) for "being influenced in the performance of any official act" (Trump's release of the aid money to Ukraine). Trump's proposal to Zelensky also appears to constitute extortion, which is essentially the converse of bribery: give me what

I want (announcement of the Biden investigation), or else I'll harm you (by withholding the foreign aid).

And Trump's conduct likely violates the federal law against "solicit[ing]" (asking) a foreign national for a "thing of value" relating to a campaign. Some defenders have argued that a bogus investigation intended to generate dirt on a potential campaign opponent might not technically qualify as a "thing of value." Why, then, does virtually every political campaign spend money on opposition research? Because it is without "value"? As one veteran political consultant said to me, "What could be *more* valuable to a campaign than a criminal investigation of your opponent?"

Trump defenders have also argued that perhaps there was no connection between the two things Trump raised on the call with Zelensky, the foreign aid and the investigation of the Bidens. But a parade of insider witnesses testified at Trump's first impeachment that his proposal to Zelensky was indeed a corrupt quid pro quo (Latin for "this for that"). What else could it be, logically? Pure coincidence, two demands relayed on the same phone call but unrelated to one another? Trump himself linked the two in his call with Zelensky. And Trump's own acting chief of staff, Mick Mulvaney, publicly blurted out that these exchanges happen "all the time," but the public ought to "get over it." (In a remarkable display of denialism, Mulvaney quickly attempted to take back his damning admission by simply claiming he had not said precisely what he had just said into a microphone.)

Making matters worse, Trump broke federal laws against witness tampering and retaliation. In February 2020, just two days after the conclusion of his Senate impeachment trial, he went on a public vengeance tour, demoting two key witnesses, Lt. Col. Alexander Vindman and ambassador to the European Union Gordon Sondland. Trump openly broadcast his corrupt retaliatory motive when he commented on Vindman's testimony, "Well, I'm not happy with him. You think I'm supposed to be happy with him? I'm not." Trump even fired Vindman's twin brother, Lt. Col. Yevgeny Vindman—who had nothing at all to do with the Ukraine scandal and ensuing impeachment—just for old-fashioned, retributive good measure.

Even before the impeachment trial started, Trump demoted one prospective witness, ambassador to Ukraine Marie Yovanovitch, after ordering his henchmen to "take her out." Just to make his intent perfectly clear, he later tweeted an attack on Yovanovitch *while she testified* during the impeachment proceedings. This was witness tampering in real time.

Despite the obvious evidence of at least potential criminality, the Justice Department under Barr conspicuously declined to even open a criminal investigation. This was a classic act of Barr's permissive myopia when it came to Trump. Barr's successor as attorney general, Merrick Garland, showed zero interest in picking up the investigative mantle when he took over. There's no evidence that his Justice Department ever did a single thing to investigate it, though all the conduct remains within the statute of limitations even now.

But I'm putting together this indictment, not Garland or Barr—I've tried my share of bribery and extortion cases, by the way—and we're including it.

COUNT 4: CONSPIRACY, OBSTRUCTION OF AN OFFICIAL PROCEEDING, AND ELECTION INTERFERENCE (2020 PRESIDENTIAL ELECTION)

"All I want to do is this. I just want to find 11,780 votes, which is one more than we have because we won the state."

Trump made this request in a desperate phone call to Georgia secretary of state Brad Raffensperger on January 2, 2021, as Trump flailed about wildly trying to find local sympathizers who might go in on a little election fixing with him. Raffensperger (a Republican) politely but firmly declined, informing Trump that based on the actual votes cast by Georgia's citizenry and a full recount, "We don't agree that you have won." He bluntly rebuked Trump's absurd claim to victory: "Well, Mr. President, the challenge that you have is the data you have is wrong."

This call to Raffensperger, it turned out, was just one particularly egregious incident in a weeks-long effort by Trump and his persistent band of lunatic enablers—private attorneys Giuliani, Sidney Powell, and John Eastman; White House chief of staff Mark Meadows; Justice Department assistant attorney general Jeffrey Clark; various Republican members of Congress—to steal the 2020 election, well after it was done and certified for Joe Biden.

Trump and his cultish cronies pressured state and local officials in other key swing states including Arizona, Michigan, and Pennsylvania to overthrow their own democratic processes. Giuliani engineered a scheme in which officials in seven states submitted fraudulent documents purporting to name pro-Trump electors, contrary to those states' actual election results and official certifications. Trump urged the Justice Department to just make stuff up about election fraud, in a quest to lend legitimacy to his fabricated claims; Clark stood ready to oblige but was thwarted by other DOJ officials who were less inclined to indulge a coup attempt. And Trump and his acolytes relentlessly pressured Vice President Mike Pence to unilaterally (and illegally) reject slates of electoral votes for Biden that had been duly certified by swing states.

Even before any of the rioters set foot in the Capitol on January 6, Trump had violated a bundle of state laws—most notably in Georgia, given his incriminating call to Raffensperger—prohibiting election interference, including solicitation of an official to count votes not actually cast, to discard votes that were cast, or to falsely certify an election result. And Trump broke federal laws that prohibit conspiracy to defraud the United States of a fair election and attempted obstruction of an official proceeding (here, the counting of electoral votes by Congress).

One federal judge found that it was "more likely than not" that Trump and others had tried to commit the crime of obstruction (a lower evidentiary bar than the "proof beyond a reasonable doubt" standard necessary for a conviction, but a notable finding nonetheless). Other judges repeatedly upheld obstruction charges against various defendants charged by the Justice Department in connection with the January 6 Capitol attack. Whether or not Trump incited a riot (or intended for violence to break out on January 6—which is a trickier case to make, as we'll address in the next count), it's enough under this law if Trump corruptly tried to interfere with the proper counting of electoral votes by Congress.

The most common defense of Trump is that he didn't possess criminal intent because, in his heart of hearts, he believed that he had won. First, even if that were true, it's not actually a defense; a person who genuinely thinks he won an election can seek a lawful recount or file a lawsuit, but he can't lean on election officials behind the scenes to throw things his way.

In any event, Trump's own words convey that he didn't actually think he had won. Here's where we get to call on that good old-fashioned common sense. If Trump truly believed he had won, why would he ask Raffensperger to "find" votes? And why precisely one more vote than he'd need to win the state, as opposed to simply counting all the votes and letting them fall where they may? And why would Trump have instructed the Justice Department, according to the contemporaneous notes of one official, to "just say the election was corrupt + leave the rest to me and the R. [Republican] Congressmen"? Indeed, multiple witnesses testified to the January 6 Committee that Trump had, at various times, acknowledged his own electoral loss.

Also, worth noting: Trump didn't win, and he either knew it or intentionally turned a blind eye to it (either of which is sufficient to show criminal intent under the applicable laws). There never is, was, or has been any actual evidence that Trump did win—a fact confirmed publicly by dozens of state and federal judges across the country; by the states, in their official certifications of their own election results; and by Trump's own chosen leaders of the Justice Department, Department of Homeland Security, and FBI. Just to drive the point home, several of Trump's own White House lawyers and advisors told him directly that there was no evidence of widespread fraud sufficient to swing the election his way.

In the end, a good-faith belief by Trump that he had actually won, based on some legitimate kernel of truth, might be marginally defensible here. But an absolute fantasy, conjured out of nowhere, explicitly recognized by Trump himself as a fiction—as a thing to be "found" or to "just say"—is no defense at all.

COUNT 5: SEDITIOUS CONSPIRACY AND INCITEMENT (JANUARY 6 CAPITOL ATTACK)

This count—which focuses on the January 6 Capitol attack itself—is a closer call and a more difficult case than Count 4, which rests on Trump's efforts to upset the election results during the weeks preceding the riot. While it's plain in my view that Trump bears legal responsibility for trying to steal the election through fraud and improper political pressure, it gets trickier proving he bears direct criminal culpability for the actual January 6 attack. He'd have a potent, though not necessarily winning, defense based on the First Amendment. Still, I'd be willing to make the case.

Let's start with seditious conspiracy. The term *sedition* evokes dramatic images of efforts to topple the government, and there's an argument that that's precisely what Trump was trying to do when he prompted his frothing, armed crowd to go to the Capitol right as

Congress was counting the electoral votes that would certify his defeat. But there's an easier path. The federal sedition law also applies to efforts "by force to prevent, hinder, or delay the execution of any law of the United States"—including, for example, the constitutionally mandated counting of electoral ballots on January 6, an event to which Trump intentionally pegged the rally. And the law prohibits the forcible takeover of any federal property. The US Capitol would, of course, qualify. The key question is whether Trump conspired to use force—specifically, the force of the crowd that stormed the Capitol—to achieve the unlawful objective.

Federal law also prohibits incitement of a riot. Taking the easy part first, January 6 was, to put it mildly (and legally), a "riot"—technically defined as a public disturbance involving an act of violence by a group of three or more people, resulting in property damage or personal injury. We've all seen the videos of the Capitol attack. Check.

The pivotal issue, then (for both charges), is whether Trump intended to inspire the crowd to commit acts of violence. Defenders have claimed that his speech was merely political rhetoric, protected by the First Amendment, and that he never specifically instructed his followers to destroy property or threaten public officials or commit crimes. The law does not, however, require that a person stand before a crowd and solemnly intone, "I do hereby instruct you to commit criminal acts," to qualify as unlawful incitement.

Remember: we can use common sense. I concede that this point is not an easy win for a prosecutor, but I'd argue to a jury that Trump's words before, during, and after the January 6 attack on the Capitol, delivered to an angry, armed, Trump-flag-waving crowd, by the most reasonable understanding, were intended to incite. Virtually every day for months leading up to and after the election, Trump cried publicly over Twitter and elsewhere that the election was rigged and had been stolen from his tens of millions of supporters, and that the future of their country was at stake: "What are they trying to hide. They know, and so does everyone else. EXPOSE THE CRIME!"; "They are trying to STEAL the election"; "MOST CORRUPT ELECTION IN U.S. HISTORY!" Trump upped the desperation behind his call to action in a December 2, 2020, address to the nation during which he declared, "If we don't root out the fraud, the tremendous and horrible fraud that's taken place in our 2020 election, we don't have a country anymore."

Then he hyped up the January 6 rally on the White House Ellipse—specifically timed to coincide with the official counting of electoral votes, which would seal Trump's fate as the loser of the 2020 election—like it was some professional wrestling event to be played out in real life: "Big protest in D.C. on January 6th. Be there, will be wild!" among others.

After all the hype, before he spoke at the January 6 rally itself, Trump angrily noted that the crowd was smaller than he had hoped, according to testimony given by former White House aide Cassidy Hutchinson to the January 6 Committee. Hutchinson testified: "He was angry that we weren't letting people through the mags with weapons. I overheard the president say something to the effect of, you know, I don't f-ing care that they have weapons. They're not here to hurt me. Take the f-ing mags away. Let my people in."

Moments after acknowledging that the crowd of "my people" was both armed and "not aiming to hurt me," Trump addressed the soon-to-be rioters. "Our country has had enough. We will not take it anymore and that's what this is all about. And to use a favorite term that all of you people really came up with: we will stop the steal." He then pointed his followers directly to the Capitol: "Now, it is up to Congress to confront this egregious assault on our democracy. And after this, we're going to walk down, and I'll be there with you, we're going to walk down, we're going to walk down." Hutchinson later testified that Trump wanted to physically accompany his supporters to the Capitol but was stopped by the Secret Service. Hutchinson's testimony on this point was backed up by Trump himself, who told the *Washington Post* in April 2022, "Secret Service said I couldn't go. I would have gone there in a minute." Trump continued at the rally, "You'll never take back our country with weakness. You have to show strength and you have to be strong." Throw in the inflammatory rhetoric that immediately preceded Trump's January 6 speech—Giuliani exhorting the crowd to engage in "trial by combat," Brooks screeching that the crowd should "start taking down names and kicking ass"—and violence became all but inevitable.

Making matters worse, at 2:24 p.m., as rioters began to overtake the Capitol, Trump tweeted a verbal attack against Vice President Mike Pence, castigating him for declining to discard certain electoral votes for Joe Biden: "Mike Pence didn't have the courage to do what should have been done to protect our Country and our Constitution." The January 6 Committee showed video evidence of rioters reading Trump's tweet out loud and immediately breaking into chants of "Hang Mike Pence!"

As Christie later put it, "I think everything that he was saying from election night forward incited people to that level of anger." Yes, Christie—former federal prosecutor and, at the time, ardent Trump apologist—concluded that Trump had incited the mob. Or take it from Trump himself. Representative Kevin McCarthy, the then–House minority leader and Trump sycophant, was captured on tape just five days after the riot stating that Trump had acknowledged at least some level of responsibility for the January 6 attack on the Capitol: "I asked him personally today: Does he hold responsibility for what happened? Does he feel bad about what happened? He told me he does have some responsibility for what happened. And he'd need to acknowledge that."

The First Amendment is, rightly, exceptionally broad—but it's not limitless. Under the leading case on criminal incitement, *Brandenburg v. Ohio*, the US Supreme Court held that speech is not protected by the First Amendment and can become criminal if it is: (1) directed at producing imminent lawless action and (2) likely to do so. Part (2) is easy; forget about "likely" to lead to criminal action, the January 6 speeches actually *did* just that, right away, and it wasn't hard to see coming. The only question, then, is whether Trump "directed" his speech at such action. Remember that *after* the pro-Trump crowd had torn apart the Capitol, Trump tweeted praise for the rioters. He called them "great patriots" and exhorted them to "remember this day forever!" That proves the riotous crowd did precisely what Trump wanted and intended.

Just to allay any lingering doubt, in a burst of revealing public candor in late January 2022, Trump reconfirmed his approval of the rioters' actions. He declared his continuing support for the January 6 attackers and promised that, if re-elected, he would consider pardoning them: "We will treat them fairly, and if it requires pardons, we will give them pardons because they are being treated so unfairly." The next day, Trump released a public statement lambasting his own former vice president, Mike Pence, because "he could have overturned the Election!" Yes, Trump said it himself: his goal was to "overturn" the election, and he was still angry, a year later, that Pence had not done so. Keep in mind, this was not some off-the-cuff, inartfully phrased remark by Trump; this was a deliberate statement, thought out and committed to writing, and issued for wide public consumption.

Taken altogether, the evidence of Trump's criminal intent is compelling, and a First Amendment defense—"Free speech" or "protected political activity"—would stand on shaky ground.

Don't just take it from me. A group of 144 leading constitutional lawyers and scholars from both political parties drafted a letter deriding Trump's First Amendment defense to his second impeachment. The group concluded that there is an "extraordinarily strong argument" that Trump's First Amendment defense would not prevail in a criminal trial for incitement.

COUNT 6: CONCEALMENT AND
MISHANDLING OF GOVERNMENT DOCUMENTS

In August 2022, the FBI executed a court-authorized search warrant at Trump's post-presidential residence at Mar-a-Lago in Florida, where agents recovered boxes of official White House documents, including classified government materials (some of which carried the highest level of official classification). FBI agents found classified documents intermingled with Trump's other personal effects, and dozens of empty envelopes that had once contained classified materials. They recovered some of the classified documents in Trump's office closet and others inside desks in Trump's office.

This search came only after officials at the National Archives and Records Administration (NARA) and the Justice Department had spent over a year trying to claw back the sensitive government documents that Trump had taken from the White House to his beach resort in Florida. Trump's lawyers at one point falsely told DOJ officials that he had returned all classified materials when, in fact, he still retained boxes of government documents containing over one hundred documents bearing classified markings.

In the paperwork in support of the search warrant, DOJ prosecutors asserted and a federal magistrate judge found probable cause that the search would uncover evidence of three federal crimes: (1) destruction, concealment, or removal of federal government documents (this particular law actually provides that, if the person removes or destroys records that were in his official custody, he is disqualified from holding any federal office in the future—though there is a legitimate question about whether this disqualification provision is constitutionally valid); (2) obstruction of an official investigation; and (3) a violation of the Espionage Act relating to knowing or intentional removal of materials that could be harmful to the national security of the United States.

In the wake of the search, Trump, his lawyers, and his supporters publicly claimed an internally contradictory slate of potential defenses. They started with the nonsense conspiracy theories: the FBI planted evidence and similar tinfoil-hat drivel. There's zero evidence to support this, and plenty to refute it, so we won't indulge it further here.

Trump and his team also claimed that he had issued a standing order declassifying the documents while he was still president. (At one point, Trump posited publicly that he had the power to declassify "even by thinking about it.") The president does hold broad (arguably unlimited) constitutional authority to declassify information. But this defense nonetheless suffers from three fatal defects. First, if Trump had declassified, presumably there would be at least some smidge of documentation or other evidence to support it. Yet no such evidence ever emerged; to the contrary, eighteen former White House officials told CNN that Trump never declassified the documents, and that the notion of a standing order was "ludicrous," "ridiculous," "a complete fiction," and "bullshit." Second, there are plenty of crimes, including all three underpinning the Mar-a-Lago search warrant, that have nothing to do with classification. And third, it's a bit contradictory to argue that documents that were somehow faked or planted were also at some point declassified by Trump; do the documents exist, or not?

Trump's primary defenses in a courtroom likely would hinge on his lack of knowledge and criminal intent. Prosecutors would of course bear the burden of proving his state of mind, beyond a reasonable doubt. They'd point to the fact that Trump had access to the documents as president; that hundreds of the documents were clearly marked as classified or otherwise sensitive; that they wound up in the resort that he owned, often in specific areas over which he had unique or exclusive access (like his closet and desks); and that he and his team refused to return the documents, and misled federal investigators, when the National Archives and Records Administration (NARA) and later DOJ demanded their return. Further, the *New York Times* reported that Trump "went through the boxes himself in late 2021, according to multiple people briefed on his efforts," before turning over some of the materials (but not all of them) to NARA.

Nor is Trump a stranger to the legalities around the handling of sensitive government information. He publicly railed against his 2016 campaign opponent Hillary Clinton, who as secretary of state had used a private email server, that "people who have nothing to hide don't bleach—nobody's ever heard of it—don't bleach their emails, or destroy evidence, to keep it from being publicly archived, as required by federal law." Trump's comments are not merely hypocritical—they're also evidence that he understood the federal laws around document retention and destruction. And in 2018, as president, Trump signed a new law increasing penalties for mishandling classified information. It's tough for a former president to claim ignorance of a statute that he himself signed into law.

Separate from the Mar-a-Lago documents, in early 2022, a spate of media reports established that Trump, while president, habitually took steps to hide and destroy evidence of his own communications and activities. He reportedly would routinely rip up documents, forcing White House aides and other government officials from the National Archives to tape them back together like jigsaw puzzles. At times, White House residence staff tasked with fixing backed-up toilets found wadded up, printed paper—not toilet paper, that is—

clogging the piping. Trump denied this, but the reporting was based on multiple sources, and was later confirmed by published photographs of papers bearing Trump's distinctive handwriting, resting at the bottom of toilets.

I'm not so concerned here with the habitual ripping up of documents. That could be fairly seen as a thoughtless habit; former Trump aide Stephanie Grisham—who became a pointed critic of Trump after she left her job—said publicly that while she was "not surprised" about the document revelations because "we had no rules," Trump would rip documents mostly as a "nervous tic." Other aides were often able to piece the documents back together. (Imagine getting a job in the White House and then spending hours taping up documents that had been torn up and thrown in the trash can by the president.) So we'll overlook the ripping habit.

But the toilet, dear friends, is different. It seems an uncontroversial, intuitive assertion, understood even by young children, that a person deposits items in a toilet and flushes them for one reason—to get rid of them and make sure nobody can ever recover them. This was a common move by criminals in my cases. Often when police arrived to make an arrest, defendants would head right to the toilet and start flushing—drugs, phones, SIM cards, papers. In one case, when the FBI arrived at a Mafia defendant's house, he started flushing documents relating to his loansharking and gambling operations. But a remarkably dedicated FBI agent scooped whatever documents she could find out of the toilet, let them dry out, and taped them back together. That particular defendant pled guilty to obstruction of justice as a result, on top of other crimes. I'd be fine standing in front of a jury to argue that when Trump wadded up presidential documents, threw them in the bowl, and flushed them, then yes, his intent absolutely was to destroy those documents and to make them unavailable to others.

COUNT 7: RACKETEERING

Finally, we come to a particularly potent weapon that prosecutors could have used to bring down Trump: RICO (Racketeer Influenced and Corrupt Organization) laws. These laws are often oversimplified and misunderstood in public discourse. I humbly submit myself as your expert guide here; I prosecuted dozens of people on federal racketeering charges, and eventually I taught the in-house training course on RICO to younger prosecutors at the SDNY.

First, a bit of background. Passed by Congress in 1970, the federal RICO laws were originally intended to help prosecutors take down organized crime syndicates. (Many states later passed their own iterations of the law.) There's a persistent rumor that Congress chose the acronym based on the character "Rico" played by Edward Robinson in the 1930 gangster movie *Little Caesar*. The law's drafter, G. Robert Blakey, has maintained publicly that the law was given a purely functional name, and has refused to either confirm or deny that he had cinematic referential intentions (but really, we all know these clever legislative acronyms are never accidental).

RICO hit its stride in the 1980s, when the SDNY used the new laws to charge and convict bosses and other members of all five Mafia families. Giuliani, who was then the US attorney for the SDNY, deserved much of the credit, and he basked in the publicity. Looking back, it's hard to fathom that the once-admired prosecutor has now become an angry con man, a dangerous conspiracy theorist, and a clownish sycophant for Trump.

Over time, prosecutors have gotten creative and applied RICO laws to other groups, including labor unions, drug trafficking organizations, corrupt government entities and public officials, and foreign terrorist groups. As an SDNY prosecutor, I charged gangsters at all levels—bosses, mid-level managers, enforcers, money men, and hangers-on—under the RICO laws. As we'd tell juries, everyone who plays a role, large or small, is part of the enterprise—just as every actor in a movie, even in the smallest role, is part of the cast.

For a prosecutor, RICO can be more complicated than other charges, but it also provides invaluable benefits. On the downside, the prosecutor has to do more work in a RICO case than in a typical criminal case. The prosecutor must prove the existence of a "racketeering enterprise"—the Gambino family, for example, or the Latin Kings, or a crooked labor union or city government. The prosecutor also has to establish a "pattern" of racketeering, meaning two or more criminal acts related to the enterprise, and related to the other crimes committed by the group. Those are added evidentiary lifts; normally, prosecutors only have to prove the charged crime, and not that it was part of some organized enterprise and that it was related to other crimes.

But if a prosecutor can make those showings, then the benefits accrue. First, the RICO laws enable prosecutors to charge older conduct that might otherwise fall outside the statute of limitations, so long as some other act occurred recently enough to fall within the statute.

For example, in 2010 the aforementioned FBI agent Ted Otto brought me a case involving two Gambino family associates who had committed a double murder. Our suspect, Onofrio "Noel" Modica, had a beef over the drug trade with a local tough guy, James DiGuglielmo. One summer night Modica drove a motorcycle with another gangster (since deceased) sitting on back with a machine gun, hunting for DiGuglielmo. They eventually found him in a crowded Staten Island parking lot and opened fire, killing him and hitting two innocent bystanders. (One bystander died and the other was hit eleven times but somehow survived.) The problem was, the murder had happened twenty-three years before, in 1987, and under federal laws in place at the time, the statute of limitations had long run out. But RICO gave us a hook. Because we could prove that

Modica was part of a racketeering enterprise (the Gambino family) and had committed other, more recent crimes, including bookmaking, we were able to charge him with the decades-old hit as well. A little bit of timely sports gambling kept Modica on the hook for a double murder in the distant past.

RICO offers other benefits, too. It lets federal prosecutors charge certain state-level laws that couldn't otherwise be brought in federal court. Your standard assault, for example, is typically a state crime, but not federal—unless it was committed as part of some racketeering enterprise. And the RICO laws enable prosecutors to charge conduct that occurred in other geographic districts, so long as the enterprise did at least some business in the district where the case is charged. I once charged a RICO case involving crimes committed almost entirely outside the Southern District of New York based on a single phone call placed by one defendant from a pay phone in Manhattan. (Kids, pay phones were those things your parents would use, where you'd drop a quarter into a public phone and then make a call.)

Most importantly, RICO laws impose criminal liability where a boss presides over an entity that he *knows* is engaged in multiple criminal acts—even if there's no smoking-gun evidence showing that the boss directly *participated* in or ordered those criminal acts. In that sense, the RICO laws seem to have been created precisely with a savvy powerhouse like Trump in mind. In a routine criminal case, including a standard (non-racketeering) conspiracy case, it's a viable defense to argue, "Maybe the defendant was the boss, and maybe crimes were committed on his watch, and maybe even for his benefit—but you can't find him guilty if he didn't directly participate." But that defense fails under RICO, so long as prosecutors can prove the boss knew at least generally what was going on underneath and around him.

The RICO laws are custom tailored to a boss like Trump. The

racketeering enterprise here would be the Trump White House (which we would define to include the presidential campaign, plus the administration). Under the law, the racketeering enterprise itself does not need to be an inherently criminal organization, like a mob family or a street gang. In fact, prosecutors have successfully charged government entities and otherwise legitimate businesses (labor unions, for example) as racketeering enterprises. The question is whether the members of that organization committed two or more crimes in connection with the entity. We've got ample basis to use those laws against Trump and his presidential campaign and administration, which engaged in the many crimes laid out above in our proposed indictment. And under RICO, we'd only need to prove *any two* of these crimes.

RICO laws would permit federal prosecutors to charge Trump with older conduct (which might otherwise be barred by the statute of limitations), with certain state-level offenses, and with conduct occurring in various geographic districts. And the primary potential benefit of RICO laws as applied to Trump is that he could be convicted if a jury found that (1) he was part of the charged enterprise, which is inarguable, and (2) he merely knew about and acceded to the criminal conduct, even if he did not commit the unlawful acts with his own hands. The typical Trumpian defense—"That wasn't me, somebody else did that, you can't put that on me, he was just a coffee boy, I hardly know the guy," and the like—would fail in a RICO prosecution.

• •

Moving beyond the scope of Trump's political career, let's take a moment to examine two sets of allegations that have long swirled around him, without criminal consequences.

TRUMP ORGANIZATION FRAUD

This one is, in my view, different from the others. Trump's conduct in the business world is distinct from his campaign for president or his performance of official duties as president. The guy was a crook, or at least his company was crooked. That matters, of course. But, in contrast to the charged crimes discussed above, the Trump Organization's offenses don't involve abuse of official power, don't undermine the integrity of our legal processes, and don't pose a threat to democracy. Nor does the available evidence conclusively prove Trump's individual criminality.

The investigation of the Trump Organization by New York prosecutors—primarily former Manhattan district attorney Cy Vance, who initiated the criminal inquiry in 2019, and New York attorney general Letitia James, who joined forces with Vance in 2021—was deeply flawed. Together, New York state prosecutors put on a public clinic on how not to run a fair and effective criminal investigation. James overtly politicized the investigation from the start by running for office and fundraising on an explicit campaign platform that she'd pursue Trump and anything around him. Both James and Vance stoked the public's appetite for justice and reveled in the resulting attention. They made bold pronouncements, in court and in the media, about the seriousness of the investigation, even as they dragged the matter out over an inexplicably long period of time. Vance spared no expense, retaining an outside expert forensic accounting firm and a former SDNY prosecutor, Mark Pomerantz, specifically to work on the case. But in the end, after more than three years of investigation, all of it—all the campaign promises, all the public braggadocio, all the time and resources—ultimately resulted in a hill of beans.

After working on the case for years, Pomerantz and another experienced prosecutor, Carey Dunne, resigned suddenly in February 2022. According to Pomerantz's resignation letter, which was leaked to the *New York Times*, he believed "that Donald Trump is guilty of numerous felony violations of the Penal Law in connection with the preparation and use of his annual Statements of Financial Condition. . . . The team that has been investigating Mr. Trump harbors no doubt about whether he committed crimes—he did." Pomerantz claimed in the letter that Vance, shortly before leaving office at the end of 2021, "concluded that the facts warranted prosecution, and he directed the team to present evidence to a grand jury and to seek an indictment of Mr. Trump." When a newly elected district attorney, Alvin Bragg, took office in January 2022, however, he disagreed. He concluded that the evidence at that point was insufficient to indict, and directed that the investigation would continue. (Disclosure: Bragg is a personal friend and former SDNY colleague of mine.)

Count me as deeply skeptical of Pomerantz's post-resignation bravado. If Vance, Pomerantz, and Dunne were so gung-ho to charge Trump, why didn't they do anything about it during the first three years of the investigation, when they could have charged at will? Yes, they had to contend with an appellate fight over Trump's tax returns, which would have caused a temporary diversion of some fragment of the team's resources, but that doesn't explain three years whittled away without an indictment.

The resignations of Pomerantz and Dunne elicited a spate of Twitter-based conspiracy theories directed at Bragg: he had been bribed, or blackmailed, or was somehow in the bag for Trump. But Bragg is a deeply experienced federal and state prosecutor who had investigated Trump aggressively during his prior tenure with the New York attorney general's office. (His recent prosecutorial experience far outstripped Pomerantz's, who hadn't charged a criminal case since he left the SDNY in the late 1990s.) And Bragg had just won a crowded Democratic primary and then a general election in a heavily Democratic-leaning county; he won 83 percent of the vote in the general election, against just under 17 percent for his Republican opponent. If anything, Bragg stood to bolster his political standing in deeply blue New York by indicting Trump.

Here's the reality: prosecutors disagree internally about whether evidence is sufficient to indict *all the time*. Some cases are easy, and everyone agrees an indictment is necessary; others plainly fall short of the mark. But there's a substantial gray area, where some prosecutors believe the evidence is sufficient to charge, while others disagree. I can't even begin to count how many times I wanted to charge a case but was overruled by a supervisor who would conclude, essentially, *You're close but you need more, so keep working*. And that's fine—it's a vital part of the process, and often leads to better charging decisions by prosecutors. Sometimes you buckle down and get more evidence and bring a charge, sometimes you don't. In this scenario, Pomerantz and Dunne seemed to believe they had enough evidence to indict, while prosecutors both above them (Bragg) and below them disagreed; the *Times* reported that three other prosecutors on the case had resigned in late 2021, before Bragg arrived, because they believed Pomerantz was proceeding too hastily and there were "gaps in the evidence." Indeed, Pomerantz acknowledged in his resignation letter that Bragg's decision was made "in good faith."

While we don't know precisely what evidence the DA's office had, it's far from clear how prosecutors would have proven their case against Trump. Remember: bosses have the substantial advantage of organizational insulation, as we discussed in chapter 5. It's simply not enough for a prosecutor to stand in front of a jury and argue, "Hey folks, look, we know there was some fraud at the Trump Org. And Donald Trump is the boss. So he must have known!" That won't cut it. You need proof beyond a reasonable doubt not only that there was fraud but also that Trump himself knew about it and blessed or participated in it in some manner.

So how might prosecutors have established Trump's knowledge of fraud at the Trump Organization? He didn't text or email, so there's no smoking-gun document. There's no known incriminating wiretap or other recording. The files surely are papered over by lawyers and accountants who blessed the transactions at issue from both sides; the financial institutions that lent millions to Trump were sophisticated players in the financial markets. And the DA's office did not appear to have a credible cooperator who could have brought the case home. Michael Cohen certainly does not qualify; as discussed earlier, he could never identify a specific fraudulent transaction, and the SDNY firmly rejected him as a cooperator for a reason. And Allen Weisselberg, who state prosecutors smartly tried to flip, didn't turn against Trump.

In the end, New York prosecutors left us with a cloudy picture of Trump's actual conduct at the head of the Trump Organization. There's little question the company itself engaged in crime, likely widespread. New York prosecutors did indict the Trump Organization as a corporate entity for a long-running tax fraud scheme and did obtain a guilty plea from Weisselberg for the same conduct, though they never managed to tie Trump to the criminal acts of the business that bears his name. James filed a civil lawsuit against Trump, his family members, and his businesses, alleging systematic overevaluation of properties to obtain bank loans and other financial benefits, but she never brought criminal charges either.

Ultimately no prosecutor ever charged Trump himself for any criminal corporate fraud, likely as it seems that he must have been involved. Alas, "must have been involved" is simply not enough in the prosecutorial world.

SEXUAL ASSAULT

Estimates vary about exactly how many women have publicly alleged that Trump sexually assaulted or harassed them. Perhaps this is the most telling: so many women have alleged sexual misconduct by Trump that it's difficult to tabulate them all and, well, *estimates vary*.

Generally, the number seems to settle at around two dozen; depending how you count, it can land in the high teens to mid-twenties. The range of alleged conduct here is astonishing. Trump has been accused of accosting women on an airplane, at hotels, at beauty pageants, at a tennis match, on the set of a television show, in a department store. Many of the allegations involve unwanted kissing and forcible grabbing of breasts and genitals; recall that Trump boasted on the infamous *Access Hollywood* tape that "I just start kissing them. It's like a magnet. Just kiss. I don't even wait. And when you're a star, they let you do it. You can do anything. Grab 'em by the pussy. You can do anything." The most serious allegation came from the writer E. Jean Carroll, who alleged that Trump forcibly had sexual intercourse with her in a Manhattan department store in the 1990s. In 2019 Carroll sued Trump for defamation when he denied the allegations and called her a liar. Trial is set for early 2023.

The legal nuances around these allegations are tricky, and we can see plainly here how the law complicates and undermines prosecution of serial sexual offenders, discussed earlier in chapter 12. There is no federal criminal law that generally covers sexual assault, so we're in the realm of various states here. Trump's alleged conduct spans five decades, from the 1970s through the 2010s, occurring across the United States in Florida, New York, California, and elsewhere—so, as we saw earlier, it would be impossible for any prosecutor to charge the entirety of his conduct, or anything close. Each state has its own sexual assault laws, and some criminal cases (including Carroll's) could be barred by the statute of limitations. Some of the alleged incidents could be fairly low-level misdemeanors ("forcible touching," as it's called in New York, for example), while the alleged Carroll assault would constitute first-degree rape, a serious felony. Most of the allegations were made publicly years or decades after the actual incidents occurred, and many were never formally reported to law enforcement. Delayed reporting should not cast doubt on the complainants—sexual assault victims commonly are fearful or reluctant to come forward immediately, for legitimate and understandable reasons—but it does limit the ability of prosecutors to investigate and develop corroborating evidence.

Big picture, it's virtually certain that Trump committed sexual assault. Many of the allegations are facially credible, and some are backed by other circumstantial evidence (including Trump's own boasting about his "grab 'em" proclivities). And there is a fundamental consistency among the women who have accused Trump of various sexual assaults. Yet in the end, no prosecutor has felt able to bring criminal charges and prove them beyond a reasonable doubt, given the legal and practical obstacles.

· ·

All told, we have an imposing rundown of Trump's criminality. Take issue at the margins, or with some of the proposed counts, if you will. I've laid out and rebutted the primary defenses, and you can judge the merits. But even if you wiped out, say, a handful of the crimes in our proposed indictment, there's still plenty on which Trump could have been charged—and most of it is still technically in play right now. (Some of the conduct, particularly that which goes back more than five years, is likely barred by the statute of limitations.)

Don't get me wrong; I'm not suggesting that a prosecution of Donald Trump would be simple, or easy. It would be a long, ugly, bloody-knuckles battle, with professional, political, and reputational casualties assured. The prosecutor would bear the burden of proving guilt beyond a reasonable doubt—the highest standard in our legal system—to the satisfaction of a unanimous jury; even a single Trump holdout juror would cause a hung jury and a mistrial, a disastrous outcome for any prosecution. On top of these atmospheric hazards, you've got a subject who is particularly adept at exploiting the deeply embedded systemic factors identified throughout this book, each of which benefits and protects bosses and other powerful people. Victory would hardly be certain for the prosecutor.

So, no, it would not be an easy task, either in the courtroom or beyond. But here's the thing: any prosecutor who takes the job hoping it'll be a breeze is simply in the wrong business. Sometimes prosecutors have to make tough decisions. Sometimes prosecutors have to take on people who are powerful, well protected, rich, even scary. That's the job. If there's a crime, and it's provable, and the case is a righteous one, you bring the charges and do the work. You don't slink away because a case looks challenging or imposing, or because a defendant is simply too powerful to pursue.

Chapter 18

THE SOUTHERN DISTRICT OF NEW YORK AND "INDIVIDUAL-1"

Post-Presidency but Still No Charge

Let's circle back to a question we posed early on in this book: What ever happened to the SDNY's investigation of Michael Cohen, Donald Trump, and others for making hush money payments to silence Stormy Daniels and Karen McDougal? We know that the SDNY charged and obtained a guilty plea from Cohen in 2018 on campaign finance charges and sent him to prison for those crimes, among others. And we know that Justice Department policy precluded the SDNY from charging Trump while he was in office. But why didn't the SDNY charge him after he was no longer president?

When Trump left office and lost his protection from indictment on January 20, 2021, Audrey Strauss was the SDNY's acting US attorney. Strauss had taken over in June 2020 after Trump and his attorney general, Bill Barr, clumsily fired the SDNY's US attorney, Geoffrey Berman, under false pretenses. Late on a frenetic Friday night, Barr announced that Berman would be "stepping down," but Berman stated publicly just hours later that he had no intention to leave voluntarily. Berman's unprecedented dismissal—just months before an election, by the very president who had appointed him—set off alarm bells that Trump and his cronies wanted to rein in the famously independent SDNY as the election drew near.

When Berman pushed back, Trump and Barr scrapped their

initial plan to give the job to their chosen successor, Jay Clayton (who had never before worked as a prosecutor). Instead Strauss, who by that point was Berman's deputy, took over as acting US attorney in the normal course of succession. Strauss was no Trump loyalist and had no discernible political bent. To the contrary, she was the prototypical veteran, nonpolitical DOJ prosecutor. She had worked at the Justice Department from the mid-1970s to the early 1980s, in administrations of both parties, and she served on the staff of the independent prosecutor on the Iran-Contra matter. She spent the next three decades in various private sector jobs before she rejoined DOJ in 2018. People who know Strauss confirmed to me that she was liberal-leaning, and certainly no political fan of Trump's.

In January 2021, starting just days before Trump's presidency ended, Strauss met with a small group of other SDNY prosecutors (some of whom had worked on the Cohen prosecution) to discuss whether the office should consider charging Trump once he lost the protection of the DOJ policy against indicting the sitting president. Although the SDNY had represented to the judge on the Cohen case back in 2019 that it had closed its hush money investigation, the prosecutorial team had never formally cleared Trump. And the team understood that reopening the investigation was as simple as ordering the files back from internal storage.

The team of SDNY prosecutors, headed by Strauss, discussed the factors that weighed against a charge. First, they understood that to charge a former president would be politically explosive, perhaps to an unprecedented extent. Fair or not, Trump supporters (and perhaps others) might perceive an indictment as the newly installed Biden administration's effort to seek prosecutorial retribution against the former president. Prosecutors strive for political independence, to be sure. But public perception and political reality matter too, and those factors influenced the SDNY's calculations. One person with knowledge of the investigation told me, "We were well aware of the prudential reasons why you wouldn't charge a president, even after he was out of office." Another pointed to the "complications" and "potential evils" of indicting a former president. The SDNY, sovereign as it may be, does not operate in a bubble.

The SDNY team also assessed the strength of its evidence against Trump. Opinions varied among the team members, as discussed earlier in this book. Some believed the evidence was more than enough to charge in an ordinary case, while others thought it was a close call, though still chargeable. Even if the evidence was sufficient to support a charge, it also wasn't a slam-dunk case in the majority view.

The team assembled by Strauss also considered the nature of the potential campaign finance crimes against Trump. The group of SDNY prosecutors, who spent much of their time working on cases involving terrorism, organized crime, billion-dollar financial fraud, and large-scale cyberattacks, viewed Trump's involvement in the hush money scheme as serious, but not the end of the world. The conduct related to a political campaign for the presidency, of course, but tangentially; in a campaign where both sides combined to spend over $2 billion, a violation involving a few hundred thousand dollars did not in itself threaten the democratic process. And, the team acknowledged, the hush money payments did not directly implicate Trump's execution of his official duties as president (though they did touch on the way he became president in the first place). Perversely, Trump's misconduct *after* the hush money payments—obstruction of the Mueller investigation, the Ukraine scandal, the effort to steal the 2020 election, his provocation of the January 6 Capitol attack— worked to his advantage, in a sense. Trump's more recent scandals made the campaign finance violations seem somehow trivial and outdated by comparison.

After multiple meetings and discussions, Strauss and the team concluded that the SDNY would not seek to indict Trump. That came as little surprise to the team members. Strauss had a reputation for caution; some saw her as a bit trigger-shy, while others noted that she tended to ask many questions and deliberate extensively before taking action on any case. She had worked on the original prosecution of Cohen in 2018, in her capacity as senior counsel to the US attorney (after Rob Khuzami, she was the second-highest-ranking SDNY official on the team), and she was keenly aware of the practical concerns around charging a former president, particularly in a case involving proof that was arguably close to the line. Recall also that Strauss had quickly overruled the frontline prosecutors who suggested, back in 2018, the possibility of wiretapping a phone that might have yielded evidence of Trump's phone calls. A wiretap would have been controversial and politically risky; an indictment would be far more explosive than that.

Even if Strauss had authorized an indictment, she would have been required by formal DOJ policy to get pre-approval from Main Justice, including the deputy attorney general and the AG himself. (As discussed in chapter 10, criminal charges against powerful subjects receive more systematic scrutiny, at higher levels, than ordinary charges.) Remember that even the most minute decision relating to Trump on the original Cohen prosecution—down to the seemingly trivial question of whether Trump should be referred to as "Candidate-1" or "Individual-1"—went to the bosses at Main Justice for review. We know that DOJ leadership micromanaged the SDNY's prosecution of Cohen in 2018 because he was Trump-adjacent, and stifled a significant part of that case, refusing to allow the SDNY to lay out its evidence against Trump in detail in the Cohen charging document. Surely, then, Main Justice—even under a new Biden administration—would apply intense scrutiny to any proposed charge of Trump himself, once he became former president.

Monty Wilkinson served as acting AG from Biden's inauguration in late January 2021 until March 2021, when Merrick Garland was confirmed. There's no practical way that a temporary placeholder like Wilkinson would approve the nation's first-ever criminal charge against a former president. And, as we'll discuss in the next chapter, there's virtually no chance Garland would have signed off either, given his paralyzing reticence on vastly more serious potential charges against Trump, supported by even stronger evidence.

Strauss held the top job at the SDNY until October 2021, when Biden's nominee, Damian Williams, was confirmed. Williams was no stranger to high-stakes, hotly contested prosecutions. Before his confirmation, he had spent nine-plus years as an SDNY prosecutor, primarily working financial fraud and public corruption cases, including the prosecutions of Republican congressman Chris Collins and the powerful Democratic speaker of the New York state assembly, Sheldon Silver.

By the time Williams took office, he faced the same landscape as Strauss had, but an additional ten months had passed since Trump left office. There's no public evidence that Williams ever meaningfully considered reversing Strauss's determination and charging Trump under the campaign finance laws. I spoke to several people inside the SDNY, none of whom knew of any such deliberations. And when I asked the SDNY whether Williams had ever held a meeting to discuss such charges, a press spokesperson declined to comment.

By the time the Biden administration and its appointees settled in, the new president had already made clear in public that he did not want his Justice Department to pursue Trump. Just two weeks after Biden's election as president, on November 17, 2020, NBC News reported that five different sources confirmed that Biden had told his advisors he did not want his presidency consumed by investigations of Trump, and that he "just wants to move on." Biden didn't make his preferences known in a formal public statement, but the man was a nearly five-decade veteran of Washington, DC; he had to understand full well that if he repeated his wishes to five advisors, word would get out somehow. (Even Biden, it seems, understood how savvy bosses can convey their wishes without stating them expressly.) Justice Department prosecutors will proudly tell you that DOJ never takes marching orders on prosecutorial matters from the president, and that's almost always true. But prosecutors also do not operate in a vacuum, and they do read the press. Whether it influenced them or not, it's a certainty that leaders at Main Justice and the SDNY knew of Biden's widely reported preference.

A year and a half later, as Garland's palpable lack of action caused growing public exasperation, the president reversed course. The *New York Times* reported in April 2022 that Biden had told two close advisors that Trump "was a threat to democracy and should be prosecuted." Biden reportedly complained that he wanted Garland "to act less like a ponderous judge and more like a prosecutor who is willing to take decisive action over the events of Jan. 6." Biden did not directly convey his wishes to Garland, or in a public statement— but, as with his prior statement to advisors about potential Trump prosecutions, he had to know full well (and perhaps even intended) that his words would leak out to the public. Biden's turnabout reflected the extent to which Garland's inaction had ballooned into a political problem.

Ultimately, the SDNY's decision not to charge Trump after he left office rested on a combination of factors. Time had passed and urgency had waned thanks to the DOJ's no-indictment policy, which protected Trump during his four years in office. While prosecutors likely had enough evidence to charge, they did not have an overwhelming no-brainer of a case. Campaign finance violations, though serious, lack the obvious punch of murder or robbery or firearms trafficking, or even bribery and other more traditional corruption charges. Even in the context of Trump, the campaign finance violations rank fairly low on his personal list of potential offenses. A prosecution of Trump would have overshadowed and drawn public focus from the other priorities of the incoming Biden administration, and the new president initially made it clear that he hoped DOJ would steer clear of a prosecution of his predecessor (before he reversed course a year and a half later). A Trump indictment, even if solidly grounded in the facts and the law, would have been cast by roughly half the country as a political vendetta, and could have sparked large-scale protests, or worse. All told, the SDNY simply had neither the incentive nor the appetite to charge Trump after he left office.

Understand how remarkable this is. The prevailing culture at the SDNY during my eight-plus years there—and surely for generations before my time, and ever since—is that its prosecutors will pursue any wrongdoer, anytime, regardless of how powerful, how intimidating, or how well connected he might be. The SDNY has a long, proud history of taking on the most imposing of bosses: crooked Wall Street traders Ivan Boesky and Michael Milken; well-connected political powerhouses like Sheldon Silver and Chris Collins; murderous Mafia bosses Paul Castellano, Tony Salerno, and John Gotti Jr.; terrorist leaders including Omar Abdel Rahman (the "Blind Sheikh") and Osama bin Laden (indicted in the SDNY, but never extradited to the United States); billionaire insider traders Raj Rajaratnam and Rajat Gupta; international arms trafficker Viktor Bout; notorious con man Bernie Madoff; sex traffickers Jeffrey Epstein and Ghislaine Maxwell; plus countless less famous but deeply feared criminal kingpins.

If anything, there's an overarching machismo to the place, and an aversion to making cases against what we'd derisively call "mopes"— hapless, low-level criminal dregs. We'd ridicule anybody who indicted a case involving only small-time players (in a drug trafficking network, or a mob family, or any corrupt organization). I once did a Russian Mafia case against a group of young lower-level hangers-on.

The judge, who was an SDNY alum, said to me sarcastically after one proceeding, "Well, Mr. Honig, I see you're really going after the heavy hitters here." I deserved that.

So now consider the SDNY staring down the most powerful person on the planet—and backing away because of complications, or prudential concerns, or policy issues. I'm not claiming the SDNY, or the Cohen prosecutors, lacked backbone or toughness. What does strike me, however, is how institutional pressures and wide-lens political concerns placed Trump so far above the law that the SDNY never got particularly close to charging him after he left office—even when prosecutors believed they had a legitimate, well-supported criminal case against him. The prevailing view in the SDNY, both when Trump was in office and afterward, was essentially this: it's not worth it. Not for *this* crime, on *this* evidence, with *this* much political risk, *this* long after the fact.

The SDNY passed on filing the first-ever charge against a former president and taking on the untold difficulty, distraction, politicization, and risk that would come with it. Call it fear, call it institutional drag, call it justified, call it some mixture of those things. The end result, to put it bluntly, was that the SDNY handled Trump differently from how it would have treated any other person on the planet.

Chapter 19

GEORGIA

The Looming Showdown

As of this writing, in late 2022, Donald Trump faces two primary ongoing criminal investigations relating to his effort to steal the 2020 election: one by the Fulton County (Georgia) district attorney and another by the US Department of Justice. We'll focus first on Georgia; in the next chapter, we'll consider DOJ.

Given the public information about the Georgia investigation, I believe chances are high—I'd say it's more likely than not—that Fulton County district attorney Fani Willis will indict Trump for his attempt to corrupt the 2020 election. This might even happen by the time of this book's publication, in early 2023. If and when a Trump indictment drops, immediate reactions will be pointed: jubilation from those who have been hoping for years to see Trump brought to some measure of criminal accountability, and outrage from those who view the indictment as the culmination of a series of vengeful, politically driven prosecutorial inquests.

But that initial burst of emotion will yield quickly to a high-stakes legal battle in which Trump holds, and will seek to exploit, substantial legal and structural edges. And the DA—partially because of her own delay in completing the investigation and bringing an indictment, and partially because of institutional factors beyond her control—will be at a decided tactical disadvantage.

Let's play this out. Assume for starters that the Fulton County DA (a county-level prosecutor who charges Georgia state-level crimes in Georgia state-level courts) completes her grand jury work and obtains an indictment of Trump sometime in early 2023, potentially for charges including election interference and racketeering.

An indictment will not catch Trump flat-footed. As of late 2022, Trump already had retained a highly regarded, deeply experienced attorney in Georgia, Dwight Thomas. A former prosecutor in Georgia told me that Thomas is a "lawyer's lawyer and a trial ace." He said of Thomas, "If you got in trouble and you needed somebody who brought gravitas to a case, he's the one you'd call. Judges like and respect him—he's a serious lawyer and he's not out to be flamboyant—and he knows how to talk to a jury." A CBS News profile of Thomas called him "one of Atlanta's most respected and influential lawyers" and noted that he had made campaign donations to several prominent Democratic politicians in Georgia. The article mentioned that Thomas "has mentored countless attorneys . . . and many of his protégés are current or former prosecutors in Fulton County." One Georgia attorney offers this telling quote in the piece: "More prosecutors here have learned the practice of criminal law through Dwight's office than I can count." Note that, when the cameras are off and there's real work to be done, Trump is less inclined toward the unhinged blowhards like Rudy Giuliani and Sidney Powell; when the stakes are highest, Trump knows to retain real-deal lawyers who can get the job done locally. (Recall how Trump hired an understated but highly effective former SDNY prosecutor, Joanna Hendon, to protect his interests during the SDNY's campaign finance investigation and the resulting prosecution of Michael Cohen.)

If you're representing Trump on a state-level charge by the Fulton County DA, your first move is obvious: get the heck out of the Georgia state courts. If Trump is indicted by the Fulton County DA, watch for Taylor and the rest of Trump's legal team to run right to the federal courts and ask them to do two things. First, Trump's legal team would argue that the state-level charges brought by the DA should be dismissed outright because he has constitutional immunity; the charges, they'd argue, violate principles of federalism (the concept of government by two distinct governments, federal and state) and federal supremacy (the notion that federal laws trump state laws). There is a colorable if untested constitutional argument that a state- or county-level prosecutor cannot indict a president or a former president for conduct that touches on the presidency—yet another of the legal doctrines discussed in chapters 13 through 16 that, if accepted, would place a president or a former president in a uniquely favorable legal posture and largely beyond the reach of the law. Our system generally does not countenance state and local officials disrupting the functioning of federal government, the claim would go, and it would impede presidents from fulfilling their official duties if, while in office, they had to worry that they could someday face charges from partisan, elected, local DAs.

On a policy level, Trump's lawyers would argue, it could invite chaos and a potentially devastating cycle of political retribution if state- and county-level prosecutors could charge former presidents. Consider, for example, a (hypothetical) elected prosecutor in a small, heavily Republican county in Arizona who decided to indict Barack Obama, after his presidency, for the Fast and Furious scandal—the aforementioned incident involving the DOJ's disastrous efforts to sell and then track illegal firearms, one of which was eventually connected to the shooting death of a federal agent. (A local prosecutor could charge a crime only if the underlying acts somehow touched on her particular geographic jurisdiction, but presidents are commonly involved in conduct that unfolds in localities across the United States.) Or what if a local commonwealth's attorney in a blue-leaning county in Northern Virginia, where the CIA is headquartered, saw fit to charge George W. Bush with a crime after his presidency for his adoption of "enhanced interrogation" tactics? We have thousands of elected county-level prosecutors across the country; some represent small counties that lean heavily Democratic or Republican, and virtually all solicit campaign donations from the public (as discussed in chapter 4). Trump's attorneys would argue that to allow these local, partisan officials to disrupt the functioning of the White House would create endless political mayhem and opportunism.

Prosecutors would likely respond, first, that state- and county-level prosecutors like the Fulton County DA represent separate governmental sovereigns from the federal government and have independent power to indict even a federal official (or former federal official) who has broken state laws. The DA also could argue that Trump's effort to steal the 2020 election had nothing to do with his official duties as president and, if anything, contravened his most basic civic responsibilities to uphold the Constitution and the law. Trump's lawyers likely would counter that the DA's argument is circular—*his conduct was illegal because we allege it was illegal*—and that he intended not to steal the election but rather to fulfill his responsibility as president to protect constitutionally mandated electoral processes. Even if one thinks he handled those duties in a ham-handed (or worse) manner, Trump's team would argue, he nonetheless was trying to do his job.

While prosecutors have the better argument in my view, it's close enough that a judge could find some rationale to call this one either way. Keep in mind, we have no precedent here; nobody, never mind a state-level prosecutor, has ever indicted a former president. So it would fall to judges to make novel interpretations of the law and decide the issue.

Which brings us to this crucial factor: the federal judicial deck is stacked in Trump's favor.

At the district court level, it's more or less a coin toss, with a slight lean toward judges nominated by Democratic presidents—but, as we'll see in a moment, this isn't where the real action will happen.

Of the eleven active trial-level federal judges currently sitting in the district, six were nominated by Democratic presidents, while five were Republican nominees (four of them Trump's). Five more district judges, all nominated by Democratic presidents, have taken senior status, which means they handle reduced caseloads. This is not to suggest that a Republican-appointed judge would surely throw out any case against Trump, while a Democratic appointee would categorically refuse to do so. (Indeed, a three-judge federal appellate panel, including two Trump nominees, ruled against him on the Mar-A-Lago classified documents case in September 2022.) But, given the choice, you can bet Trump would want to draw a conservative judge that he or another Republican president had nominated, while prosecutors would hope for the opposite.

So the federal district court leans slightly against Trump, on the surface. But far more importantly, the district court's rulings are subject to review by the intermediate appellate court, the Eleventh Circuit Court of Appeals, which has jurisdiction over federal cases originating in Georgia, Alabama, and Florida. Of the country's thirteen federal circuits, the Eleventh is widely regarded as the second-most conservative, behind only the Fifth, which covers federal cases arising in Texas, Louisiana, and Mississippi. As of this writing in late 2022, there are eleven active judges on the Eleventh Circuit. Seven were nominated by Republicans, including six by Trump, while only four were Democratic nominees. Another nine judges (five Republican nominees and four Democrats) hold senior status—bringing the total to twelve to eight in favor of the GOP. (Joe Biden nominated Nancy Gbana Abudu to the circuit in December 2021; if she is confirmed, the balance would become twelve to nine.) Typically, a federal appellate panel is comprised of three judges selected randomly, so odds are Trump would have an edge there. And in rare circumstances where a case presents an issue of enormous consequence, the court of appeals can choose to hear a case *en banc*—meaning all the active judges sit together on one large panel. If that happened, the court would, as a certainty, be Republican-majority. There are few if any federal circuits in which Trump would rather be than the Eleventh.

Moving up a level, we come to the US Supreme Court, where conservative, Republican-appointed justices currently hold a commanding six-to-three advantage, with three of the six nominated by Trump himself. No doubt, the court has rebuffed Trump in several high-profile cases, including disputes over his tax returns and his spate of frivolous challenges to the 2020 election. But we need to consider whether this particular group of jurists would sit back and allow an explosive, all-consuming, politically divisive criminal trial of Trump to proceed in a state-level court, or whether the court would engineer some way to toss out the case on technical legal grounds and spare the entire country the trouble. Put it this way: given how aggressive the conservative majority was during the 2022 term—including its reversal of the nearly fifty-year-old protection of abortion rights first established in *Roe v. Wade*—I'd bet they intercede as necessary to blunt any potential prosecution of Trump. Or, easier still, if the Eleventh Circuit has already ruled in Trump's favor, the Supreme Court could simply decline to hear the case and leave that ruling in place as the final word.

Even if Trump fails on this count and the federal courts decline to dismiss the charges altogether, he's got a potent fallback: he'll seek to have the case "removed" (a legalistic way to say "moved") for trial from Georgia state court over to federal court, specifically the US District Court for the Northern District of Georgia (within which Fulton County is located). A rarely used federal law permits such a move if the defendant was a public official acting in his official capacity in the course of committing the alleged crimes. Once again, then, the parties would argue about whether Trump's conduct touched on his official duties as president; once again, we come back to the favorable judicial lineup for Trump in the federal courts.

Trump's legal team would try to get state charges tried in federal court for two reasons. First, as discussed above, he'd likely have the benefit of a favorable judicial lineup in the federal courts—which would preside over his trial (at the district court level) and then review any guilty verdict on appeal (at the Eleventh Circuit and possibly the US Supreme Court). Even if he were to be convicted by a jury in a federal trial court, the Eleventh Circuit and the Supreme Court would still have the opportunity to strike down the verdict if they saw fit.

Second, a trial jury would be drawn from a far better jury pool, from Trump's perspective. Remember the defense lawyer's admonition to me, when I was a young prosecutor: *Jury selection isn't just a big moment, it's the whole ball game.*

Let's do the math. If Trump were tried in Georgia state court, his jury would be drawn entirely from Fulton County, a heavily Democratic area that voted for Joe Biden over Trump in 2020 by a margin of 72.6 to 26.2 percent. At first blush, if you're a prosecutor aiming to convict Trump, that sounds pretty darn good. But if we run the numbers, despite Biden's electoral blowout in Fulton County, there's nonetheless approximately a 98 percent chance that at least one of the twelve jurors would have voted for Trump in 2020. Even in solidly blue Fulton County, there's an 86 percent chance that a jury would include at least two pro-Trump voters, and a 64 percent chance that at least three Trump voters land in the jury box.

And remember: a jury trial isn't an election, where a majority vote wins. It's unanimity-or-nothing. A prosecutor must convince all twelve jurors, beyond a reasonable doubt, of Trump's guilt. Anything less—even the prosecutor's nightmare, the eleven-to-one jury with one holdout preventing conviction—is a hung jury and a mistrial, which would be a triumph for Trump and a disastrous result for prosecutors. (A mistrial would likely spell the end of any prosecution; while prosecutors theoretically can retry a case that hangs, there's little practical chance for that to happen here, given the chaos and the calendar, which we'll discuss in a moment.) No, it's not certain that a Trump voter would find him not guilty (or vice versa), and yes, a judge would instruct the jurors to put aside their personal views and to decide the case based solely on the law and the trial evidence. But let's be real here: Can you see a political supporter of Trump voting to send him to prison, or a Biden voter choosing to spare Trump?

If anything, the latter scenario seems more plausible when we consider the role that fear might play in influencing any individual juror, regardless of political leanings, in a potential trial of Trump. As we discussed in chapter 8, jurors—normal civilians, chosen at random from the population—naturally approach jury service with trepidation. It's a scary thing to serve on any jury, particularly where a juror fears the potential consequences of a guilty verdict against a powerful defendant—like the aforementioned Juror #5 in the murder trial of the Genovese family gangster Angelo Prisco, who worried about potential fallout from a guilty verdict. No, a Trump juror likely wouldn't fear a late-night knock on the door from a shadowy mob figure with bad intentions. But any juror in a Trump trial would surely be aware of the risk that a guilty verdict might spark violent civil unrest. We don't like to think that a juror might be so colored by extrajudicial considerations, of course. But any juror who saw what Trump's extremist supporters did on January 6, 2021— and who heard him urge his followers in January 2022 to stage "the biggest protests we ever had" against "vicious, horrible" prosecutors who are "not after me, they're after you"—might think twice before voting to convict. Remember: a single holdout juror would cause a hung jury and a mistrial.

So, even before a state court jury, the outlook is ominous for prosecutors. But if Trump manages to get the case into federal court—forget about it. Now the jury pool looks even better for him, and borderline impossible for prosecutors. If Trump is tried in the federal Northern District of Georgia, the jury could be drawn from any of the forty-six counties that comprise that federal district. While Fulton County is the most populous (and hence would likely contribute the highest percentage of potential jurors to the jury pool), more than three-fourths of the counties in the district voted for Trump in 2020—many of them with over 70 percent of the vote going Trump's way. It's mathematically a near-certainty that such a jury pool would contain multiple jurors who voted for Trump in 2020; the jury could well end up majority pro-Trump. Try getting all twelve jurors in any of those scenarios to vote unanimously to convict.

Further complicating the case for prosecutors is the reality of the calendar, and the problems caused by the galactically slow pace of the DA's investigation. The centerpiece of the Georgia case—the infamous phone call in which Trump beseeched Georgia secretary of state Brad Raffensperger to "find" just enough votes for Trump to win the state—became public in early January 2021. And while District Attorney Willis announced that she would investigate Trump's potential election interference in February 2021, she then waited nearly a full year—until January 2022—to request a special purpose grand jury. (Normally, prosecutors convene a grand jury right away, to make full use of its power to issue subpoenas and compel testimony under oath.) The DA then waited another four months, until May 2022, to begin selecting grand jury members. As a result of the DA's own deliberate pace, and the inexplicable whittling away of a year and a half, we're now looking at a potential indictment toward the end of 2022 or early 2023 at the soonest.

But keep in mind: an indictment is just the start of a criminal case. We'd then have to go through legal motions to dismiss and to transfer the case to federal court (including appeals, as laid out above), plus discovery and pretrial motions. Trump's legal team would no doubt seek to maximize delay in the courts, filing as many motions as conceivable to push the case back on the calendar; recall Trump's successful delay strategy, discussed in chapter 14, which enabled him to run out the clock on post-Mueller congressional inquiries.

At this point, if Trump is indicted in Georgia, and if the case ever does reach trial, that won't happen until late 2023 or, more realistically, 2024. By that time, the 2024 presidential campaign will be in full swing. Trump may well be the Republican front-runner nominee by then, or even the nominee.

Consider what the political landscape will look like at that point. As a prosecutor, you're already asking a jury of twelve people (including, almost certainly, at least one and likely multiple Trump voters) to unanimously find a former president guilty of a crime, for the first time in American history. Now imagine upping the stakes to where you're also asking the jury to send to prison one of the major party's nominees, or presumptive nominees, for the upcoming 2024 election. And, again: this isn't an election, where majority vote prevails—this is a jury trial, where you need the votes of all twelve jurors. One dissenter, and the prosecution is cooked.

All of which leaves us here. The Fulton County DA's office might indeed indict Trump. I suspect they will. But when you combine all the relevant factors—the DA's bafflingly slow pace, the constitutional principles that could preclude local prosecution of a former president, a favorable judicial lineup, and the practical difficulties of trying and convicting an enormously polarizing political figure— the likelihood of Trump's ultimate conviction in Georgia is remote.

Chapter 20

WAITING FOR GARLAND

There's this great scene in the Ben Affleck movie *The Town* where, moments after they've committed an armed robbery, four Boston-area thugs jump out of their getaway SUV, holding bags of money and long guns, all wearing identical scary-nun masks. Suddenly, a uniformed Boston police officer in a marked squad car, seemingly on a routine patrol, unwittingly pulls up next to them. The cop looks at the armed robbers, quickly calculates what's happening, and then turns his head away from them in an "I'm gonna just pretend I didn't see anything here" manner. Moments after the near confrontation, as members of the heist crew flee the scene, one asks, "What the fuck was that?" Another answers, "He didn't wanna end up on the wall of the VFW." The bad guys know that the cop understood his predicament: I can tangle with these guys, but it's going to be ugly, and difficult, and dangerous—or I can just pretend nothing happened, turn away, and go about my day, safe and unbothered.

The cop in that scene makes me think of Merrick Garland.

..

When he became attorney general in March 2021, Garland was best known as President Barack Obama's 2016 Supreme Court pick, whose nomination was blocked by Senate Republicans on the premise that a president should not get to select a new justice in an election year. Four years later, Senate Republicans had no problem when President Donald Trump chose Justice Amy Coney Barrett to fill the vacancy created by Justice Ruth Bader Ginsburg's passing, even later in an election year. Garland became an object of liberal affection and sympathy—the soft-spoken, well-qualified career public servant who deserved the job but got screwed by Republican hypocrisy, yet stayed quietly dignified through the whole ordeal.

Even without a seat on the high court, Garland has had an extraordinary career. He served as a federal judge on the US Court of Appeals for the District of Columbia Circuit—commonly regarded as the second most powerful court in the country, after the Supreme Court itself—from 1997 until his confirmation as attorney general in 2021. Less known but perhaps more relevant to the task before him as attorney general, Garland also was an accomplished Justice Department alum who had worked on the prosecution of the 1995 domestic terrorist bombing of a federal building in Oklahoma City, which killed 168 people, including 19 children. As attorney general, Garland seemed primed to take on high-pressure, high-stakes prosecutions; cases don't get any bigger than Oklahoma City, after all.

Whether he wanted the burden or not, Garland bore the hopes of Democrats and others who looked to him as a vehicle for truth and justice, the one who would address the wrongs of the Trump era and set things right again. But it was never an easy fit, given Garland's mild demeanor and judicial inclination toward circumspection.

Still, expectations ran hot. Garland suggested early on that he'd be up to the task, making clear during his confirmation hearing that he fully appreciated the seriousness of the January 6 coup attempt and was ready to take action: "If confirmed, I will supervise the prosecution of white supremacists and others who stormed the Capitol on January 6—a heinous attack that sought to disrupt a cornerstone of our democracy: the peaceful transfer of power to a newly elected government." Others expressed their hopes that he would take down Trump and his confederates who tried to engineer an election-stealing coup. Former Democratic senator Claire McCaskill said

Garland would either "rise to the occasion or go down in infamy as one of the worst attorney generals in this country's history" if he did not prosecute Trump.

As the one-year anniversary of the January 6 attack approached, with few overt signs of action from the DOJ toward Trump or other coup plotters, Garland sought to reassure his public detractors. On January 5, 2022, he solemnly vowed in a formal speech to hold "all January 6 perpetrators, at any level, accountable under law—whether they were present that day or were otherwise criminally responsible for the assault on our democracy." Over the following months, Garland and his top brass intoned the familiar mantra about fearlessly kicking down the doors of power and bringing to justice the powerful people who drove the coup attempt. In a March 2022 press conference, deputy attorney general Lisa Monaco proclaimed, "Let's be very, very clear—we are going to hold those perpetrators accountable, no matter where the facts lead us." Seemingly for dramatic emphasis, she added: "No matter what level." When asked in July 2022 by CNN's Evan Perez whether the Justice Department would prosecute "anybody who was involved, at all levels," FBI director Christopher Wray declared, "We're going to follow the facts wherever they lead, no matter who likes it."

Yet here we are, two years after the coup attempt, and the Justice Department has done—let's be blunt—nothing of the sort. Yes, federal prosecutors swept up over eight hundred Capitol rioters, all told. These were important and necessary prosecutions, and it's a big deal to charge over eight hundred people who tried to topple democracy. And Garland made waves in January 2022, days after his anniversary speech, when DOJ charged eleven members of the extremist Oath Keepers with seditious conspiracy—a rare and serious charge applicable to any person who plots to use force to topple the government or obstruct the execution of any law. But those defendants, like the others, were still (quite literally) at ground level; all of the charged

Oath Keepers were at or near the scene of the Capitol building on January 6. In March 2022, DOJ indicted Proud Boys leader Enrique Tarrio for conspiracy and other crimes relating to the Capitol attack; in June 2022, prosecutors added seditious conspiracy charges against Tarrio and members of the extremist Proud Boys. Notably, Tarrio was the first person charged who was not physically present at the Capitol on January 6. He was, however, in direct contact with people who stormed the building.

Even the Justice Department's prosecutions of the people who were at the Capitol were, in certain respects, soft and inconsistent. Garland's Justice Department brought seditious conspiracy charges in about 2 percent of all January 6 prosecutions (sixteen charges out of over eight hundred cases total, as of this writing in late 2022). Far more Capitol rioters were charged with trespass and other petty misdemeanors.

Several federal judges had choice words for the Justice Department about its January 6 prosecutions. The chief federal district judge in Washington, DC, Judge Beryl Howell, called the DOJ's approach to the January 6 cases "schizophrenic," "baffling," "puzzling," and "peculiar." Howell blasted the Justice Department for "fostering confusion" by charging lowly misdemeanors like "the parading, demonstrating, or picketing charge," which could create a false public perception that January 6 was a legitimate political demonstration. In another case, Howell criticized prosecutors for seeking insufficient monetary penalties against rioters. Another federal judge in Washington, DC, Tanya Chutkan, rejected DOJ's probation recommendation and sentenced a Capitol rioter to 45 days in jail, noting sharply that "there have to be consequences . . . beyond sitting at home." A third judge, Emmett Sullivan, called out DOJ prosecutors for undercharging a case against a defendant who boasted on videotape after the Capitol attack that she was looking for House Speaker

Nancy Pelosi and wanted "to shoot her in the friggin' brain, but we didn't find her."

Federal judges do, fairly routinely, criticize prosecutors for being too aggressive. (I've been there.) Judges sometimes opine that a prosecutor has overcharged a case, or has made unduly aggressive arguments to a jury, or has sought an excessive sentence. But it's extraordinarily rare to see the converse—a federal judge (never mind several of them) calling out the Justice Department for being *too lenient*.

Here's the reality: Garland had every opportunity to achieve meaningful justice against Trump and his confederates who plotted the coup attempt from a safe physical distance. (Recall how smart bosses know to stay away from the crime scene.) The investigative circumstances could not have been more favorable. When Garland took over as AG in March 2021, many of the obstacles that had prevented or inhibited prior Trump investigations and prosecutions had vanished. Most importantly, Trump was out of office and no longer protected by the DOJ policy against indicting a sitting president. Any claim of executive privilege he might raise as a former president would be strained, at best, and would likely fail in court. Trump no longer held the pardon power, which he had skillfully deployed to reward potential witnesses who kept quiet. And his conduct was brand-new, still well within the statute of limitations and fresh in the public and political memory, even as prior scandals receded into the history books.

Garland's failure is particularly unforgivable because he had a healthy head start. By the time he took office as attorney general in March 2021, Trump's second impeachment had already provided compelling proof of his effort to steal the election and to spur his rally-goers toward the Capitol. And the January 6 Select Committee would soon uncover far more evidence that plainly demonstrated Trump's central involvement in the plot to steal the 2020 election through fraud and, ultimately, the Capitol attack. Yet despite these built-in advantages, Garland has come up mostly empty on Trump and his powerful inner-circle advisors for their effort to execute a coup.

. .

Starting in early 2022, around the one-year anniversary of the January 6 attack, a public dispute began to boil over: Was Garland even investigating Trump at all?

Oh yes, he's on it, claimed the Garland faithful. *He's a stealthy prosecutorial ninja,* they proclaimed, and—despite the passage of time since the January 6 attack and the conspicuous absence of overt indicators of a Trump-focused investigation—*he's coming after the boss.* Besides, they'd argue, *This is complicated and these things take time and he's being super-careful. Garland's gonna nail Trump, just you wait.*

I fell in the other camp, as you might have surmised. The pro-Garland crowd claimed that every sign of life from the DOJ was proof positive that Garland was a man on a mission. But this straw-man construction wrongly presupposed that the skeptics believed Garland was doing *nothing at all.* Plainly, Garland invested massive resources in DOJ's January 6 investigation, and the department brought hundreds of prosecutions. And in the summer of 2022—after the January 6 Committee obtained public testimony from former White House insiders who exposed Trump's malfeasance, many of whom had not yet spoken to federal prosecutors—the Justice Department stepped up its investigation and subpoenaed key players from inside the Trump administration, including former White House counsel Pat Cipollone, former White House aide Cassidy Hutchinson, and Marc Short and Greg Jacob, both former advisors to Vice President Mike Pence.

No doubt DOJ leadership could declare plausibly and technically correctly that everybody was in play, at all levels, including Trump himself. Garland and his top brass reminded the public at every opportunity that they would follow the evidence wherever it took them, no matter how high. And, eventually Garland did set his sights on the White House, and Trump's inner circle.

The problem, however, was that Garland took far too long to focus squarely on Trump—and even then, he behaved more like a tepid bureaucrat than a determined prosecutor. The *New York Times* reported in July 2022 that—consistent with the period of conspicuous public inaction from DOJ that stretched through 2021 and into 2022—Garland "never seriously considered focusing on Mr. Trump from the outset." As a result, the Justice Department "had not even opened a case targeting fake electors by early fall 2021, months after details of the wide-ranging scheme were known publicly."

Why, we can fairly ask, would the attorney general decline to focus from the start on the person who sat atop the hierarchy of power behind the coup attempt? Instead, Garland structured his investigation in an impossibly bureaucratic and paralyzingly myopic manner that was essentially predestined to never reach Trump or the true power players at all. Garland could have gone right for the jugular; instead, he poked at each individual capillary.

Garland first tipped his hand about this approach during a subtly telling exchange at his confirmation hearing in February 2021. Senator Sheldon Whitehouse asked whether Garland was "willing to look upstream from the actual occupants who assaulted the building, in the same way that in a drug case you would look upstream from the street dealers to try to find the kingpins, and that you will not rule out investigation of funders, organizers, ringleaders, or aiders and abettors who were not present in the Capitol on January 6th." Garland responded, "We begin with the people on the ground and we work our way up to those who were involved and further involved and we will pursue these leads wherever they take us."

On the surface, this sounds like an unremarkable response. Every prosecutor routinely intones that the job is to follow the facts and the law and pursue any leads wherever they may go, typically working from lower-ranking players up the hierarchical chain. But that approach, as applied to the coup attempt—particularly Garland's suggestion that the only way to reach the true power sources was to "begin with the people on the ground"—was virtually guaranteed to fail.

As we discussed in chapter 5, it takes hard work and good luck for any prosecutor to climb from the bottom all the way to the top of any hierarchical pyramid. Savvy bosses like Trump understand the advantages of holding power, and they can exploit their positioning atop the organizational pyramid to their advantage. So as a prosecutor, you typically need to flip not just one cooperating witness but several, each one taking you a step higher on the organizational flowchart. The more layers you need to climb, the lower your chances of ultimate success. As we saw earlier, in a typical narcotics case, you might flip a few dealers and move up the ranks a couple rungs to the serious traffickers, but you'd still fall well short of El Chapo or other top magnates. Similarly, in some of my mob cases we got lucky, flipped a few guys, and rounded up some mid- or even upper-level players. But we often still fell short of the boss.

Now apply that to the model of January 6. Let's take the Oath Keepers indictment, which was widely hailed upon its announcement as the Justice Department's most serious charge against the biggest players, the "Mission Accomplished" moment for the Garland believers. Let's say some of those defendants had flipped—perhaps even the top person charged, Oath Keepers leader Elmer Stewart Rhodes. (Indeed, some of the charged Oath Keepers reportedly did cooperate with federal prosecutors.) Now: Would Rhodes or any other Oath Keeper realistically have had information that prosecutors could have used against Trump? Or even information that could have led to somebody else who, in turn, might have flipped and gotten to Trump? How many layers stood between the ground troops who actually stormed the Capitol and Trump himself?

It's not at all clear that there was any chain of command from the Oath Keepers or other on-the-ground forces, up through intermediaries, and eventually to Trump himself. Remember that Trump has shown over the years that he's smart enough to limit his contacts, particularly with the rabble who carry out his wishes and instructions. Trump would no sooner meet directly with an Oath Keeper than a Mafia boss (like Artie Nigro, in the aforementioned murder of Al Bruno) would meet with a low-level hired gun (like Frankie Roche, who actually shot Bruno). Yet, as Trump also has demonstrated, he knows how to mobilize his supporters to criminal action without quite saying so explicitly, as we assessed in chapter 6.

Not every criminal conspiracy has neat ranks and job titles that can be expressed in one pyramid-shaped diagram, like the mob with its associates-soldiers-capos-consiglieri-underboss-boss structure. With respect to the coup attempt and January 6 attack, for example, prosecutors seemingly were dealing with not one unified criminal enterprise but rather several overlapping conspiracies. Trump and his close advisors tried to steal the election by spreading a lie and through fraud: pressuring local election officials to throw some extra votes Trump's way, trying to install a loyalist as acting attorney general and enlisting DOJ to falsely validate claims of election fraud, pressing state legislators to override the will of the voters, drafting up slates of fake Trump electors for states that had voted for Biden, and intimidating the vice president to illegally throw out electoral votes. Meanwhile, members of numerous separate but overlapping conspiracies (inspired by Trump's overheated public rhetoric about a stolen election, but seemingly not formally or legally connected to one another or to Trump) stormed the Capitol and wreaked havoc. Even among the foot soldiers, we saw not one singular conspiracy but many—the Oath Keepers, the Proud Boys, plus other groups (some with formal names, others without) and individuals at ground level on January 6. They blitzed the Capitol because of Trump's lies, but not necessarily in a legally cognizable criminal conspiracy with one another, or with Trump. The Capitol attack was not a single, unified conspiracy; it was a mass of different conspiracies—some small, some large, some simplistic and others sophisticated—motivated by and acting toward the same broad goal.

So, using Garland's investigative model, even if the Justice Department had reached the top of some pyramid—say, the top of the Oath Keepers, or even a step or two beyond—federal prosecutors likely still would not have gotten to Trump. The way Garland structured his investigation and set the bar for himself, DOJ would have needed to get extraordinarily lucky, many times over, to even approach the real bosses. And even if prosecutors had flipped all the people they charged, it's still far from certain there would have been an available pathway to implicate Trump or his top advisors at all.

It's worth asking whether Garland took this ultimately futile approach because he genuinely believed it was the optimal and most efficient way to build a case against the real power sources, or because he knew on some level that such a strategy was unlikely ever to result in a prosecution of Trump, with all its attendant political risks and complications. In the end, Garland's chosen strategy enabled him to invoke the rote mantra of "facts and law, facts and law"—*I simply followed the facts and the law, and here's as far as it got me*—while never having to meaningfully grapple with a potentially explosive, uniquely difficult prosecution of the most powerful and combative target on the planet, Donald Trump. (I repeatedly requested through the Justice Department an interview with Garland or any of his top advisors for this book, and was denied or ignored.)

• •

The futility of Garland's stubborn, bottom-up approach to investigating the January 6 Capitol attack came into stark relief as the

House January 6 Committee unveiled its findings to the American public in a series of hearings during the summer of 2022. Even though DOJ had a monthslong head start on the committee (which wasn't formed until the end of June 2021), and even though prosecutors hold massive investigative advantages over Congress (prosecutors, unlike Congress, can issue grand jury subpoenas, obtain wiretaps and search warrants, and use the threat of prison time to flip cooperating witnesses), it quickly became clear that the committee was well out ahead of the Justice Department.

In April 2022, the Justice Department formally requested that the committee share transcripts of all interviews it had conducted or would conduct. By that point, the committee had spoken to over a thousand potential witnesses, including insiders from the Trump White House and campaign. One committee member, Representative Jamie Raskin, responded with a hint of gloating that fearsome DOJ prosecutors had to come hat in hand, begging for help: "The interviews in the possession of the committee are the property of the committee. I imagine that the committee will want to see any relevant evidence used with any relevant legal context." The committee's chair, Representative Bennie Thompson, similarly rebuffed prosecutors who lagged behind his panel's investigative pace: "We can't give them full access to our product." The committee did eventually begin to parcel out documents to DOJ, but only those of the committee's choosing, and on the committee's own timeline.

It got worse for the Justice Department. When former White House staffer Cassidy Hutchinson testified publicly before the committee in June 2022, she blew the roof off the Trump White House. She testified that Trump knew that the crowd of his supporters that had gathered at his January 6 rally was armed; that, after he directed that mob to march to the Capitol, Trump desperately wanted to join them there, but was prevented from doing so by the Secret Service; that at Trump's direction, White House chief of staff Mark Meadows on January 5 had contacted Michael Flynn and Roger Stone, both of whom had contacts with domestic extremist groups that would storm the Capitol the next day; and that Meadows and Giuliani had asked for presidential pardons after the riot occurred.

It turned out that, as Hutchinson delivered her seismic testimony, Garland's prosecutors were watching on television, mouths agape, along with the rest of the American public. The *New York Times* reported shortly after Hutchinson's testimony that "federal prosecutors working on the case watched the aide's appearance before the House committee investigating the Jan. 6, 2021, riot and were just as astonished by her account of former President Donald J. Trump's increasingly desperate bid to hold on to power as other viewers." Somehow, the committee had managed to obtain damning testimony from a highly credible, well-placed White House staffer, while the Justice Department sat by in stunned silence.

Hutchinson's testimony rang an alarm bell of sorts within DOJ. According to the *Times*, Hutchinson's "electrifying public testimony . . . jolted top Justice Department officials into discussing the topic of Mr. Trump more directly, at times in the presence of Attorney General Merrick B. Garland and Deputy Attorney General Lisa O. Monaco." It apparently was mildly taboo even to mention Trump's name within Justice Department headquarters in front of the big bosses; "overt discussion of Mr. Trump and his behavior had been rare, except as a motive for the actions of others," according to the *Times*. Yet in a telling reminder of Garland's implacable inertia, the surprise and embarrassment of learning about Hutchinson's testimony along with the rest of the American public spurred DOJ only to permit prosecutors to make slightly more explicit mention of Trump's name when kicking things around inside headquarters.

• •

Garland's inaction extended beyond the January 6 Capitol attack. Let's not forget that Garland could have charged Trump, or at least investigated him, on other crimes for which he could have been prosecuted once he left the presidency on January 20, 2021. But Garland took no concrete prosecutorial action at all.

For example, Garland's failure to do anything about Trump's obstruction of the Mueller investigation remains unexplained. As of this writing, Garland has never publicly addressed the Mueller investigation or his refusal to do anything about it. The prosecutorial nonfeasance here is particularly baffling because Mueller all but wrote a prosecution memo and indictment of Trump on obstruction charges. In his final report, Mueller laid out the evidence of eleven separate instances of "potentially obstructive acts" by Trump and, for each, proceeded legal element by legal element to explain how the evidence fit the definition of the charged crimes. In at least four of the outlined incidents, Mueller concluded with little to no stated reservation that all the legal elements of obstruction had been met.

Garland did stand mildly impeded by his predecessor, Barr, who had blithely (if incorrectly) concluded in his dishonest, inaccurate letter summarizing the Mueller report that "the evidence developed during the Special Counsel's investigation is not sufficient to establish that the President committed an obstruction-of-justice offense." So Garland would've had to reverse his predecessor, which is politically tricky, though not at all impossible as a technical legal matter. Yet he apparently was perfectly content to let Barr's indefensible home-cooked clearance of Trump stand undisturbed.

In the final calculus, Trump will, somehow, never face any consequences for his audacious effort to derail Mueller's investigation. Congress never impeached, or even meaningfully investigated. (House Democrats' ham-handed post-Mueller investigation, led by the comically inept Representative Jerry Nadler, barely got off the ground and ultimately went nowhere.) And then, once Trump left office and was subject to indictment, Garland sat idly by, saying nothing, as Trump's criminal liability quietly evaporated with the passage of time. At this point, the five-year statute of limitations has expired for most of Trump's obstructive conduct.

Garland also had ample basis on which to open a criminal investigation on the Ukraine scandal. Congressional investigators on Trump's first impeachment had unearthed compelling evidence, including damning witness testimony, texts, and other documents, and had presented their case in trial-like fashion to Congress and the American public during impeachment proceedings. There's some wiggle room to argue that Trump's conduct, though disloyal and abusive of his power, didn't quite match up squarely with the federal laws prohibiting bribery, extortion, and solicitation of foreign election assistance. And Barr's original determination that no crime had been committed and DOJ should not investigate, while not binding, did pose a practical obstacle for Garland. Yet there's no public indication that he ever even took a look at potential criminal charges—bribery, extortion, or solicitation of foreign election assistance—in connection with Ukraine. Once again, Garland seemingly opted for the easy way out.

. .

I need to say this much for Garland, and it's important. He has, in key respects, restored the most vital foundational principles of the Justice Department.

During his tenure as attorney general, Garland has given the public no serious cause to question his truthfulness or credibility. He hasn't said much publicly, and he tends to default to clichés and generalities, but he hasn't lied to us. An honest attorney general shouldn't be a big deal, normally. But Garland stands in stark contrast to his predecessor, Barr, who lied about issues large and small to Congress and the American public and was repeatedly caught in the act by his own Justice Department employees, by lawmakers, and by federal judges.

Garland also has taken pains to re-establish, both in word and deed, that the Justice Department must act independent of politics. During his confirmation hearing, Garland vowed to reaffirm "the norms that will ensure the Department's adherence to the Rule of Law: Policies that protect the independence of the Department from partisan influence in law enforcement investigations; [and] that strictly regulate communications with the White House." In contrast to Barr, who politicized the Justice Department to serve the president's political agenda, Garland regularly sounded the theme of prosecutorial independence: "Political or other improper considerations must play no role in any investigative or prosecutorial decisions. These principles that have long been held as sacrosanct by the DOJ career workforce will be vigorously guarded on my watch, and any failure to live up to them will be met with strict accountability."

Garland has backed up his rhetoric on this count. For example, in October 2021 CNN's Kaitlan Collins asked President Joe Biden whether, in his view, people who defied subpoenas from the January 6 Select Committee ought to be prosecuted. The president responded, "I do, yes." Biden crossed a line here by publicly expressing his view on how the Justice Department should exercise its prosecutorial power. (Trump, of course, constantly declared in public that DOJ prosecutions of his political allies were unjust while calling for indictment and arrest of his perceived enemies—with little to no pushback from Barr or his other attorneys general.) But Garland and the Justice Department promptly fired right back at Biden. In an extraordinary but necessary public statement, DOJ reminded the American public, while casting a glance up Pennsylvania Avenue at the White House, that "the Department of Justice will make its own independent decisions in all prosecutions based solely on the facts and the law. Period. Full stop." Garland's rejoinder forcefully confirmed that politicians—even the president—do not dictate prosecutorial outcomes.

The problem is that, in seeking to recalibrate DOJ and restore its political independence, Garland has gone *too far*—or at least has misconstrued the mission. It's one thing to do the job without regard to politics. But it's another to contort ordinary prosecutorial judgment to avoid doing anything that might even be perceived as political or controversial. Yes, it's important to keep politics out of prosecution. But that doesn't mean prosecution should never touch on anything political, if the prosecution is otherwise justified.

In fact, the *Justice Manual*, which guides all DOJ prosecutions, specifies that "where the law and the facts create a sound, prosecutable case, the likelihood of an acquittal due to unpopularity of some aspect of the prosecution or because of the overwhelming popularity of the defendant or his/her cause is not a factor prohibiting prosecution." In other words: federal prosecutors should not hesitate to charge a case where the defendant is widely known, or broadly loved, or deeply hated (all of which apply to Trump)—even if that defendant's fame (or notoriety) might make it difficult or impossible to convict him. Rather, the prosecutor's job is to bring charges that are just and righteous and supported by the evidence, and then let the process—ultimately a jury—dictate the outcome. The *Justice Manual*'s instruction is a technical codification of the colloquial prosecutor's credo that the job is to pursue justice without fear or favor.

Too often, Garland crossed that line between making nonpolitical decisions and making decisions engineered to avoid anything that might ruffle political feathers. At a certain point, if a prosecutor focuses primarily on staying clear of turbulence, he simply isn't doing the job. Sometimes prosecutors have to take on tough fights. And sometimes those fights implicate powerful political players.

..

"Let us do something, while we have the chance! It is not every day that we are needed. . . . To all mankind they were addressed, those cries for help still ringing in our ears! But at this place, at this moment of time, all mankind is us, whether we like it or not. Let us make the most of it, before it is too late! . . . Yes, in the immense confusion one thing alone is clear. We are waiting for Godot to come."

This quote, as the closing line reveals, comes from the 1950s-era Samuel Beckett play *Waiting for Godot*—now perhaps better known for the 1996 movie satire *Waiting for Guffman*, in which members of a community theater group anxiously anticipate the arrival of an influential producer who, of course, never shows up. The punch line is that the protagonists cling to hope, even as it becomes increasingly obvious to the audience that they'll be waiting in vain for the savior to arrive.

Merrick Garland could have set things straight on Trump. But he failed; worse yet, he seemingly didn't even investigate in any manner reasonably aimed at the top of the power structure, or properly reflecting the urgency of the moment. Even after it became plain that he was not up to the task, he still had his believers. The Garland faithful clung to the hope that he was working slowly but meticulously behind the scenes. One commentator theorized hopefully on national television that Garland had intentionally "lulled" Trump by his inaction and that Garland was known for the "slow build." But that's just wrong. In the highest-profile case of Garland's career, the 1995 Oklahoma City bombing, the lead perpetrator, Timothy McVeigh, was first charged by federal authorities *two days* after the attack; the DOJ team supervised by Garland then procured an indictment less than four months later. Maybe a stubborn few still hold out hope for action, even today. But at this point, it's obvious that anyone waiting for justice to arrive might as well wait on Godot or Guffman as Garland.

Let me be clear about this: Garland and DOJ might well still indict Trump in, say, early 2023—relating either to January 6 or to the Mar-a-Lago documents, which Garland permitted to remain in Trump's private residence for over a year and a half, while playing a prolonged game of patty-cake with Trump's lawyers, before executing a search warrant. The problem is that it'll be too late as a practical matter. As we discussed in the prior chapter, given the extensive discovery and the inevitable pretrial motions and appeals, a trial wouldn't realistically happen until late 2023 or, more likely, 2024. Trump could well be the Republican front-runner or nominee for the 2024 presidential election by then, which would enormously complicate the already difficult task of convincing a jury to unanimously return a guilty verdict. It's even possible that, by the time Garland's prosecutors get through trial, sentencing, and all levels of appeal (including the intermediate court of appeals and, potentially, the US Supreme Court), it could be January 2025 or later, and we might have a new president in office; a newly elected Republican could well choose to exercise the pardon power on Trump's behalf. When considering Garland's glacial pace, a line from the 1993 chess prodigy movie *Searching for Bobby Fischer* comes to mind: "You've lost. You just don't know it yet."

The Justice Department would've had a realistic chance to convict Trump if they had charged him in, say, late 2021. But by now, the task has become impossibly complicated by politics and the passage of time. The primary benefactor of Garland's paralyzing reticence has, of course, been Donald Trump. And the American people, and our democracy, have sustained the concomitant damage.

Let's assume for a moment that Trump did in fact commit at least one crime while running for the presidency, or while in office. We've got only three potential outcomes: (1) the former president is indicted and convicted; (2) the former president is indicted but not convicted; and (3) the former president is not charged at all. None of these options is pain-free; all come with serious and inevitable costs. But which is the worst?

The downside of options (1) and (2) is mostly the same. The primary concern is essentially that prosecuting a president is just *too political*. A prosecution of a former president, particularly one as simultaneously popular and unpopular as Trump, would be uniquely and potentially dangerously polarizing. Over 70 million Americans voted for Trump in 2020, while over 80 million voted against him. And it's safe to say that feelings about Trump tend to run hotter than toward, say, Jimmy Carter or George W. Bush. A criminal charge against Trump would infuriate an enormous swath of the American public, and the outcome of the case would either further inflame that group (if the end result was a conviction) or the other half (if the case ended in anything but conviction—dismissal of charges by a judge, a not-guilty verdict from a jury, or a series of hung juries resulting in eventual dismissal by a prosecutor). Trump recognized and exploited this vulnerability, explicitly urging his supporters at a January 2022 rally in Texas to take to the streets if he were someday indicted.

Beyond the risk of large-scale political opposition and potential civic unrest, there's also a prevailing sense that it simply doesn't *feel* American to slap handcuffs on the former president. Only other countries—less stable ones, we like to think—lock up their fallen leaders, their vanquished political adversaries. We just don't do that here in the United States. Despite the prevalence of jaunty memes featuring Trump in an orange jumpsuit, the image of a former president serving time in prison would be difficult for many to stomach, regardless of party affiliation.

But plenty of other stable, developed countries have brought criminal charges against former presidents or prime ministers in recent years, and they've survived just fine.

Former French president Nicolas Sarkozy was prosecuted and convicted twice after he left office—once in March 2021 for bribery and influence peddling, and then in a separate case in September 2021 for criminal violations of France's campaign finance laws. Sarkozy's predecessor, Jacques Chirac, was charged in 2010 and convicted in

2011 for embezzling funds while he was mayor of Paris, before he became president.

In 2019, Israeli prosecutors indicted former prime minister Benjamin Netanyahu (once a close friend and political ally of Trump's) on bribery, fraud, and other charges. In 2015, former prime minister Ehud Olmert was prosecuted and convicted for bribery, and served sixteen months behind bars. And in 2011, former Israeli president Moshe Katsav was convicted on rape charges; he served five years in prison.

In Italy, former prime minister Silvio Berlusconi was charged, tried, and acquitted in 2021 for allegedly paying a witness to make false statements about an underage prostitution case. And he was found guilty in 2013 of paying an underage girl for sex and abusing public office. In 2009, before Berlusconi's prosecution, Italy's highest court overturned a law that had been passed during his tenure in office that protected the country's prime minister, president, and other top officials from prosecution—a broader, cross-continental variation of the US Department of Justice's policy against indicting a sitting president—beyond the official's term in office.

Also since 2000, former presidents and prime ministers have been criminally charged and convicted in South Korea, South Africa, Taiwan, Brazil, and Iceland.

Circumstances vary case by case, and each country has its own laws and political considerations. But the common through line is this: prosecutors in developed nations across the globe have in recent years criminally charged their country's own former democratically elected leaders. Each time, the criminal justice processes played out, verdicts were rendered, and in some instances the former leaders went to prison. None of these countries collapsed or devolved into chaos or civil war.

In the final calculus, we have to ask: How do the negative consequences of prosecuting a former president compare to doing nothing at all? How does a criminal prosecution that promises to be difficult, controversial, and polarizing stack up against a convenient turning of the head, like the cowardly cop in *The Town*?

I'll stipulate that the answer there depends to some extent on the nature of the crime, and the strength of the evidence. Perhaps we are capable of gliding past it, of simply gritting our collective teeth and moving on, if the evidence of a crime is less than ironclad, or if the crime itself doesn't directly threaten the future of the republic. Despite widespread anger, after all, we survived the pardon of Richard Nixon, and we got along just fine when Bill Clinton wasn't indicted for perjury.

So let's assume momentarily, for the sake of argument, that some of Trump's conduct—campaign finance violations, obstruction of justice, extortion of Ukraine—somehow just isn't worth it, at least not this long after the fact. Still: Trump's effort to steal the 2020 election is different. It goes to the heart of our constitutional democracy. The proof is substantial enough to justify a charge—we laid it out in chapter 17—and the crimes could hardly be more serious. Trump's conduct is amply documented. This isn't a whodunit; he took most of his actions in plain public view, and much of his behind-closed-doors conduct has now been exposed. Trump tried to steal the election through lies and political pressure and, in the end, the violent acts of his extremist supporters. To simply turn away from that conduct, as Garland has done, is to permit by inaction a grave injustice against our democracy.

· ·

I reject two common lines of argument against Trump.

First, I reject the call for criminal prosecution as a sledgehammer to address all manner of perceived wrongs. Not every abuse or misuse of power is criminal, or appropriately remedied through indictment. But we've seen ridiculous "hot takes" from well-known commentators calling for criminal prosecution of Trump for everything from manslaughter charges over his mishandling of Covid-19 to criminal election obstruction for his public comments opposing certain funding to the US Postal Service.

Second, I reject the "somebody's got to nail this guy" approach. As popular as he is among his supporters, Trump also is widely despised, perhaps with a ferocity never seen before in the United States—certainly in recent history. That lends itself to a certain paranoia, an obsession with seeing him getting his comeuppance, somehow, some way, and I-don't-care-what-for: *They got Al Capone on taxes, after all, so let's just lock this guy up on whatever might be available.* Trump's ability to slip away from law enforcement, time and again, has stoked that fire.

While I empathize to a degree, I also reject this approach. First, it's simply not how prosecutors ought to operate. We don't single out a person who is politically unpopular, or boorish, or even dangerous, and then try to find some way to, well, lock him up. As distasteful as Trump can be, the principle transcends any individual. After all, it's not a principle if we abandon it when we dislike the outcome.

On a practical level, Trump-fixated prosecutorial quests haven't been particularly effective, either. Witness the futile effort of New York State prosecutors to nail Trump for his pre-presidency business and financial affairs, after years of public vows to bring him to justice, somehow, some way. New York authorities ultimately brought a civil lawsuit, but if they had indicted Trump, he would have had a ready-made defense based on what lawyers call "selective prosecution"—meaning, essentially, that he was specifically singled out for political reasons. That defense almost never succeeds, but New York prosecutors gave Trump plenty of ammo. I took a quick poll of three deeply experienced prosecutors, none of whom are Trump fans, asking if they'd ever seen a stronger "selective prosecution" defense than Trump would've had if he had been charged criminally in New York State. None had.

So, no—I'm not on board with going after any person, including Donald Trump, because, well, *somebody's got to get him for something.* It's not what prosecutors are supposed to do, and it's ultimately self-defeating.

But I do embrace the notion that we cannot simply glide past monumental, democracy-threatening, criminal abuse of power and hope for the best, simply because it would be too difficult and too risky to prosecute.

..

The Justice Department does have a special responsibility here. It's unfair and suboptimal to depend on elected, county-level district attorneys—in Manhattan or Fulton County or anywhere else—to take on the daunting task of charging a former president for conduct relating to the office.

For one thing, DOJ has far more resources and expertise at its disposal than even the biggest and best DAs. The Justice Department has about 117,000 employees, including about 12,000 federal prosecutors, plus the FBI, DEA, ATF, US Marshals Service, and Bureau of Prisons, with an annual budget of over $30 billion (plus easy access to other federal, state, and local agencies). An attorney general would have the luxury of tapping the absolute best of the best from an enormous pool of talent, both on the prosecutorial side and the law enforcement side, with virtually limitless resources and support. By contrast, the Manhattan DA—commonly regarded as the most powerful district attorney in the country—has about 550 prosecutors, while Fulton County has only about 70. County prosecutors simply don't have DOJ's firepower.

Second, the Justice Department is better positioned, legally, to bring the nation's first-ever charge against a former president. As we discussed in the prior chapter, there is a legitimate constitutional argument, based on the principles of immunity, federalism, and federal supremacy, that a state- or county-level prosecutor cannot indict a former president for conduct that touches on the presidency. The issue has never been formally raised in a court—no former president has been indicted in the first place—so we don't know how it might come out. We do know, however, that this argument would be available to Trump, or any other former president, against a state AG or a county DA, but not against the US Department of Justice.

Finally, and perhaps most importantly, DOJ has unique institutional standing to take on a prosecution of a former president. The Justice Department stands alone in this country. It is our only nationwide prosecutor's office, and it is by far the largest and the most esteemed. The US attorney general is nominated by the president and confirmed by the Senate—which provides some insulation from local, partisan electoral politics—and the vast majority of DOJ's lawyers and other staff are nonpolitical public servants. To put it plainly: only the Justice Department has the institutional heft, political ballast, and established credibility to take on a contentious prosecution of a former president. In that sense, Garland's failure as attorney general is even more acute.

In the end, Garland simply didn't do the job, or didn't do it well enough. He could have brought criminal charges, but he didn't, at least not in a timely manner. He talked the talk and went through the motions, sort of, but ultimately he was wary to the point of paralysis about causing political dissension. Trump is a remorseless street brawler; Garland plays by Marquess of Queensbury rules. It was a mismatch from the start. As many advantages as the system gave to Trump, and as aggressive and effective as he has been in exploiting them, Garland still could have achieved some measure of justice, if he had just done his job.

..

Daniel Marino—the Gambino family powerhouse who sanctioned the murder of his own nephew—has a few things in common with Donald Trump. They're roughly contemporaries, born a few years apart in the 1940s, both in the outer boroughs of New York. Both men ruthlessly pursued power as they rose to the top of their chosen cutthroat professions—Marino in the mob and Trump in business and politics. Both understood and leveraged money, status, and fear to protect their own interests and to silence or destroy anyone who posed a threat.

In other key respects, of course, Marino and Trump are quite different. Both were willing to break the law, and did so prodigiously, as discussed in chapter 17—but Marino, unlike Trump, was an outright murderer (an obvious distinction, but an important one). And while Marino was a notorious Mafia powerhouse, he has no bearing on our national public life. Trump, by contrast, is the most influential national political figure of the past decade, and perhaps longer.

So I understand the limitations in comparing my (highly imperfect) effort to bring Marino to justice to the varied prosecutorial pursuits of Trump. It's not apples to apples. A trial of Daniel Marino would have riveted the Mafia world, and maybe the New York City tabloids, but the stakes wouldn't have gone much beyond that. A prosecution of Donald Trump would capture international attention, with implications for our democratic republic.

But both of these powerful men posed daunting subjects for law enforcement. Both were elusive, savvy, cold-blooded operators who fought like mad to build their power and dodge accountability.

The difference, in the end, comes down to this: we took a shot at Marino. No doubt, it would have been easier to turn away than to tangle with him. Ted Otto, the intrepid FBI special agent on the case, and I had taken down all the players around Marino, and we could have called it a day and declared victory, even if we came up just short of the top guy. We understood that Marino was an extraordinarily difficult and elusive target, and we knew that our evidence of his criminality was close to the line, perhaps even a smidge short of what prosecutors ordinarily hope for. We took a real risk in prosecuting Marino. And in the end we settled for an outcome (the five-year guilty plea) that felt less than fully satisfying or just.

So, yes, Marino wound up with a relatively light sentence. Like I said up front, it still bothers me, and I still question whether I did everything right in that case. But I take solace in this: we didn't let Dan Marino get away with it. He didn't stroll away from the murder of his nephew—a cruel act for which he was responsible, in both the legal and moral sense—utterly unchallenged. We indicted him. We brought a criminal case captioned *United States v. Daniel Marino.* He took a plea. He admitted his guilt. He went to federal prison, for years. The first paragraph of his obituary will say that he conspired to murder his own nephew, and he was charged for it and convicted in a court of law. We gave Frank Hydell's surviving relatives some degree of clarity and closure.

So as much as I still relive the Marino case even now, years later, I take solace in this: we took on a difficult fight because we knew it was the right thing to do. We felt we *had* to do it. Any prosecutor who aims to jump from one easy conviction to another, or dallies over a case until it reaches a point where the proof is utterly undeniable, doesn't really understand the job, or perhaps just isn't up for it.

It's not a matter of courage, really; it's a matter of humility. It's a willingness to take on an imperfect case, and perhaps even to absorb a "loss" of sorts, to promote and protect the greater good. Sometimes you have to take on the tough battles, including those that may seem at once necessary and just, but also potentially unwinnable. Sometimes the fight itself is worth it. And imperfect justice is preferable to no justice at all.

ACKNOWLEDGMENTS

This book is the work of a small but sturdy crew. Thanks to Eric Nelson at HarperCollins for rolling the dice on me and for your willingness—eagerness, perhaps—to challenge glib conventions. From the start, all you ever told me was to be gutsy and to say it plainly; I couldn't ask for more than that. Hannah Long's editorial input was invaluable, and helped shape this book in large ways and small. Thanks also to James Neidhardt, Miranda Ottewell, Tracy Locke, and Tom Hopke.

Yaffa Fredrick remains unequaled as an editor, fact-checker, and general commonsense-bringer. (I know that's not technically a term.) Your talent and vision are unique.

Thank you to Jess Graham and Anu Chugh for your research and for your support and enthusiasm. I take quasi-parental pride in all that you do, and I look forward to you both making your marks in the real-world legal profession.

I am eternally grateful to the people of CNN, who have taught me so much and have unfailingly encouraged me to pursue and speak truth. Thank you to Chris Licht, Ramon Escobar, and Becky Schatz for your guidance and support for this and other projects. Thanks to Jeff Zucker, Rebecca Kutler, and Mitra Kalita for giving me a shot and for helping me understand and grow in this strange industry. Thanks also to so many others: Jim Acosta, Christiane Amanpour, Robert Aouad, John Avlon, John Berman, Victor Blackwell, Wolf Blitzer, Kate Bolduan, Pam Brown, Erin Burnett, Ana Cabrera,

Alisyn Camerota, Laura Coates, Kaitlan Collins, Sam Feist, Mike Figliola, Jenna Fratello, Randi Furman, Richard Galant, David Goodman, Alli Gordon, Nyja Greene, Eric Hall, Poppy Harlow, Alli Hedges, Bill Hinkle, Laura Jarrett, Athena Jones, Brianna Keilar, Don Lemon, Marie Malzberg, Lauren Mensch, Javi Morgado, Michelle Moryc, Izzy Povich, Joanna Preston, Shimon Procupecz, Meredith Richards, Kara Scannell, Jessica Schneider, Jim Sciutto, Michael Smerconish, Sara Sidner, Rahel Solomon, Gena Somra, Maria Spinella, Jake Tapper, Adam Thomas, Mariella Vaudo, Laura Vigilante, Emily Welch, Elliot Williams, Susie Xu, and Jamie Zahn-Liebes, to name just a few.

Thanks to Preet Bharara for your friendship and mentorship, and to Tamara Sepper and the entire crew at CAFÉ and Vox Media for somehow managing to do important work and have fun at the same time. Thanks also to Dan Abrams for always making time to help and advise.

I'm grateful to Jen Campanile and Lia Aponte at UTA for your loyal guidance and support.

I've had too many great teachers to ever list here, most of them in the New Jersey public school system. If you happen to read this, I'm sorry for being a pain in class, and I hope that whatever pride you feel in a former student writing a book can help make up the debt that I owe you. In particular, thanks to Mr. Schultz for challenging me to think beyond accepted wisdom, to Mr. Carr for inspiring me to write boldly, and to Professor Milt Heumann for sparking my interest in the law.

None of this can happen without family. Thanks to Mom and Dad for your unfailing, unconditional love and support in all things. To Pete, Erica, Ben, and Dana: I never take for granted having two brothers (and two sisters-in-law) by my side. To Alice and Molly (I'm putting your names in this book whether you like it or not), and to Micah and Ethan, maybe you'll write your own books someday.

I think you can, and I hope you will. And a remembrance of my Grandma Janet, a copy editor at a time when very few women were in the business; my Grandma Gusta, whose determination and ferocity live on; and my babysitter Gloria Mastripolito, who encouraged me to write when I was a kid, and once bought me a set of pencils engraved "Elie Honig, Future Author."

Finally, thanks and love to Rachael, for putting up with and supporting, well, me and all of this stuff. And to Aaron and Leah: maybe you'll read this someday, I don't know (probably not, realistically). If you do, I'll use this final line to sneak in an embarrassing message about how we love you and how it already makes our hearts hurt a bit to know that you'll be out of the house and building your own lives at college, all too soon.

INDEX

ABOUT THE AUTHOR

ELIE HONIG worked as a federal and state prosecutor for over fourteen years. He prosecuted and tried cases involving organized crime, public corruption, human trafficking, and other offenses. Honig is now an Emmy-nominated CNN senior legal analyst. His first book, *Hatchet Man: How Bill Barr Broke the Prosecutors' Code and Corrupted the Justice Department*, was a national bestseller. He writes a weekly column for CAFÉ and Vox Media, where he also hosts two podcasts, *Third Degree* and *Up Against the Mob*. Honig graduated from Rutgers University (where he now teaches undergraduates) and Harvard Law School.